Bitten by Wolves

Bitten by Wolves

Stories from the Soul of Molineux

Johnny Phillips

First published by Pitch Publishing, 2019

Pitch Publishing
A2 Yeoman Gate
Yeoman Way
Worthing
Sussex
BN13 3QZ
www.pitchpublishing.co.uk
info@pitchpublishing.co.uk

A CIP catalogue record is available for this book
from the British Library.

ISBN 978 1 78531 614 2

Typesetting and origination by Pitch Publishing

Printed and bound in the UK by TJ International

CONTENTS

For Mum and Dad,
and Daniel

ACKNOWLEDGEMENTS

THAT FIRST memory of Wolves is still a vivid one. After alighting at Rock Ferry railway station following a short journey from my home city, Liverpool, a British Rail football special train pulled up alongside the next platform and hordes of Wolves supporters disembarked. It was the crowds, the noise and the excitement in the air, walking down the platform, that left an indelible mark. We were off to an FA Cup third round match at Tranmere Rovers. It was January 1983, and a small child was hooked forever.

Writing this book has perhaps been a long time coming, then, but it needed the help of many people. All those who have spoken to me, not just the interviewees in these pages, have shed light on the Wolves story and I really appreciate their time. The many supporters, staff and former players and managers who I have chatted to down the years have helped paint a picture of this unique club too. Meeting other fans and listening to their stories is never a chore. Wolves has given me many lasting friendships down the years, I am thankful to every one of them, they know who they are.

At the *Express and Star*, I'd like to thank my sports editor Russell Youll for offering me the opportunity to write a weekly column three years ago, which reinvigorated a passion for writing, and deputy sports editor Derek Bish who helped facilitate access to the newspaper's archive. I first wrote about the club as a student in the pages of *A Load of Bull*, the much-loved Wolves fanzine. To that end I owe founding editor Dave Worton and his successor Charles Ross my gratitude for the opportunity. Dave's good friend Simon Smith was great company during the many lifts he gave me to Molineux whilst living in Leeds throughout much of the 90s. Paul Berry, another former contributor to its pages and a brilliant Wolves writer, has been a source of advice over the past year.

The management and players of the Wolves All Stars, the club's former players' charity team, have welcomed me into their fold. Apart from enjoying an occasional appearance as a ringer, it has been great to chat to so many ex-players from different eras.

I chose Matt Murray to write the foreword because, in many ways, his career is classic Wolves, marked by such highs and lows. In the space of two successive games in 2003 he went from the unadulterated elation of the play-off final success in Cardiff to a 5-1 defeat on his Premier League debut. There is nobody better placed to talk about the contrasting emotions of professional football at this club. Since his early retirement he has become a good friend and trusted colleague on *Soccer Saturday*.

I'd like to thank my employer, Sky Sports, for giving me the creative freedom to cover the club so extensively. My interviews in this book with current Wolves players and management are extracts from original Sky Sports features and documentaries.

The Lych Gate pub kindly hosted our interviews with some of the stars of Airwolf 90 – many thanks to Dave and Hayley for their hospitality.

Mike Watkins is a long-standing family friend and Wolves fan who drove Dad and I to many a game in my youth, and he helped build a picture of the rich history of the club on those long car journeys from Liverpool to Molineux. As a kid, the Wolves talk over a (soft) drink in pubs pre-match with his friends Richard Preston, Bob

Munn and George Murray was always a highlight of a matchday.

Closest to home, my parents, John and Terry, continue to be a fantastic support. Their proof-reading and editorial advice as each chapter was written was invaluable. My wife, Michelle, had to bear the brunt of the many evenings I was sat tapping away on the laptop neglecting family duties. I will be forever grateful for her sacrifices and patience.

FOREWORD
Matt Murray

WOLVES IS a special club and Molineux is an amazing place. Every now and then, there has been a reminder of this when I least expected it. I remember one occasion a few years ago when I was on holiday with Robbie Keane, who was the superstar at the time playing for Liverpool. We were chatting to some football fans at a bar. They all knew who he was and which club he played for. One fan asked where I was playing, and his mate said, 'He only plays for Wolve's. And the other fan replied, 'Only? Wolves is massive.' That drummed it in really. I knew anyway, but it brought it home to me just how important this club is.

I was nine years old when Wolves came into my life. I was training with Lichfield Colts. My manager, Don Astle, was a big Wolves fan who had experienced the worst times, the moments you wouldn't wish on any supporter. He donated his wages when Wolves almost went bust in the 1980s. He worked in a factory, he loved the club and he made donations of his wages to help save Wolves.

In 1990 a few of us were invited down to training one day, when Graham Turner was manager at the club. There was no centre of excellence then, it was before the academy had started. My friends at school were impressed, they were saying, 'Wolves are famous!' We went down to a place called

East Park and trained on the artificial turf. It was a four-week trial. I remember at training on the Monday nights you could hear sounds of the speedway from Monmore Green in the background. People like Rob Kelly and Tony Painter were developing the youth system, but it was just schoolboy stuff then. I got taken on for a year, and then each year after that I would be kept on again. There was myself and a boy called Claudio Coleman who stayed right to the end. He was a brilliant player of Italian heritage, a real talent.

Once we got taken on full time, we used to get two tickets left for us on a matchday, so I saw all the redevelopments happen in the early 90s. I remember the old standing terrace behind the goal, the South Bank, and the John Ireland Stand, as it was then, was such a long way from the pitch. Gradually they redeveloped the place. While they were building the Billy Wright Stand, there were Portakabins in the corner where the players would get changed, so my mate Gaz Astle and I would wait by the fence and if we were there at the right time we'd see Stowelly [goalkeeper Mike Stowell] go out to do his warm-ups. We used to love watching him run out with all his goalkeeper gear. All I ever wanted to do was be a footballer.

I was lucky that the youth side I grew up with were a special bunch of lads. I was only 11 years old when I met Lee Naylor; he always had a hammer of a left foot even back then. Joleon Lescott came in a bit later; he was the year below me. We had Adam Proudlock and Keith Andrews too, they were really good prospects at the time. It was when we first went over to a tournament in Holland that I first met Robbie Keane. It was my GCSE year, Keano had just won the golden boot for the youth team and he was doing stuff in training that made us realise he was really special. He won player of the tournament; he tore up Ajax and Sampdoria on that trip. That was the last we saw of him as kids, he went straight into the first team the season after that.

Back then we all just lived in the moment. In some ways I wish that I could be back in those times, where we all just lived in the moment. We thought we could beat anyone as a youth team. I remember when we used to change at Molineux and then go down to the training ground, we had all just passed our driving tests, and so many of us signed professional terms for the first time, we just lived the life. We thought it would last forever, and we were all so proud of our mates when they broke through into the first team. Keano was the first to step up, then Joleon. There was no jealousy, everyone was so pleased for the team-mate who stepped up, and we pushed each other all the way. I was probably the last one to come through – everyone else had made their debuts, but even at a young age I'd had a few injury problems that held me back.

The first-ever time I was named in the senior team was an unreal moment. It was for a Wimbledon away game on 31 August 2002. I'd been at the club from the age of nine, and to actually stand there in the tunnel about to make a first-team debut, wow, what a feeling. It was strange because we had more fans in the ground than they did. The first home match was against Reading, and it was a really emotional moment. The fans were singing my name, and it was a case of taking it all in. I'll never forget that, even though we lost the game. The first win came in the next game at home to Preston North End, when I made a few saves, which meant a lot. The roar from the crowd whilst stood on the Molineux pitch when we scored was indescribable, it was such a good feeling.

Back then there was nothing better than playing away on a Saturday afternoon. We'd just spent the week training hard, then we'd be coming back to Wolverhampton on the team bus in such good spirits if we'd got a result. Seeing the big RAC building around junction nine on the M6, we knew the night was ahead of us. They were the best of times, there were no camera phones or anything, so we didn't have to worry too much about enjoying ourselves. We played and partied together. And when you play for Wolves it's special. When you've come through the youth set-up the supporters give you more time, they encourage you, they forgive the odd mistake. I can't explain to the fans how helpful that was to so many of us. The thing I miss most is the matchday with the adrenaline pumping. Pulling up outside the ground and seeing someone wearing a shirt with your own name on the back. Going out to do the warm-ups, then standing there in the tunnel seeing the seats filled in the stand opposite, where I used to sit. Then just before kick-off they're all singing 'Hi Ho Silver Lining'. Standing in the goalmouth in front of the North Bank or the South Bank and hearing that roar, the hairs stand up on the back of my neck now just thinking about it. That's where you feel so privileged because you know every single person in that stadium would give anything just to experience that once.

If you could give me a few games to experience again, then there's a handful that stand out. The FA Cup third-round match when we beat Newcastle United 3-2 in January 2003. Everything about that was sensational, the atmosphere inside Molineux that day was incredible. It was awesome playing against Alan Shearer at the top of his game and other players of that calibre. It kick-started our whole season and we ended up winning promotion on that amazing day in Cardiff in May. Obviously the play-off final itself was unreal. I really knew the history of the club. I'd been there as a kid when we were beaten by Bolton Wanderers over two legs, I was there when we got turned over by Crystal Palace a couple of years later. I was in the schoolboys team then, and I felt the hurt throughout the whole club.

I knew promotion was such a massive deal for Wolves as we hadn't been in the top division for so long – I understood what it meant to get to the Premier League. So to get to the final was amazing, and to go up and be a part of it, for that to be my debut season in the first team, capped everything.

Even now, 16 years later, there are so many fans of a certain generation who still come up to me and say that was the best day, it was so good.

I only played in that first game of the following Premier League season, so that was a real disappointment. If we're really honest, as a squad and a club, our preparations were not the best. It's a regret that we didn't do ourselves justice. I went into that season not fully fit after having a hernia operation, which should have been nothing. If I'd met Steve Kemp (Wolves' head of medical, 2008–12) earlier I believe I'd only just be finishing my career now. Instead, I only got 90 minutes of Premier League football.

I finally got back to full fitness for the 2006/07 season. Every time my contract was coming to an end I ended up playing, and that is where Wolves is a particularly caring club because they backed me in the bad times. Jez Moxey, our former chief executive, still believed in me, telling me to keep working hard and to get right.

The 2006/07 season was special in a different way to 2002/03. There had been a mass exodus of players. The manager, Glenn Hoddle, had left just before the season started, but we still had really good people in the building, like coaches Bobby Mimms and Terry Connor, unbelievable people who cared so much. But all the big players had gone: Paul Ince, Kenny Miller, Mark Kennedy and Joleon. We went to Spain for a pre-season tour and then Mick McCarthy came in. What a guy he is. It was unbelievable the way he brought players in, got the maximum out of everyone, brought together a whole club, and bought into the ethos of the club.

The thing that sticks out most about that season is when we got beaten 6-0 at home by Southampton and we got a standing ovation from our fans as we left the pitch. That is something that will live with me for the rest of my days. I had my pen pal over from Germany, who I'd been writing to since I was a kid. I got the golden glove for the most clean sheets in the league that season, yet the one game I fly a guy in from Germany for, who I hadn't seen since I was 15 years old, I let six in! I knew exactly where he was sitting in the stand, and I had to take him out for food later that evening. I felt like I was choking on every mouthful of that meal.

I felt right back at it that season, thinking I was finally over the injury nightmares. The fans were right behind us too, but then I broke my shoulder the day before the play-off semi-final against West Bromwich Albion. I landed on my shoulder going for a corner in training, it was just bad luck, so I had to work hard all summer to get back. I had a good pre-season, secured the number-one shirt again, and was thinking I'm going to play. Then I did my cruciate ligament in my knee for the second time and missed the whole season. It was just one setback after another. I ended up going to Hereford United on loan three months into the 2008/09 season. The first game I played for them was one of the best games I ever played in my life, a 3-0 win against Cheltenham Town. I was back up and running and thought I'd be pushing Wayne Hennessey and Carl Ikeme for a first-team spot. Then in my third game for Hereford, away at MK Dons, I struck a routine back pass with my left foot, and as I put my standing right leg down I ruptured my patella tendon. I lay there on the pitch and just cried.

As I was being taken off the pitch, one of the medics asked me if I was in pain and if I wanted gas and air. I told her I wasn't in pain even though my kneecap was half way down my leg. It was just all the emotions coming out. My wife at the time was pregnant with our second child, my Nanna was on her deathbed, the landlord who I had lived with from the age of 16, when I first went full time at Wolves, had had a stroke. It all just completely consumed me after that one moment on the pitch. My stepdad came and met me at the ambulance. I knew I was struggling, I'd worked so hard and I just couldn't get fit. I remember all the lads at Wolves ringing me. They'd just won a game at

Sheffield United but they'd heard I'd got injured so I was getting lots of calls from them, Terry Connor, Mick, and others in the management team.

I knew I was done, but when you get told the words that you are no longer a professional footballer any more, I can't explain what that sounds like. The bit that kills me is that I can't even have a kick-about today, I can't play in any of the charity games. But first and foremost, I wanted to be a dad, so I could do things with my kids and do a bit of coaching, so I knew the most important thing was not to do any further damage, even if that means not playing now.

There was also a sense of relief that I hadn't quit, that someone had done it for me. They put me out of my misery. But it was scary, it was all I'd ever known, it was part of my identity. My family were great, the club was great, they gave me an ambassador role, and they paid up my contract. Richard Skirrow [then club secretary] and Jez gave me a testimonial, the fans were overwhelming, the club was just amazing. I'm not going to lie, it was a dark and daunting moment. Professional clubs get stick over things like this, but from the fans, players, management, board – everybody – they were great at Wolves.

If you speak to Robbie, Joleon or anyone else who spent time here they'll tell you why Wolves gets hold of you. That's why we do these former players' nights – some of them you'll read about in this book – because coming back to Wolves is unique, especially if you have come through the system here.

I see it as a working man's place. You always knew the club was the pillar of the town, now the city, as it had a massive influence. It gives a lot of pride to so many. As long as you give your all they forgive an honest mistake. Yes, the expectations are high, but whenever you go on holiday you always see a Wolves fan, and there's a reason for that, it's because of the teams Billy Wright and Bert Williams played for back in the 1950s. And it's because, even in the bad times, Wolves represents so much.

I think of George Elokobi, who is one of those Johnny spoke to about his time here, and he became a cult hero because he played with his heart on his sleeve. George realised he was doing the best job in the world and that he was privileged. You always felt all those fans would do anything for the club, they had this committed passion. Matt Jarvis is another, a different character, but he gets so much respect as well because he understood the club. He loved coming to Wolves and strived to be the best he could be. When Jarvo used to be out after training, working on his left foot, his right foot, getting better and better, playing for England and becoming a household name, the Wolves fans were so proud. Just like they were proud of Steve Bull when he did it all those years earlier. It's the same with Jody Craddock. Jody said to me that when he retired he was ready because he knew he had been the best he could be, he had got the maximum out of his career. Supporters appreciate that.

When I was playing I remember Mick saying to us all once, 'You guys do the community visits and appearances. And if you do one second under an hour I'll fine you because those events with the fans, the schools and everything else, you're meeting fans who spend all their cash on going to watch Wolves, or buying the kits, and without them there's no us. I'll be there, so you be there.'

For any new signing coming to this club I would say, 'Go to the museum because then you'll understand where the club has been and why it's such a great club.' It's a unique place. At the moment I think they've still got the balance. They are going to another level and looking to get into that top six, but they've got the balance of what Wolves is about. And it's a club the fans believe belongs to them. It's not a commercial thing. Some clubs have gone that way, but Wolves have proper fans in the stadium, it's not just a day out. They work all week for that game.

It's a big club with a lot of history, a sense of identity. We haven't always been the most technically gifted – although that's starting to change – we like flair wingers, playing with width, but with real fight. That's where that song comes from, 'Fight, fight, wherever you may be'. You had to show you had fight. It got you up, when the supporters were behind you singing that. I'd get home at night and notice a big graze on my body or another knock and be wondering where it came from, but while we were playing the adrenaline came from that song.

It is amazing what is happening here now. I think the owners have come in with a real ambition, real vision, and they're backing the team. They're not here for the short term. But then I can still pop down to the training ground and see familiar faces. And then there's Nuno, who I think is a bit of a genius, with his brand of football and what he has done with the players, in particular Conor Coady and Matt Doherty. The style of football is incredible and the fans love it. This is the best Wolves team I've ever seen and the best brand of football I've ever witnessed at Molineux.

I hope they don't lose sight of what makes Wolves the club it is, though. They've got to tap into the commercial side, of course, and build the brand. But they've still got to know what the fabric and the identity of the place is. Wolves means the world to me, there's no club like it.

INTRODUCTION

'Change'

ON 21 July 2016 Wolverhampton Wanderers confirmed that they had been bought by Chinese investment conglomerate Fosun International. 'Our goal is crystal clear,' said the Championship club's incoming chairman, Jeff Shi. 'We will do our very best to help take Wolves back to the Premier League as soon as possible and to stay there. We believe the club and the fans belong at the top of English football and getting there is our first and top priority.'

It was the beginning of another chapter in the history of a club that, perhaps more than any other in this country, has been through both the best and the worst that professional football can offer.

For more than a quarter of a century Wolves had operated under the ownership of two British businessmen. Under their watch, Sir Jack Hayward and Steve Morgan ensured that the club would never return to the chaotic days of the 1980s, a period of time where its entire existence was threatened on more than one occasion. Such stability came as a blessing. Supporters could enjoy attending matches at Molineux without the concerns and fears they held throughout much of that decade.

When Sir Jack acquired the club in May 1990 from Gallagher Estates, it heralded a bright new era off the pitch. The new owner was a hugely popular local man who invested millions of pounds of his own money in rebuilding the ground, after Jack Harris and Dick Homden had formed a consortium four years earlier to rescue the club from administration with the help of Wolverhampton Council. Three sides of the ramshackle ground were knocked down and replaced. Molineux was transformed into a stadium fit for the Premier League. Meanwhile, manager Graham Turner's team, spearheaded by Steve Bull, had rebuilt Wolves on the pitch.

But it was also a long period of missed opportunities. Shi's comments were not the first time such ambitious words had fallen on the ears of eager supporters.

'Let's make Wolves the leading club in Britain once more,' said Sir Jack on his takeover 26 years earlier, in those days before the Premier League was formed. 'We want to get into the First Division and then win the First Division title, and we want to win the FA Cup. The name of Wolverhampton Wanderers is known all over the world and we want to make sure that continues.'

The 1990s, in particular, turned out to be a soul-destroying period of under-achievement. Supporters watched through gritted teeth as modestly resourced clubs like Oldham Athletic, Notts County, Swindon Town, Barnsley, Bolton Wanderers and Bradford City were all promoted to the top flight ahead of Wolves. Sir Jack eventually oversaw a promotion to the Premier League in 2003 but it turned out to be just a fleeting visit.

Under Morgan's tenure, a further three years at the top were secured. Grand plans were drawn up for another Molineux rebuild and land was secured to develop the club's training facility. The new Stan Cullis Stand was ready for the start of the 2012/13 season as part of a planned three-sided redevelopment, but the remaining two structures were never built. In 2014 the Category One status academy was officially opened at the club's Compton Park training base.

Both men left behind legacies off the pitch to be proud of. But at the end of the 2015/16 season, Morgan's final one as owner, Wolves occupied 14th position in the Championship with 58 points. It was virtually a replica of Sir Jack's very first season as owner. Back in 1990/91 Graham Turner's Wolves finished the campaign two places higher in the same division, with the same 58 points tally. In more than a quarter of a century of their ownership, Wolves spent just four years in the top division. They had, effectively, stood still.

Yet when Fosun arrived there was much scepticism about the new foreign ownership. Change is not always embraced. There was a stumbling start to the new regime. After publicly backing the manager in place, Kenny Jackett, it became clear that there had been manoeuvrings from the owners behind the scenes to bring in the former Porto coach Julen Lopetegui. But at the 11th hour Lopetegui accepted the job as Spain's head coach. Fosun's 'Plan A' was in tatters with the start of the new season just days away.

Jackett had known for some time that he was a dead man walking, but remained in his post for a week as speculation mounted about his future. He was eventually dismissed on 29 July 2016. A day later the club announced Walter Zenga as the new head coach, exactly a week before the season's opening game away at Rotherham United. It was the former Italian goalkeeper's 16th managerial post in just 18 years.

It represented a tumultuous beginning to Fosun's ownership. The words, at the time, of Wolves' much-loved vice president Rachael Heyhoe Flint echoed the fears of many supporters. 'Let us never forget the proud history and legacy of Wolverhampton Wanderers and respect all its traditions.' Fosun had upset the status quo.

The football industry makes a great play of traditions. Heritage is important to the identity of any club. But when examining the past, it is not always the case that history is represented as accurately as it should be. Wolves' traditions include three league titles, four FA Cups and two League Cups. The club played a key role in the birth of European club competition and produced many a home-grown international, including England's longest-serving captain, Billy Wright. But the last major honour was won four decades ago, in 1980, and memories of it are the preserve of an ageing band of supporters.

Just as important to Wolves' heritage and traditions are those days when the club could barely cobble a team together, when two sides of the ground were shut and another stand sat marooned like a beached whale 50 yards from the pitch. All this under an absentee ownership, the Bhatti brothers, who ran the entire operation into receivership. Wolves, at various times, has been both the pride and embarrassment of the city. Supporters fell in and out of love with the club too.

Yet it never died. Owners, managers and players can only be responsible for their own periods of time at a club. They represent the pieces in a jigsaw that is never finished. Fans carry the puzzle with them throughout a lifetime of support. *Bitten by Wolves* is an exploration of the different moments and eras in the club's history that have contributed to making it what it is today. It is a rich and colourful history. These changes that have taken place at Molineux over the generations have helped make it one of the most distinctive clubs in English football.

Fosun's opening three years at Molineux were, in many ways, a microcosm of the wider Wolves story. Hindsight has shown that they were willing to learn quickly from a muddled first season. Zenga enjoyed a promising start to the 2016/17 campaign, with two wins and two draws from the opening four games. But it was not long before serious concerns spread. Behind the scenes all was not running smoothly as overseas recruits failed to get to grips with the Championship. Zenga and general manager Andrea Butti rubbed many of the backroom staff up the wrong way with their new approach and abrupt style. 'Bacon Butti' was one of the less flattering nicknames to be overheard amongst some of the staff.

The approach to recruitment was different to anything the club had previously experienced, with an influx of unproven European players who appeared ill-equipped for the demands of second-tier English football.

In the event, Zenga's time at Wolves was brief even by his own track record. On 25 October 2016, after just 14 league games of the season, the Italian was dismissed with Wolves occupying 18th place in the Championship table. Zenga's 87-day tenure represented a chastening first few months in charge for Fosun. First-team coach Rob Edwards, assisted by under-23s coach Scott Sellars, was put in temporary charge while Fosun plotted their next move. Edwards remained in position for just two games before Paul Lambert was introduced as the club's third permanent manager in the space of little over three months.

Lambert masterminded a headline-grabbing FA Cup run, including a famous third-round victory against Jurgen Klopp's Liverpool at Anfield, but there was little progress in the league. It took a pair of impressive victories on the road in west London at Brentford and Fulham in March to lift the club away from any relegation danger.

There is no doubt Lambert would have expected another crack at the job for the following season. In April 2017, Shi gave an endorsement of the manager in an interview to the *Express and Star* newspaper: 'I like him very much – I chose him. When we choose a coach we think the character and personality is important,' he said. 'For Fosun our culture is about working hard, commitment and entrepreneurship. That's the culture in our group and also the formula for being successful all over the world as a company. For the club it's the same thing, we need a head coach to have the same genes as us.'

But the reality was that, as with Zenga before him, Lambert was only ever a stop-gap appointment. And as with

Jackett's dismissal a year earlier, the manner of his departure left a bad taste. Wolves were gaining a reputation as a 'hire and fire them' outfit. The consensus in the media was that Sir Jack would be 'turning in his grave'.

On 1 June 2017 Nuno Espírito Santo became the club's fourth permanent manager in less than a year. As the media gathered ahead of the press conference that morning in the Sir Jack Hayward Suite on the first floor of the Billy Wright Stand, the talk was along the lines of, 'Here we go again.' What was the next move going to be for a club whose reputation was becoming tarnished? What muddied the waters further was that the new head coach was the very first client of football agent Jorge Mendes.

In November 2015 Mendes had sold a 20 per cent stake in his Gestifute agency to a subsidiary of Fosun, Foyo Culture and Entertainment. When Fosun bought Wolves from Morgan in July 2016, they had gained Mendes as an adviser in their recruitment process. For months the British media had been questioning the ties between Mendes and Wolves' owners, despite that relationship being approved by the Football Association as far back as December 2016. There was a jingoistic tone to much of the coverage, suspicious of a foreign owner with an enviable contacts book.

Now Nuno was in the firing line. 'I am a client of the best agent in the world,' he explained at his unveiling. 'He does his job, I do my job. Being at Wolves, for us, is a big challenge as coaches. We know after the big clubs we have coached before with success that we had options, very nice options. But we are here to work and make Wolves a better team. So this is important, that the people who are here physically – day by day at the club – these are the people who are going to make Wolves a better club, and a club that can proudly regain the success of the 50s and 60s. This is what we hope to do.'

With his coaching team watching on from the back of the room, Nuno outlined his vision further. 'We will bring commitment and we will try to make the players better each day. We are a coaching staff that really looks to develop the players. We can bring hard work, organisation, good planning and strategy. Things that we believe can make Wolves a better team and a winning team. We believe that our idea can succeed.'

Shi's commitment to making a success of the club was illustrated by his decision to move his family from their home in Shanghai, China, and set up residency in Wolverhampton. The mistakes made during the first season of Fosun's ownership were recognised and acted upon. But not even the most optimistic Wolves supporter could have imagined the journey the team would go on between August and May of the 2017/18 campaign. The Championship title was secured playing a style of football that had never before been seen at Molineux.

Nuno and his team had captured the hearts of a fan base. Supporters took ownership of the success. The appetite to share experiences and memories grew as the season progressed. Fans proudly showed off this new identity that had been bestowed upon them. Wolves finished the season in style, celebrating the Championship title with a thumping 4-0 win at Bolton Wanderers in front of almost 5,000 visiting supporters in late April.

On the first Bank Holiday Monday of May, the whole city was able to show their appreciation of the team. Tens of thousands lined the streets of Wolverhampton for an open-top bus parade that headed to West Park for a promotion party in front of another 30,000 supporters. The club entered the summer on an incredible high. Never before had a Premier League season been so eagerly anticipated. Fosun's short tenure had reinvigorated a whole supporter base. Word from Shanghai was that the international conglomerate now regarded Wolves as 'the jewel in the crown' of their overseas investments.

In 2018/19 the most expensively assembled team in the club's history left its mark on the Premier League, qualifying for Europe for the first time in almost 40 years. It was clear, as the season progressed, that the club was changing before our eyes. Changing again.

The stories documented in these pages were collected during Wolves' first year back at the top under Fosun's ownership. This is a club that has taken on many guises since its heyday as champions of England. Here are the accounts of those who have played unique roles in observing or shaping Wolves over several decades, from the glory days of the 1950s that Nuno referred to at his unveiling, to the darker moments and sometimes forgotten times.

No other club in England has experienced such a broad spectrum of highs and lows. This collection of interviews, stories and events paints a picture of how Wolves have become the club of today. Supporters, former heroes, staff and others have shared their own individual tales. Including behind-the-scenes insight from the current management and players, *Bitten by Wolves* is a journey through the soul of an iconic football club.

Chapter 1

THE HISTORIAN

'Every club needs a Graham Hughes'

WOLVES SUPPORTERS are walking up to Molineux for the opening game of the 2018/19 season with a sense of anticipation not witnessed here for generations. It is the first season of Premier League football under the ownership of Fosun International. Navigating the close season is always easier when there is nothing to look forward to. No hope or belief. But this was a summer that tantalised like no other, filled with so much expectation.

The memorable Championship winners' promotion parade around the city is still fresh in the mind, when over 80,000 lined the streets of Wolverhampton and West Park on that May Bank Holiday. The new kit, the new Premier League fixture list, the new players. Most of all the new players. Fosun backed up the previous season's expenditure with another round of squad-strengthening. Mexican striker Raúl Jiménez arrived on loan from Benfica. Full-back Jonny Castro Otto came in on loan from Atletico Madrid. The club-record transfer fee was broken when capturing Spanish winger Adama Traoré from Middlesbrough for £18million.

But it was the signing of Portuguese star João Moutinho that genuinely stunned supporters. The 31-year-old arrived from Monaco on a two-year deal for just £5million. The midfielder stands as the third-most-capped player in Portugal's history, after Cristiano Ronaldo and Luis Figo. In addition to 113 caps for Portugal, he was a key member of the team that won the European Championships in 2016. He also has three Portuguese league titles, three Portuguese cups, the Europa League and a Ligue One title on his curriculum vitae.

All around, there are signs of change. The infamous subway underneath the city ring road, once a congregating point for crowd disorder in the 1970s and 80s, has been given a bright and colourful makeover. An admirable collaboration of club, university and council. A timeline of images, from the club's formation in 1877 to the current team of Championship title-winners, adorn the walls.

The Civic Centre piazza has been transformed into an inner-city beach, playing host to a pre-match entertainment roster of events such as penalty shoot-outs, football darts, table football and face-painting. Local radio station, Signal FM, have brought their roadshow to the event, with live music being performed. Street food stalls and a bar ensure the hundreds of supporters who have been drawn to the fan park are fed and watered. It is not everyone's cup of tea, but it is a thoughtful and concerted effort by the club and city council to put something more into the matchday and modernise a day out at the football.

Yet Wolves are unable to escape their history. It is all around them. The Billy Wright Stand and Stan Cullis Stand are the two largest structures of the four stands. Statues of the two giant figures of Wolves' glorious past watch over fans as they wander up to the turnstiles. At the worst of times it has weighed heavily on the subsequent custodians, almost a shameful reminder that the club should be doing better. At its best, the club's illustrious past acts as a guardian, as if watching over owners, management and players, checking that they are aware of what has been achieved here, inspiring them to aim higher. History is strange like that.

The seemingly unattainable benchmark for any success at this club is the 1950s. Wolves ended the 1949/50 season as the second-best team in the country, missing out on the league title, on goal difference alone, to Portsmouth. They finished the 1959/60 season lifting the FA Cup at Wembley, pipped to a league and cup double by Burnley by just a single point.

During the ten years between those points, under the iron-fist management of Cullis and led on the field by the England captain Wright, they won three league titles. Wolves were the pioneers of international club football during this time, hosting prestigious floodlit friendlies against the top sides in Europe, which in turn led to the inception of the European Cup in 1955.

A museum at Molineux, inside the Stan Cullis Stand, charts the history of the club from its inception to the present day. There is also a smaller display of artefacts in the reception area inside the main entrance of the Billy Wright Stand. On any given matchday, the club's current custodians will walk past this display on their way to the first-floor boardroom. Jeff Shi is the Wolves chairman, appointed by the owners Fosun International. Occasionally he will be accompanied by Guo Guangchang, chairman of the Chinese conglomerate itself. Jorge Mendes, football's widely tagged 'super agent' and unofficial adviser to the owners, also checks in from time to time.

On hand to greet the owners, officials and the steady stream of guests who walk through the doors each matchday is Graham Hughes. Although, sometimes, he will have to take a seat and watch the arrivals go by. The years have taken their toll on Graham, who walks with the aid of a frame now. Aged 86, he has seen more than most. First as a supporter, and later as an employee, Graham carries with him more than just the history of the club. He holds some of its secrets too.

Graham began his job as the club's dressing room attendant 30 years ago, although that job title does not do justice to the roles he has undertaken at the club, which have ranged in variety from running the post-match baths, stadium maintenance, sorting the post, tending the pitch and arranging players' tickets. 'Every club needs a Graham Hughes,' said former manager Mick McCarthy during his time here.

'I used to help out here back in the 1981/82 season and then I went full time in 1989,' Graham recalls. 'Everybody mucked in. The motto in those days was, "If the job wants doing, do it."'

But his association with the club began much further back. 'The first game I can remember is against West Bromwich Albion in the 1941/42 season,' he says. 'It was the semi-final of the wartime League Cup. That was when Billy Wright broke his ankle and he had to come off. In those days they used to open the gates about 20 minutes before the end, so, as we had no money, we used to come in. Sometimes we'd sneak in, but one day we got chucked out by one of the directors. To work here now, well, it's a privilege and an honour.'

When the club built their museum in 2012, Graham played an important role. 'Being a collector as well, it's great,' he adds. 'There's over 25,000 items in it. The earliest thing we've got is from 1730, a brass kettle from the Molineux Hotel.' Graham points to an old sheet of paper that has been delicately laid out in his reception display. 'This is the wage book for the 1888/89 season.'

Graham was a teenager when the country's post-war football boom began. Wolves' attendances would regularly break 50,000 as the club swiftly established itself at the top. Christmas Day 1948 is etched in his mind – not for anything that happened on the pitch, more for the unconventional build-up to a home fixture with Aston Villa, during an era when games were played on 25 and 26 December, usually against the same team.

'We cycled in from Codsall, which is five miles away, with my brother on the crossbar,' says Graham, recounting the story with a smile. 'He put his foot in the front wheel and I went straight over the handlebars, there was blood everywhere. We were about 200 yards from the village doctor. So I got into the surgery and he patched me up. My wheel was wobbling away, but we still got to the match.'

In the 1990s, as a member of staff, Graham was knocked off his bike again. This time the players had a whip-round to buy him a new one, along with a high-visibility jacket. He saw the funny side, continuing to cycle in to work until the years caught up with him more recently.

Back in those halcyon days as a supporter, it wasn't just the bike he relied on to get to the ground. More often than not he would bump into the heroes who helped Wolves become one of the giants of the English game. Wright, the man who captained England on 90 occasions, was one of those who would join supporters on their journey to Molineux.

'He was on the same bus that we got to the match,' Graham explains. 'Five past one bus from Codsall. Billy Wright used to get on halfway and it was always packed. He'd walk through with all the supporters, who'd be shouting, "Have a good game Billy." And he'd reply, "And you enjoy it."'

Graham reveals that when Wright was made captain of England the news was broken to the player on the bus.

'He was coming back home from the match one day, on the bus, and the conductor said, "Congratulations, you've just been made captain of England." It was in the stop press of the *Express and Star*, but he didn't know about it.'

Wright is regarded as the club's greatest player. He was made captain of Wolves in 1947, taking over from Cullis, who became assistant manager to Ted Vizard before taking the managerial reins a year later. After captaining England in the 1950 World Cup, Wright won the Footballer of the

Year in 1952. He was the inspirational leader on the pitch during the club's three title wins, making 541 appearances before his retirement in 1959. A colossus of the game, who caught a bus to the match with the supporters.

'Wolves were the first club to sign a television deal, you know,' Graham continues. 'When they played Honved. They only had two cameras, like. They agreed on a match fee of £600 to televise the second half of the match. I've still got the letter that Sir Stanley Rous had written down.'

The floodlit friendlies are as much about European football history as they are about Wolves'. In 1953 the club installed floodlights at Molineux at a cost of £10,000. A number of friendlies were organised against international opposition, including Racing Club Buenos Aires, First Vienna, Spartak Moscow and Honved. They captured the public's imagination at a time before the advent of European club football.

The Honved fixture, on 13 December 1954, broke new ground. A crowd of 54,998 packed inside Molineux for the game. Wolves wore a specially made shiny satin shirt, designed to stand out under the floodlights for the benefit of millions of television viewers, who were watching live night-time football for the first time.

The match took place a year after England had been stunned by Hungary at Wembley, losing 6-3 to a Ferenc Puskas-inspired side, and just six months after the Hungarians had routed England 7-1 in Budapest. Honved were the champions of Hungary and their side contained five of the 'Mighty Magyars' team who finished runners-up in the 1954 World Cup Final. Wolves were champions of England, scoring 96 goals on the way to their first league title under Cullis.

The game was billed as a European club final by the international press. When Wolves came back from 2-0 down to win 3-2, the British press was enthralled. Peter Wilson, a widely respected Fleet Street sports journalist, wrote in the *Daily Mirror*, 'I may never live to see a greater thriller than this. And if I see many more as thrilling I may not live much longer anyway.'

Headlines such as 'Hail Wolves – Champions of the World' and 'Wolves The Great' were written. This reaction was greeted with scepticism in the European press. It set in motion a chain of events that led to the formation of the European Cup.

In France, *L'Equipe's* football editor, Gabriel Hanot, a former French international and long-time proponent of a European club competition, wrote, 'Before we declare that Wolverhampton are invincible, let them go to Moscow and Budapest. And there are other internationally renowned clubs, Milan and Real Madrid to name but two. A club world championship, or at least a European one, should be launched.'

L'Equipe produced a format for a European club competition, to be considered by UEFA. The UEFA congress of March 1955 saw the proposal raised, with approval given in April. The first-ever European Cup competition was held in the 1955/56 season. But Wolves could not retain their title. Instead, it was Chelsea who won the First Division, only to be barred from entering the tournament by a Football Association concerned that their participation would affect domestic midweek attendances. The FA relented the following season, and Wolves entered the competition for the first time in 1958, after securing their second league title of the decade.

By then, Wright's career was drawing to a close and his half-back colleague Bill Slater was emerging as the natural successor as captain. Graham recalls, with great fondness, the time Slater walked through the Molineux reception doors ahead of Manchester City's match here in 2003.

'He had his grandson with him. I saw him in reception and Bill asked if it was possible to get some Manchester City players' autographs, because his grandson was a City fan,' Graham explains. 'As it was early, I just knocked on the away dressing room door. Kevin Keegan, who was their manager, opened the door. I said, "Bill Slater would like some autographs." He said, "Bill Slater? Bring him in." So he came in with his grandson and had photographs taken with all the players.'

Four months into the 2018/19 season, in December, Slater passed away at the age of 91. There are very few more iconic photographs in the history of Wolves than the one of Slater holding up the FA Cup at Wembley in 1960, sat on the shoulders of Ron Flowers and Peter Broadbent. Slater was a unique figure in the history of Wolves. His was a career that was fulfilled just as much away from the game as in the throes of title battles and cup finals. Slater was the last of the great amateurs.

His move to Wolves happened purely because of a posting in his professional day job. He was appointed as a lecturer of physical education at Birmingham University in 1952. His early career with Blackpool and Brentford had always played second fiddle to his academic studies. When he was posted to Birmingham he wrote to Cullis asking for a game. On signing, he received a stern rebuke from the disciplinarian manager because he had politely asked only for a match with any of the club's teams. Cullis told him that he wanted men with ambition whose only desire was to play for the first XI.

Two months after signing amateur terms, Slater made his debut in October 1952, replacing Wright, who was playing for England that day. It was an unforgettable experience as Wolves thumped Manchester United, the champions of England, 6-2.

The three league titles Slater won in the 1950s owed much to the strength in depth of the half-back positions. He earned an international call-up for England, along with team-mates Wright, Eddie Clamp and Ron Flowers. It was Slater, Clamp and Wright who made up England's half-back line on three occasions at the 1958 World Cup finals, on one occasion famously shutting out eventual champions Brazil, who averaged three goals a game in their other matches.

Incredibly, Slater's trip to represent his country left him out of pocket. He was given leave of absence by the university but his wages were docked accordingly. The Football Association's own expenses for players representing their country did not quite cover the loss of earnings. Cullis persuaded Slater to turn semi-professional during his time at Wolves. His ten-pound signing-on fee came with the player's stipulation that he be allowed to carry on teaching at Birmingham University.

A young Alan Hinton joined the club in 1957 and, on hearing of his passing, recalled the dedication Slater showed to his football: 'He often ran alone around Molineux in afternoons when he missed normal Wolves sessions due to his university lecturing job,' Hinton revealed. 'He always pushed himself to keep his fitness. A real gentleman.'

Graham, and all those who knew him, describe a man of great humility and dignity. Cullis himself acknowledged as much during a dinner at the Victoria Hotel in Wolverhampton, held in Slater's honour, in 1963. 'I know of no one who created a greater impact on the players at Molineux than Bill, with his self-discipline, good behaviour and sportsmanship. I wish we had many more like him.'

After leaving Wolves, a short second spell at Brentford followed, before Slater retired from football and went on to become director of physical education at Liverpool University. As well as his academic post, he became warden of McNair hall of residence and enjoyed his time participating with students in the competitive halls league each week. There he earned a reputation for never crossing the halfway line unless McNair were losing, in which case he would amble forward and invariably come to the students' rescue.

His successful career continued as he later took a role on the National Olympic Committee, before becoming president of the British Amateur Gymnastics Association. In 1982 he was awarded the OBE and in 1998 he received a CBE, both for services to sport.

But that iconic portrait at Wembley is a fitting way to remember his talents on the pitch. To become captain of one of the very finest teams in England was a monumental achievement. He was named Football Writers' Association Footballer of the Year the season he lifted the cup, as Wolves finished just a point away from a league and cup double. Slater's passing breaks another tie with that golden age, but he will be remembered as a true great. Only the senior generation of supporters can recall what it was like to follow Wolves in that golden age, but the stories have been handed down by men like Graham.

Back in 2012, the club held a retirement reception in Graham's honour, not because he was retiring – he'd never do that – but just to mark three decades of service as he approached his 80th birthday. Graham Taylor, who managed the club in the mid-90s, was one of those who paid him a fitting tribute. 'He's a first-class man. All my memories of him are good ones,' said the former England manager. 'As a manager I always considered it important to be surrounded by good people and you knew he was very loyal. You never had to worry about him talking behind your back or saying something out of place.'

Goalkeeper Mike Stowell, who joined the club before the redevelopment of the ground in the early 90s, remembered how players became reliant on him. 'There would always be leaks from the home dressing room roof when it rained, sometimes so bad that we had to stand on the benches to get changed,' he added. 'Hughesie never complained though. He'd just get his mop and bucket out and clean the place up. They were character-building days and we looked on him as our one luxury.'

Even now, he is known to wander out on to the pitch while the groundsmen are mowing the grass to take over the lawnmower for a few steps. 'He is the life of Wolves,' says one of the ground staff, Chris Lane. 'I don't think that there is one member of staff here who he doesn't know.' Graham's work on a matchday is restricted to a meet-and-greet role these days. He retains a sharp sense of humour. When asked how he is feeling ahead of kick-off, he replies, 'I don't think I'll make it, my pace has gone.' John Bowater, one of the club's directors, takes Graham in to his executive suite to enjoy the match now that he no longer has the mobility to work in the dressing rooms.

Years after most people are enjoying retirement, Graham continues to devote his life to Wolves. He has had other jobs, and national service of course, but none of them quite compare to this. 'I used to be in the heating trade in the south-west, working all over that region,' he adds. 'But it's just great being part of the club that I've supported since 1941. It's a privilege and an honour. I still get the buzz now. We get people from all over the world coming to see us. I remember an American chap who came here. He'd come over to London to go to university. He was walking through London Euston station and he saw one of the platform destination signs reading "Wolverhampton", so he said to his mate, "I'll see you later." He just got on the train and came here. He signed the visitors' book in reception. They come from all over the world.' And when they arrive, Graham Hughes is on hand to tell them everything they need to know.

Chapter 2

DEVOTION

The Travels and Travails of Wolves Supporters

London Wolves

The 08:43 train to Edinburgh Waverley has just pulled out of platform six at London Euston. Thirty-three of the passengers sat in coach F were given their own escort to their seats from station staff. They are, after all, some of Virgin Trains' most loyal customers. Long before the west coast mainline was taken over by the franchise, members of the oldest Wolves supporters' club in the country were making their regular weekend pilgrimage along this route to Wolverhampton. On this particular Saturday morning, in mid-December, they are heading to Molineux to watch Wolves host Bournemouth.

London Wolves were founded in 1966. Secretary Dave Slape has been with them from the start. 'There were about ten or 12 of us travelling independently on the trains from Paddington and we used to bump into each other,' he explains, in between passing a 'Guess The Scores' card around the carriage. At one pound a go, it is not going to make anyone a millionaire, but it is a valuable way of raising funds.

'We just got together and decided to form a club. We put out a few flyers at football games and we got enough people to put on a coach. It was ten shillings [50 pence] to go and if there were a few less it would be 15 shillings. When it started tailing off a bit by the 1968/69 season it was getting too expensive, and then we ran a train trip to the Burnley cup game in January 1970.'

That third-round FA Cup tie ended in a 3-0 defeat at Turf Moor. But the consolation for London Wolves was that they had found a discounted way of travelling by rail, through British Rail's group booking offer.

The brains behind the travel operation today is Peter Woodifield. He has been the travel secretary since 1987. Armed with an A4 logbook, he is patrolling the carriage collecting fares from members ahead of today's match against Bournemouth. It has cost the supporters a bargain £23 each for a return ticket, although Woodifield did manage to secure a trip for just £16 earlier in the season, which is no mean feat when up against a private rail franchise in this day and age.

'The beauty about moving to the trains was that you only had to get ten people to do a trip. You don't have to worry about filling a coach up,' Slape continues. 'We easily get that. We ran a coach to Man City in 1968/69, it was a night game that we lost 3-2, and it cost the equivalent of £2.50 each. That was a third of a week's wages at the time. We spent all that money to go to one away game.'

'The coaches were getting smashed up at games in those days, too,' adds Stuart Earl. 'We used to park at West Park for home games and once the coach got mistaken for an away supporters' coach and the Wolves fans smashed it up. Then there was the time we bumped into Millwall fans at a service station on the M1, which was trouble.'

Earl has been the chairman of London Wolves since 1985. Now in his 70th year, he admits that Woodifield and Slape are the two who put the hard yards in.

'I've formed lifelong friendships. Dave was best man at my wedding,' he adds. 'The dedication of Dave and Peter is incredible, they are so trustworthy. They run the club on their own. Stef and I just pop our heads in every now and then.'

Stef Leonard, the vice chairman, is another regular on these trips. There is hardly a Black Country accent in earshot, as the members explain how they became hooked on Wolves. Most are genuine Londoners. Stef was one of the few members born in Wolverhampton, but he only lived there with his Polish parents until the age of two, before moving to London's East End.

'When I was five, in 1953, I came home from school one day and my mum asked me what I had been doing,' he explains. 'I said I had played football in the playground and had been Wolves. My mum said, "Well you are Wolves, you were born there." And of course, in 1953/54 we won our first title. My first game was away to Arsenal in the 1957/58 season. It's been a lifelong love since that day in 1953.'

'I've always lived around Norbury and the Croydon area,' Slape adds. 'It was just the colours, that kit, that got me hooked. I was given a cigarette card book as a boy. Everyone in it was wearing red, white or blue except for one team – Wolves. Crystal Palace were in the book but nobody said I should follow them. They were only one stop down the line and I could have watched them every week.'

'I remember the Honved game on black-and-white television,' Earl says. 'Wolves were the only team we saw back then. And I'd pick them out in the paper reports. So I thought that when I could afford to see them I would go, it was mainly in London. Travel was a lot longer then. When we went to Molineux the train would leave Paddington at 9:15 in the morning and get into Wolverhampton Low Level station at ten past one. I can practically recite the old British Rail timetable.'

From the outset, the football club took London Wolves under their wing. 'We got to a game really early one day and the gates were open so we just walked in and had a look around,' says Slape. 'Jack Howley [then Wolves secretary] saw us and asked what we were doing so we explained ourselves and he said whenever we came up he'd make sure we got in.'

'Jack introduced me to John Ireland [then chairman] and told him that as we'd travelled all that way we shouldn't have to pay for tickets,' Earl adds. 'From then on I just phoned Jack in advance and told him how many of us were coming up and the tickets would be there. In the end it got a bit embarrassing so we agreed that they'd just reserve the tickets if it was a sell-out, but we started to pay for ourselves.'

At its peak the club had over 400 members. The record for members travelling on one trip stands at 108, for the 1981 FA Cup semi-final at Hillsborough against Tottenham Hotspur. The hardest times came around just four years later, with Wolves sliding down the divisions.

'When we went down to play in the Third Division [1985/86], I'd say that was the worst season,' says Woodifield. 'Although we had two seasons after that in the old Fourth Division, you could see we were going back up by then. That Third Division season took some doing.'

It is the lengths London Wolves go to while following the team that best illustrates their dedication. During their first season of trips there was a memorable day at Huddersfield in March 1967 when they didn't arrive until half an hour into the match. 'It was with a firm called Cresta Coaches. They were the only company we could get as all the other ones wanted a deposit in advance,' Earl recalls. 'It was a small operation in Hounslow and they agreed that as long as we paid the driver before we got on they'd take us. We broke down several times on the way there and eventually the coach conked out the other side of this big hill on the way in to Huddersfield. We pushed it all the way up to the top, then all got back on and the coach driver free-wheeled down to the ground.'

'After the game we were playing football in the Huddersfield car park and one of the Huddersfield directors came out and asked us what we were doing,' Woodifield adds. 'We told him we were waiting for a replacement coach so he invited us back into the boardroom while we waited. The coach never came. He offered to lend us the fare for train tickets back to London if we promised to send him the money back. We ended up going home by train. We all paid him back.'

The rail network has not always proved reliable either. After a win at Sunderland in September 1993, a game notable for a wonderful solo goal from Geoff Thomas before he suffered a season-ending injury late in the match, the train back to London took several hours longer than expected to reach its destination.

'We had two signal failures on the way back and then the train caught fire,' Woodifield says. 'We got as far as Welwyn Garden City and were just stuck there for four hours. Eventually we carried on to Kings Cross, where they laid on cabs to get everybody home as it was Sunday morning by then. We won that one so we weren't too bothered, although there were a couple of Sunderland fans on the train who weren't too happy.'

'They've all been great adventures,' Earl concludes. 'The journey is half the battle. It's great having a few drinks and a game of cards. We can't do that as much these days because of the layout of the trains. The old British Rail coaches had individual compartments where you could get eight in together and put a table up in the middle. It was a more social sing-song in those days.'

Today's train is on time, which is just as well as London Wolves need to squeeze in their Christmas party at a local pub before taking in the Bournemouth match. There is one trip that has gone down in folklore, though. In 1979 Wolves had a midweek fifth-round League Cup tie away at Grimsby Town to negotiate on a typically uninviting, cold December evening. It coincided with the birthday of then treasurer Terry Peachey.

'We had 38 going on a night game to Grimsby, where we didn't get back to London till half six the following morning,' Slape proudly recalls. 'The trains were brilliant in 1979. We were told we couldn't get off at the local station for Grimsby Town, which was New Clee, but they stopped the train anyway. The guard got off and wandered down the track with a lantern and we all followed him. He opened a side gate for us so we could all get off the tracks and go on to the game.

'After the match we had to go to Cleethorpes station, though. We got on the train and it was full of Wolves fans. There was a party atmosphere because of Terry's birthday. Lots of drink going around and it was a really happy time, no trouble or anything. Then we changed at Doncaster and had an hour and a half wait for the London train, so we just went out of the station and found a local disco.'

A disco in Doncaster on a Tuesday night in December. The stuff of away-day travel dreams. So how did the match finish? 'Oh, it was 0-0.'

Odin Henrikssen

The rain is persistent and falling at a near horizontal angle, making it difficult to look too far ahead. 'This is Bergen, on most days,' says Odin Henrikssen, as he hurries across the airport parking bays to the sanctuary of his car. We jump in the vehicle and begin the short drive to Hop, a smart suburb in the south of Bergen, no more than 15 minutes from the city's airport. 'We had bright sunshine yesterday,' he explains, apologetically. 'But this is a typical day in Bergen. It rains a lot here.' On average, 240 days each year.

Bergen, on Norway's west coast, is overlooked by the Seven Mountains, making it a picturesque location on a clear day. But on this cold, wintry afternoon, with thick clouds hanging over the bays and inlets along the rocky coast, there is no view to enjoy. Bergen is the second-largest city in Norway, after Oslo, and it is here that one of Wolves' most devoted supporters has built something special.

Odin's day job is as an engineering project manager for Equinor, a broad energy company that develops oil, gas, wind and solar energy. But he works to live, and he lives for Wolves. Odin is a season-ticket holder, despite the impracticalities of travel to home matches at Molineux. Born in 1962, he has been following the club for almost 50 years. As we drive along the near-empty rain-lashed roads, Odin explains how he became hooked on Wolves.

'It started back in the early 70s. My uncle, Atle, went to Wolverhampton in 1966 to attend university there. He stayed until 1972, but he would come home with pictures and autographs of the players. So that's why I'm a Wolves fan. He got to know the players. He was studying to be a physiotherapist and he went down to Molineux to work with the players. That was it, when he came home and told me about all this I really liked his stories, and the colours of the team. I became a fan, and I have been ever since.'

Odin is a member of Viking Wolves, a 200-strong Norwegian supporters' club, who make regular pilgrimages to the United Kingdom to watch their team in action.

'I don't remember it, but the first live game ever shown in Norway was in November 1969. It was Wolves against Sunderland, Hugh Curran scored the goal, and they won 1-0,' Odin adds. 'Halfway through the broadcast they had to abandon showing it, I think they had a lot of technical problems. But that's why a lot of Norwegians are Wolves fans, it was the first game ever shown here. Many of the fans are my age because there wasn't a lot of live football on television then, but we had the English games on television and Wolves were one of the teams. I saw the two League Cup finals [in 1974 and 1980] live on television.'

As he turns the car into his driveway, Odin explains that we will not be entering the house through the front door, but by a special entrance he has had built around the side of the building. Walking along the side of the house, there is still no clue as to what lies ahead, until he opens a side door to reveal the club's wolf head badge on the inside of the door. 'Welcome to my museum.'

Through a short hallway, we walk into a large room that has been converted into a shrine to Wolves. There are shirts hung all around the walls. There are photographs, paintings, programmes, books, badges, boots, newspapers and much more. Large cabinets house a lifetime's collection of artefacts related to the club. A screen in the corner is showing Wolves matches from the 70s. This museum would not look out of place at Molineux, yet here it is in the basement of a suburban house on Norway's west coast.

'It started when I was around ten or 11 years old,' Odin explains. 'I remember getting my first scarf. I kind of started to collect things without knowing it in a way. It just grew more and more over the years. I ended up keeping so much stuff in boxes and cupboards. We moved into this house four years ago, and when we moved I had so much stuff packed up, a whole room full of this stuff. Then Cecilie, my wife, said that we should make it into a Wolves museum. I thought, "Why not?" We moved here in June 2015 and had a big house-warming party in August, so we worked the whole summer to get this room ready. My wife was the brains behind how to present it all.'

Odin's two grown-up sons, Jonas and Fredrick, are Wolves supporters, as is his stepson, Sander, from his marriage to Cecilie. She is a Liverpool supporter, though, but has been slowly encouraged to share her allegiances with Wolves, travelling over to matches with Odin a couple of times each year.

'It's fantastic, I admire his passion for it,' Cecilie says. 'He's really protective of his collection and it has a value.

He showed me some of the things and I said he should put everything on display, it's too good to be stowed away. I like his old scrapbooks from when he was a kid. He was so thorough, it's amazing he has kept them for so long.'

Odin began compiling his scrapbooks at the start of the 1973/74 season. A large Norwegian newsagent, Narvesen, sold English newspapers at the time.

'One kiosk wasn't far from my home where I took the school bus,' he adds. 'So, every Monday, I would look at all the papers on the stand. Sometimes I would be told off by the vendor for spending too long there without buying one. But I wanted to make sure I found the one with the best pictures and the largest article about Wolves, and then I'd buy that. I started to write down all the scores and cut out the reports in the papers. They wrote a lot about English football in the sports pages here.'

Of the estimated 160 shirts in his collection, at least 60 of them have been match-worn by the players. Odin counts a reserve shirt from the 1980 League Cup Final and the last-ever shirt worn by former striker John Richards – signed, of course – as his favourites.

Growing up, a trip to England to watch Wolves play was never an option, but eventually, in 1984, the family holidayed in Wales and Odin's dream of a visit to Wolverhampton became a reality.

'We took a ferry from Bergen to Newcastle and went to Wales, but my father had promised me we would go to Wolverhampton,' Odin says. 'So in the end, just before we went back home, we went there and I watched them train at Castlecroft. It was fantastic, I remember coming into Wolverhampton and seeing the sign for the town, it was unbelievable!

'I went to Castlecroft to watch them train on a very nice summer's day. I met Tommy Docherty, the manager then, I've got a picture with him in my scrapbook. They had just been relegated to the Second Division; it was the start of the dark period. I spoke to the Doc, he asked me if I played football, and he said I could have trained with them as they had so few players. The only player left from the 70s was Geoff Palmer.'

Nowadays, home matches are a regular event in the Henrikssen calendar. 'I leave home before six o'clock in the morning and take a plane from Bergen direct to Gatwick that leaves at ten past seven. Then I get the train up to London Victoria station, get the Victoria Line tube up to Euston and take a train from Euston that arrives in Wolverhampton at 12:37pm, to be exact.'

Once in England, Odin is at the whim of the country's rail network, but more often than not his travel is hassle-free. Then, after the game he stays at a hotel in Wolverhampton before heading back down to Gatwick for a Sunday morning flight home. There have been occasions when all has not gone to plan, though.

'I was going on a business trip to Denver, Colorado, and I didn't tell my wife at the time that I was going to stop in Wolverhampton on my way home,' he explains. 'It was a really tight schedule, going from the United States to Amsterdam and then to Birmingham and back to Norway the next day. The schedule was so tight that when I landed at Birmingham International it was already 2:30pm on Saturday afternoon. I had everything planned. I was in seat 1A on the plane and I had a backpack with no other hold luggage, so I just ran off the plane and straight into a taxi, and shouted "Molineux" to the driver.

'I arrived at the ground 20 minutes into the game, but I still didn't have a ticket. So I went to the ticket office and picked one up. I missed the first half hour, but it was still 0-0. We actually won 1-0, against Manchester City, and it was our first-ever victory in the Premier League. It was in October 2003, we still hadn't won up to then.

'There have also been games that have been postponed. Last season I went over for the Reading game, and Wolverhampton was like Norway in the middle of the winter. There was a snowstorm and the game was called off, so we went to see Leicester play Bournemouth instead.'

As we wander around the museum admiring the artefacts in display cabinets, a half-eaten cake covered in pink icing with a large Wolves badge in the centre stands out.

'It is getting a little bit pink now,' Odin admits. 'But it was gold a couple of years ago. It is my wedding cake from two years ago, made by my stepsister. No one dared eat the logo so I kept it. It's hard as a stone now.'

Odin's love of Wolves is almost all-consuming. 'Many people have asked me how much money I've used on Wolves, I really don't care,' he says. 'It's a passion, it's a lifestyle, it's not so important for me, it's worth it, absolutely.'

Later this year, Odin and Cecilie will host Viking Wolves' 30th anniversary party, when Norwegian Wolves fans from all over the country will congregate at their home. Several supporters from England are due to travel over to the event as well as some of the players Odin idolised growing up, including Kenny Hibbitt, John Richards and Steve Daley.

But before the party, there was a significant date at Wembley to arrange, as the 2018/19 season drew to a close. Odin and Cecilie joined 40-odd members of Viking Wolves in north London for the club's first FA Cup semi-final in 21 years. The match against Watford on Sunday, 7 April ended in an agonising defeat. With just 11 minutes remaining, and leading 2-0, Wolves looked to be heading to a first FA Cup Final since 1960. But, uncharacteristically, they conceded two late goals, including a penalty in added time. Watford completed the comeback in extra time with a decisive third.

Typically, Odin's journey to the match was not a straightforward one. He travelled on Sunday morning from Copenhagen after an unavoidable work excursion, only collecting his tickets on arrival at the ground. It might have been a difficult trip for some, but for this Wolves supporter there is no such thing as an arduous journey when Wolves are involved.

Chapter 3

SEVENTIES ICON

A round with Kenny Hibbitt

AN EARLY morning haze is lingering over the western edge of the Cotswold Hills, the sun not yet high enough to burn the autumn moisture from the air. There is the odd flutter of wings between the trees, but nothing else to disturb the stillness as Kenny Hibbitt prepares to tee up. Without even bothering to go through the motions of a practice stroke, he addresses his ball. One elegant swing later and his drive is flying straight as an arrow down the middle of the first fairway. It is a hard act to follow, but the former Wolves midfielder is the easiest company over the next three hours as we plot our way around the stunning Cotswold Edge Golf Club, his home track.

Hibbitt was a central figure during the last period of time when Wolves could be regarded as a force in English football. Between 1968 and 1984 he made 574 appearances, placing him second on Wanderers' all-time list. The club's fourth-place finish in the 1970/71 First Division season would earn a Champions League berth these days, but back then it was qualification for the UEFA Cup. It was one of three top-six finishes for Wolves over the next ten years, which also included two League Cup triumphs and a UEFA Cup Final.

Only a relegation in the middle of the 70s blotted the copybook. There was great strength throughout the side during this period, from Phil Parkes in goal, the towering presence of Frank Munro in the heart of defence, alongside John McAlle, with full-backs Derek Parkin and Geoff Palmer either side. The midfield was perhaps the strongest area, with Hibbitt joining Mike Bailey, Dave Wagstaffe, Willie Carr and Steve Daley. Whilst front men Derek Dougan and John Richards could frighten any defence in the land.

Hibbitt's enthusiasm for sport rubs off immediately. He may be 67 years old, but the competitive edge that helped make him one of the Black Country club's greatest-ever players is a big part of his character.

'Without a doubt. I played in a darts team down here at the club and I was competitive at that,' he points out. 'My children were never allowed to win anything. My wife used to give me some stick because I said that they had to learn how to win, how to be successful. If you keep allowing them to win then they don't learn how to do it.'

True, but most dads are not professional footballers. 'I know, I know! But even my grandchildren now, they have to learn how to compete.'

A two-handicapper, Hibbitt reveals that it was during Wolves' time in European competition during the early 1970s that he learnt the game of golf, when manager Bill McGarry took him for a round on days off after European midweek fixtures.

'He was a four-handicapper, a good golfer, who had a straight back and hit it straight through the swing, right down the middle. He used to take us to courses around Wolverhampton the day after the midweek games, that's how I got into it. I used to hold it like a baseball bat and smash it with a slice that would start out wide and come back over to the middle of the fairway. That's how it all started.'

That slice has long been cured. The opening few holes pose few problems for him today, but there are one or two shakes of the head after a couple of missed birdie putts as the sun begins to burn off the mist, revealing the rustic colours of the trees on the hills around. Hibbitt also represented Yorkshire schoolboys at cricket and counted the former England wicketkeeper David Bairstow amongst his peers. But it was football that won out in the end, as he followed the path of his older brother Terry into the professional game.

'As kids we played this game, long shots, stood 20 yards apart where we drilled balls at each other and we both had goals to protect,' he explains. 'We just did it for hours and hours and hours. It all started there really, we were just totally focussed on trying to make it as footballers. It got quite competitive at times but Terry was always the winner. There were three years between us and when he went to Leeds United as a 15-year-old, I was just 12 and still at school.'

Hibbitt junior got a move to Bradford Park Avenue as an apprentice when he too reached the age of 15, before Wolves came calling with a £5,000 transfer fee two years later. But the move to Molineux was not a simple one, given some tragic family circumstances.

'I'd recently lost my father. He was only 40 when he had a heart attack and there was no way back from it. I was only 17 at the time of the move and he died when I was 16. I wasn't sure if I wanted to go, I didn't even know where Wolverhampton was.'

It was Hibbitt's older brother who sought the counsel of Leeds manager Don Revie for some advice about what path his younger brother should take. Hibbitt admits it was an extremely tough period for the family.

'Oh it was, because my brother was living away from home at Leeds so it was just my mother and sister living at home. It was a big choice I'd made. My mother said it was a dream of my dad's to see me and Terry play in the

First Division. Terry spoke to Don and he said to him that I should go, so he had an input in that. Eventually mum persuaded me to go but I still had to send as much money back as I could to help pay her mortgage.'

Hibbitt endured a cartilage injury early on during his time at Molineux, but when the chance came to step up to the first team he took it in style. 'I was 19 and Bill McGarry gave me the opportunity. I made my debut against Chelsea in September 1970. We had some great players and they really supported me. It was down at Stamford Bridge in the pouring rain and I scored the first goal. A corner came in, Peter Bonetti came out and pushed it to the edge of the box, and I drilled it in with my left foot. It was a dream come true, being a young lad. I never thought I'd get to play at stadiums like Stamford Bridge, Old Trafford, Anfield and Elland Road.'

After a brilliant first season for Hibbitt, making 30 league appearances, Wolves entered the newly formed UEFA Cup at the beginning of the 1971/72 campaign. It was a competition that took Wolves to Portugal, Holland, East Germany, Italy and Hungary. 'That was a fantastic period. As a young boy the furthest I ever went was Blackpool and Morecambe for the day,' he recalls. 'But there I was on these aeroplanes travelling all over Europe and going behind the Iron Curtain. It was an experience for us as we had quite a few youngsters in the side. We were young lads learning not just about football but about life as well.

'We went to Juventus who had the great John Charles, and he took us around Turin. Everywhere he took us, people would stare open-mouthed and some even bowed. He took us to all the shops so we could buy some Italian clothes. That was an education, things like that. Maybe people take that for granted now, but I was thinking how lucky I was, it was massive for me.'

The final against Tottenham Hotspur was a tight contest over two legs. A 2-1 defeat at home was followed by a 1-1 draw at White Hart Lane. Hibbitt acknowledges that Wolves came up just short against a team which was that little bit better over the two games. There was no sense that this was a big opportunity missed, though. Wolves were regularly competing in the latter stages of cup competitions throughout the decade. The two League Cup triumphs in 1974 and 1980 would help make up for the one that got away in Europe, but one of Hibbitt's most memorable moments came in the FA Cup in April 1981, also against Spurs. With Wolves trailing the semi-final 2-1, at Hillsborough, referee Clive Thomas gave one of the most controversial penalties in the history of the game.

Hibbitt smiles. 'People don't talk about the other 89 minutes, they never talk about my goal. Nobody mentions about the knock-down from Andy Gray and my volley into the bottom corner with my left foot, it's always that 90th minute! I'd run all the way from our half, I think it was Norman Bell who gave me the ball, and made my way into the box. I went past Steve Perryman and I was ready to pull the trigger. Then Glenn Hoddle came in from the side, slid in and put the ball out for a corner.

'There was this massive cheer and I thought, "That's a hell of a cheer for a corner," then John Richards came running up to me shouting "Hibby, Hibby, get up, it's a penalty! Get up, you're taking it." I was so surprised that Clive gave it. There was no way I was taking that, I bottled it. Glenn made a really good tackle but it must have looked like a penalty from Clive's angle. We were happy coming out of it at 2-2, but I remember all the fuss afterwards.' A furore was whipped up in the Sunday papers and Hibbitt had to deal with some unpleasant hate mail from Spurs fans who accused him of diving.

Wolves went on to lose a one-sided replay 3-0 at Arsenal's Highbury, with Spurs going on to lift the trophy thanks, in part, to Ricky Villa's wonder goal in a Wembley final replay against Manchester City. 'I felt for our fans travelling all the way down from the Midlands to London in midweek when Spurs fans just had to go across town. I was a bit surprised the FA allowed that to happen, but on the night we didn't play well and we didn't deserve to go through.'

Hibbitt is just one over par at the end of our front nine. As the course dips into the valley heading west, overlooking the market town of Wotton-Under-Edge, the Severn Vale and across to Wales, talk turns to the demise of a great club. The season after that infamous semi-final, Wolves were relegated. After a decade of challenging for trophies, they had hit on the hardest times.

'Losing that semi-final, we never really recovered from it when you think about it. It was an indifferent time for the club after that and it never really got better. It just went downhill. I put it in the press at the time that if it was me who needed to move on to make way for younger players then I'd accept that. We all grew old together and were never replaced and I think that was the start of the demise. The only time I had any inclination that there was financial trouble was when Ian Greaves came in.'

Greaves arrived as manager in February 1982 after John Barnwell resigned. He took over a team that had just lost six league games in a row. 'His first game came around and we were 6-1 down at Tottenham, we got battered! We got to the end of that season where he nearly kept us up, but we got relegated. It was then that he said there were real problems at the club on the financial side. That's when I went out to Seattle Sounders for the summer, on loan for three and a half months while it all calmed down.

'I said to Ian that I wasn't really interested in going but he said I needed to get away, and that worried me a lot. But in the end I thought, "Why not?" Steve Daley was out at Seattle. Others, like Alan Hudson and Roger Davies, were playing in America. It was a difficult time for my wife really because we had two youngsters. It was on and off a few times and we kept on packing and unpacking. It was never going to be a permanent move but in the end it went very well. We ended up winning the league and getting to the Soccer Bowl. It was a very happy period for us but the club back home was desperate. They got me off the wages as I was one of the top earners, I suppose, and it helped them.

'Derek Dougan and the Bhatti brothers took over while I was out in Seattle. Derek wanted me back immediately but I was under contract in Seattle until the end of their season. I was pleased he wanted me back. I was a long way from home when I found out how severe the trouble was, and then for someone like Derek to come in and take charge, I was only too pleased to come back. I returned and signed a two-year contract with them and of course we got promotion.'

An immediate return to the top flight as runners-up in the Second Division in the 1982/83 campaign was followed by a bottom-place finish in the 1983/84 season, the first of three successive relegations. There was turmoil off the pitch, too, with the club going bankrupt and fending off winding-up orders. The ground was also closed on two sides for lack of a safety certificate. Hibbitt moved to Coventry City in 1984 but watched on as his old team suffered.

'I would have stayed again, but Jim Barron took over as caretaker-manager and with the deal they offered he just said, "You either take it or leave it," and he threw it on the desk. I didn't expect to be spoken to or treated like that, the way they went about it. He said I was on the top wages and I understood that, but even so it didn't feel right. I went to Coventry City on the same money they offered me at Wolves. I had two really happy years at Coventry but I didn't want to leave Wolves. I was looking from the outside in and it broke my heart to see them dropping down into the Third and Fourth Division.'

Several weeks before our round in the Cotswolds, Hibbitt was back in the Molineux spotlight for a supporters' tribute dinner. It was the second dinner organised by the author of *They Wore The Shirt*, a book by fan and memorabilia collector Steve Plant, chronicling the history of the Wolves strips and those who wore them. It followed on from a 2017 celebration of record appearance-maker Derek Parkin's career. Over the course of the evening, many of Hibbitt's former team-mates took to the stage to share their memories.

For the younger supporters, who never saw Hibbitt play, his former room-mate Carr drew a modern-day comparison: 'The nearest thing to Frank Lampard.' All those who played with him or watched from the terraces speak of his unerring ball-striking ability, with either foot. So it was a cause of much amusement in the room when his opening goal in the 1974 League Cup Final against Manchester City is recalled as a terrible mishit that skewed fortuitously into the top right-hand corner.

'Kenny blamed me for that one,' said Richards, scorer of the winning goal in that Wembley final. 'He said, "If you hadn't distracted me it would have gone in the top left corner." It probably would have done.'

It is a source of similar amusement to his old team-mates that Hibbitt, infamous amongst them for having a whinge to referees during his playing days, has gone on to join their ranks as an assessor in his retirement. 'He was the biggest moaner at referees you've ever seen,' Parkes revealed. 'Now he's looking after them.'

Hibbitt enjoyed his night immensely and is still chuckling at some of the comments his old pals came out with, particularly that observation from Parkes. 'I've been doing it for 15 years, I love it. You get to feel how difficult refereeing is and I look back now and think what an idiot I was. I have so much respect for them now. Their fitness levels are fantastic, they get tested every three or four weeks. They go through an awful lot to get to the level they're at.'

So many of Hibbitt's peers spoke of not just a great footballer, but a decent human being who knows the value of others. Barry Powell had lost touch with his former team-mate but the pair bumped into each other 20 years on from their playing days when they both applied for the Hednesford Town manager's job in 2001.

'My only job in management had been at Aberystwyth Town. Kenny had been to Cardiff, Walsall and Bristol Rovers,' Powell explained. 'I was sat there waiting in reception when this door opened and Kenny Hibbitt walked through. "Alright Baz, what are you doing here?" he said. I was shocked, I just said, "I think we're in for the same job, Ken."

'We hadn't seen each other for so many years, we exchanged numbers and went our separate ways. Then a couple of days later I got a call from Kenny. He said, "Barry, I've got the job, how do you fancy coming in as assistant manager?" That's unheard of in football, if you're both going for the same job you don't invite the other fella to come in as assistant. He gave me a fantastic opportunity.'

It is a story that sums up the class of the man. Powell touched on another side of Hibbitt's character as their time with Hednesford drew to a close – his optimism.

'We didn't do too well to be fair. He phoned me up one night and said, "Baz, the chairman has invited us in for a chat tomorrow." I said, "Oh my God Ken, what are we up to?" Ken said, "No, no, we'll be alright." We got there and the chairman was just faffing about saying this, that and the other and I'd had enough.

'I just got up and said, "Ken, we're gone." Ever the professional, Ken just said, "No, Baz, we can work this out," but I just got up and left. About an hour down the motorway I received this call on my mobile from Ken. "You were right mate, we're gone!"'

Richards, another great friend, holds Hibbitt responsible for opening his eyes to other pleasures in life. 'A year after I joined Wolves he introduced me to something which probably changed my life. It was the Lafayette,' he said.

Club Lafayette – The Laff, as it was known locally – was something of a Wolverhampton institution. For a time, in the 1960s and 70s, the Thornley Street venue became the place to be seen in the West Midlands. Led Zeppelin, Stevie Wonder and The Sex Pistols all walked through its doors. 'We were those annoying people who got to go to the front of the queue and didn't have to pay to get in,' Richards continued. 'There was an incident that involved Ken and myself at the Lafayette that was the closest we ever got to falling out. It was after a midweek game and the coach got back to Wolverhampton just before midnight. A group of us were hungry, and in those days the Lafayette was one of the few places you could get something to eat at midnight.

'So we went up there to their restaurant and everybody ordered steak and chips. When it came to me putting the tomato sauce on I heard this gasp, looked around, and Kenny – who was wearing this light brown suit – was covered in tomato sauce. The bottle top might not have been put on properly! It was like a scene from the chainsaw massacre. He looked at me like he looked at any referee he disagreed with. I just said, 'Do you fancy a pint?' and I got away with it. We never fell out, we played together in the reserves and first team for 14 years. Highs and lows, winning League Cups, relegation and then coming back up again.'

'What he didn't say was it was a new cream suit I had on,' Hibbitt says, as he recalls Richards' version of the story. 'We didn't realise when we asked for the bottle that it was loose, he shook it all over my cream suit. He's right, in all those years we have never had a cross word. We might have exchanged something on the pitch, but off it we have never had a bad word between us.'

Club Lafayette would draw a crowd from miles around at a time when Wolves had some colourful characters in their ranks. 'We didn't live in there but it was heaving every Saturday night we went,' Hibbitt adds. 'Peter Knowles used to go quite a lot and the other senior players. We just joined on the back of that. I wasn't a big drinker or somebody who went on many dance floors.'

Knowles remains one of the most fascinating players in Wolves' history. He was a hugely gifted forward who ended his career just a few games into the 1969/70 season at the tender age of 24, in order to become a Jehovah's Witness.

'The crowd loved him, he used to have a yellow MGB sports car with "PK" on the side,' says Hibbitt. 'He regrets all that, and playing football. He used to say he couldn't believe that he went around kicking people. But he's the most contented man I've ever met now. He just came in one day and said he was packing football up. He had a Bible under his arm. We said, "Yeah right Knowlesy, we've heard that before."

'And we never saw him again. We were all shocked. He was a super player and Wolves missed out on a top player, and England did as well. But that was what his beliefs were and he stuck with it and he is a very nice man. I have a lot of admiration for him.' Knowles has been asked to tell his story on numerous occasions since his early retirement, but has always shunned publicity since leaving professional football behind.

Hibbitt's round comes to a close in tidy fashion. The highlight of his back nine is a birdie on the tricky par four 15th, with its tight, banked fairway and lofted green. The conversation ends with talk about the current team and their hopes of emulating, and maybe even surpassing, the achievements of the 70s players.

'We've now got a team that is solid in all departments,' Hibbitt adds. 'It's great to see the English lads doing well too, Conor Coady in particular. It's nice to see him getting some recognition. It's so exciting to see Wolverhampton sparkling again.'

And would he like to play in a midfield with Neves and Moutinho? 'I don't think I'd get in it. You've got Neves, Moutinho, Costa. Great players. I've seen them against

Burnley and Southampton this season and I'd like to see them more often. We've got the slow build-up and then we can attack at pace as well. It's crazy what is happening here now. Wonderful, but crazy as well!'

Chapter 4

THE BHATTIS

A reporter's story from the darkest days

ON 1 October 1980 striker Mel Eves scored for Wolves in a 1-0 win over PSV Eindhoven at Molineux in the second leg of a first-round UEFA Cup tie. The previous season, Wolves had lifted the League Cup at Wembley, beating European champions Nottingham Forest. They had also finished sixth in the First Division under manager John Barnwell, a single point behind Forest. Just a little over a year and a half after that win against the Dutch in Europe, Wolves had gone into receivership, been declared bankrupt and ceased trading. The receivers, appointed in July 1982 to sort out the administration, set a four-week deadline for a buyer to come forward and save the club from going out of existence.

It was an astonishing decline. But it was only the beginning of the most shambolic period in the club's entire history. Between 1982 and 1986 Wolves stumbled from one crisis to another, bringing embarrassment to supporters.

At every home fixture, by the matchday press entrance to Molineux, situated at a doorway in the Billy Wright Stand just a few yards from the main entrance, works a man who reported on it all for the town's newspaper.

Growing up in Tipton, Dave Harrison was introduced to Wolves by his granddad. 'He was a miner, and a massive supporter of the club. He always called them "The Wanderers",' says Harrison. 'I caught the end of the 50s, my first game was against Villa in 1957, and we got our first television for the 1960 cup final [when Wolves beat Blackburn Rovers 3-0]. It's in your blood isn't it? It's there and you never lose it. Although I drifted around various journalism jobs, and I covered West Brom's tour to China in the 70s, Wolves was in the DNA.'

Harrison started off as a junior reporter at the *Walsall Observer* in 1975 covering courts and inquests. He later moved to the *Birmingham Post* and *Birmingham Mail* before taking the job of deputy sports editor at Wolverhampton's *Express and Star* in 1982. After leaving the newspaper in 1986, he went to work for the nationals, until his recent retirement at the end of Wolves' Championship-winning season, a campaign he marked by writing the last of his many books, *Nuno Had A Dream*.

'I'd decided I was going to stop reporting for the Sunday papers and I was going to buy a season-ticket and become a proper fan again, after all these years,' Harrison explains. 'Out of nowhere, Max Fitzgerald [Wolves' head of media] rang me up and said, "Come and work for us on a matchday," so I get to see the games still. I do a bit of handing out press tickets, meeting and greeting, hovering around the media lounge in case there's any problems that need sorting out, all that type of thing.

'We get some of the wives and families of the players coming through the media entrance to the executive boxes. Ryan Bennett's family are an absolute delight. John Ruddy, what a guy he is; even though he's been marginalised on the pitch, he's at the core of it. The Moutinhos are lovely. They came through with their daughter one day to go up to the executive box, she's only about 11 or 12, and I said, "Where do you prefer living, Monte Carlo or

Wolverhampton?" She said, "Wolverhampton, there's a lot more to do here." It's good to feel a part of the club, if only a marginal part.'

Just one of Molineux's four stands remains in situ from Harrison's time covering the club for the *Express and Star*. Opened in 1979, the Molineux Stand – later renamed the John Ireland Stand before being changed again to the Steve Bull Stand – was the source of all Wolves' troubles in the 1980s.

It was built to replace the ageing Molineux Street Stand and, for its time, was an impressive two-tiered structure with some of the first executive boxes in the country. It was constructed the best part of 50 yards from the pitch, with chairman Harry Marshall's intention being to redevelop the entire ground towards that side of the new stand in order to create more space for a new Waterloo Road Stand, which was hemmed in by the busy road up to the town centre.

But in 1982, three years after the Molineux Stand was opened, the club was struggling to pay off the Lloyds Bank loan secured to build the structure, which became known locally as 'Marshall's Folly'. The financial difficulties sparked off a bitter boardroom battle. An extraordinary general meeting was called on 8 June 1982 to try and oust Marshall and his vice-chairman Wilf Sproson. Wolves' former FA Cup-winning goalkeeper Malcolm Finlayson and former Aston Villa chairman Doug Ellis were presented as boardroom candidates in the event of Marshall's departure. A shareholders' vote saved Marshall, but he had seen enough dissent and resigned from his position on 16 June. Ellis was soon appointed the new chairman, but it proved to be the shortest of boardroom reigns at the club. One of his first acts was to request that Lloyds Bank, the club's major creditor to the tune of £1.85million, call in the receiver. On 2 July he released this statement, on behalf of the board, outlining the dire financial straits at Wolves:

When Malcolm Finlayson and myself were invited to join the board 14 days ago we promised that a full investigation of the club's financial affairs be carried out. We immediately requested the club accountant to prepare the club's draft accounts to 31 May 1982, and to prepare a financial forecast to 31 May 1983.

In addition we appointed the international firm of chartered accountants, Peat Marwick Mitchell and Co., to examine these figures and produce a viability report on the financial affairs of the club. For the last season alone these figures revealed a trading loss of £725,000 which even after a donation from the Development Association produced a NET loss of over £650,000. For next season, as members of the Second Division, the accountants projected a further loss of £540,000.

The figures also show that the club had in excess of £2.5million of liabilities as at 31 May 1982, and could not continue to meet its debts as they fell due. In view of the revelation of the seriousness of the financial position shown by the club's accountant's figures, supported by the independent accountants' investigation, our bankers felt they could no longer support the club. Under these circumstances the board has been legally advised that it cannot continue to trade. It is therefore, with extreme regret, that the directors have had no alternative but to formally request the bank appoint a receiver.

We announced shortly after our appointment that, in view of our initial concern over the club's possible financial position, your directors were not prepared to accept monies for season tickets which might have been lost in the event of a receiver being appointed and no football being played next season. That money is deposited in a separate bank and a further announcement will be made as soon as practicable.

You will appreciate that it is with deep sadness that this course of action has had to be taken, but you may rest assured that I and fellow directors will do everything in our power to assist the receiver and to ensure that league football will continue to be played at Molineux if that path is available to the receiver or in accordance with his wishes.

It was front page news at the *Express and Star*, which ran with the headline 'WOLVES HAVE GONE BUST' alongside a photograph of Ellis reading out his statement. The players appeared stunned at the news. Striker John Richards, who was the club's all-time leading goalscorer at the time, said, 'The players have just got to hope for the best. Wolves are one of the biggest clubs in Britain, and were one of the biggest in Europe. It was a great shock to hear of today's developments. It would be a tragedy if they went out of business. Everyone in Wolverhampton and all those connected with football will be hoping the club pulls through.'

Finlayson's dejected outlook seemed to capture the horror of the demise. 'It's 100 years down the drain,' said the man who had played his part when Wolves were the country's leading light.

It was not just the club and its supporters who felt the pain. Predictably, many local businesses suffered too, with Wolves being so ingrained in the community. One of the smallest creditors was a local carpet firm, R & W Carpets, who had recently fitted out the Molineux reception on the Waterloo Road. Owner Robin Rawson was left with a £2,400 debt that he was struggling to cope with. 'I was pestering the club every week for the money,' he told the *Express and Star*. 'Because, being a small business, I need it. Each time I was told it would be coming soon.'

'It was a ridiculous fall from grace, but it was all about this Marshall's Folly,' Harrison says. 'In one way it was an amazing time, I always say it was the best period of my journalism career, it was so alive. I was at the World Cup in Spain in 1982 when the receivers were first called in, so I had to work from there covering the World Cup and the Wolves story. By the time I got back from the World Cup after England had gone out, I came back right into the eye of the storm.'

Over the course of July a number of candidates from different backgrounds expressed interest in gaining control of the club, including Wolverhampton Town Council; a consortium led by Ellis and Finlayson; another involving former chairman Marshall and Walsall chairman Ken Wheldon, a scrap metal merchant; and a third consortium led by Ken Hollinshead, an insurance broker from Tettenhall. More unlikely interest came from Essex businessman and nightclub owner Anton Johnson, who had a controlling stake in Rotherham United at the time.

Midway through the month, Sir Jack Hayward flew back from his Bahamas home to meet with interested parties about a rescue deal, but no concrete offer materialised from the future owner of the club. On the Saturday before the receiver's deadline of Friday, 30 July, the players took matters into their own hands.

Despite having been relegated to the Second Division they organised a bus tour of Wolverhampton to sign autographs for fans and raise money for the revival fund. Meanwhile a local nightclub, Eves, put on a fundraiser with appearances from Bev Bevan, drummer of the Electric Light Orchestra, and Roy Wood, lead singer of Wizard.

It was on 24 July, six days before the deadline, that the *Express and Star* first reported on a new consortium of businessmen bidding to save the club. Fronted by former striker and crowd favourite Derek Dougan and Scottish property developer Douglas Hope, it involved financing from mystery investors based in Manchester.

'Derek Dougan, myself and our backers from Manchester met the receiver yesterday and we felt it was a very good meeting,' said Hope at the time. 'We have been talking about this matter for some time but have decided to keep quiet about it until we had something definite to say.'

The investors were a firm called Allied Properties, owned by two brothers, Mahmud Al-Hassan Bhatti and Mohammed Akbar Bhatti. Over the next few days the *Express and Star* reported on the changing landscape as the various consortia jockeyed for position.

'It turned into an auction to see who would buy the club,' Harrison recalls. 'It went right up to the deadline of 30 July. I'd written two stories – one that Wolves had gone to the wall and one that it had been saved. The paper was waiting to press the button on one of these two stories, the editor and managing director wondering which one they should go with. It had gone to press earlier in the day, but they were doing a special run at five o'clock because of Wolves, that's how important it was. They were holding the paper until the fate of Wolves was known.

'There were no mobile phones in those days. So I had to sit in the office with my two stories and monitor the situation. The meetings were happening in Birmingham with Peat Marwick and Mitchell, the accountants who were the receivers. The only way of finding out what was happening was by ringing the Football League. The guy there was a good contact, Andy Williamson. He was the press officer and I had a good relationship with him because there were all sorts of stories going around with Wolves at the time. I was ringing him every 15 minutes. It got to about quarter to five and he said, "Nothing's happening Dave, I think you're probably going to go to the wall."'

I rang again five minutes later and there was no reply. So it was ten to five and with no answer at the Football League, I thought Andy had gone home and Wolves had probably gone to the wall. I frantically started trying to get hold of other people. I tried Peat Marwick and Mitchell, then made one more call to the Football League a minute before five o'clock, and Andy picked up. I said, "Where have you been?" and he replied, "Oh I just went to get my coat because I'm going home now. You're alright, they've been saved." I said, "Who has saved it, is it Dougan's lot?" He said he couldn't tell me as there was a confidentially agreement, so I said, "If it's Dougan's lot put the phone down," which was an old technique we used. The phone line just clicked and went dead so I knew we'd got the story to press the button on the paper. We printed 30,000 copies after five o'clock and they sold out in the town.'

The official receiver, Alastair Jones, revealed that talks broke down at 4:30pm, only to restart a few minutes later allowing a deal to be completed at 4:57pm, just three minutes before the deadline. 'It was really touch and go to the very last,' Jones admitted. 'But, thankfully, we have managed to secure a very favourable deal for the creditors of Wolverhampton Wanderers.'

'WOLVES GO ON PLAYING' announced the headline in the *Express and Star*, but the saviours were referred to only as 'a mystery Manchester consortium', with speculation that the main backer was the Co-operative Wholesale Society, hoping to do a supermarket deal on a large plot of land behind the North Bank stand. Hope said, on completion of the takeover, 'A supermarket or leisure complex are the types of development we are likely to explore. But I must stress that it will not be at the expense of league football.'

'They were very secretive, we couldn't get to the bottom of it,' says Harrison, looking back. 'Derek Tucker was the chief reporter on the paper; he did a lot of investigations, dug them out and found out that they were the Bhatti brothers. He still never spoke to them, not once. So I was dealing with The Doog [Derek Dougan].'

'The Doog' was one of Harrison's playing heroes from the 1970s. A hugely talented forward and a larger-than-life character with a fiery temperament, he was desperate to step in and help the club. Hope was one of Dougan's long-time acquaintances. In Harrison's 2008 biography of the player, *The Doog*, Hope explained the strange location of the first meeting between the Wolves hero and the two businessmen.

'We met at a very luxurious Portakabin,' said Hope. 'They had a business called Grosvenor Aviations, which was based on a factory estate at Manchester Airport. That was the only time I saw the Bhattis dressed in traditional Arab dress. Derek talked to them at length and told them what he had in mind. He stressed all along that if Wolves could be saved there was a property deal there and we were looking at the land on the North Bank car park as a possible supermarket site.'

That land deal was the key to everything that followed. The planning application for permission to build a supermarket development on the land owned by the club behind the North Bank was turned down by Wolverhampton Council. The financial situation at Wolves soon began to collapse.

'There was a story every day. Gradually you started to realise that the whole success of Allied Properties depended on planning permission for the plot of land behind the North Bank,' says Harrison. 'Doug Hope, who was the link between Allied Properties and Dougan, said they'd been given the nod by the council that planning permission would be granted, which was all they were interested in really. It all hinged on the planning permission, which they didn't get.'

In *The Doog*, Harrison revealed that there was a suspicion of racism from at least one senior figure surrounding the planning veto. Roger Hipkiss, who became a Wolves director soon after the takeover, told Harrison, 'It wasn't obvious and, of course, no one would admit it, but I reckon there were racist undertones. Don't forget Wolverhampton was the constituency of Enoch Powell [MP for Wolverhampton South West, 1950–74], author of the

famous 'Rivers of Blood' speech, and I believe there was
still an element of those sentiments prevailing throughout
the town. They were dark-skinned outsiders and a lot of
people in the community didn't like that. The Bhattis had
a raw deal – no question about it. They had been promised
everything and ended up with nothing.'

Dougan was named chairman and chief executive of
the club, and he stamped his mark on the place early on.
'He sacked Jack Taylor, who was the commercial manager,
Phil Shaw, who was the long-serving secretary, and then
sacked Ian Greaves, the manager,' Harrison explains. 'I
think it was the *Daily Express* who ran this cartoon that said
"Dougan sacks himself". He was a strange character, such a
contradiction. I had a good working relationship with him
when he was chairman and chief executive of Wolves. He
appointed Graham Hawkins, who was assistant manager
at Shrewsbury Town and who I became very friendly with,
and Jim Barron as his assistant.

'The place was in ruins, you'd walk in in the morning,
open the dressing room door and a load of cockroaches
would come crawling out. Graham did a fantastic job, they
finished runners-up in the Second Division in his first
season [1982/83]. When he got the job he was told money
would be available but he ended up using a load of kids.'

The team for the first game of the Second Division
season, at home to Blackburn Rovers on 28 August 1982,
included four teenage debutants: Ian Cartwright, Paul
Butler, Billy Livingstone and David Wintersgill, who was
a 16-year-old plucked straight from school. But there was
still a sprinkling of senior talent, with Geoff Palmer, Kenny
Hibbitt, Andy Gray and Mel Eves playing their part guiding
the youngsters through.

'All these stories emerged about a lack of money; they
couldn't afford to pay the milkman at one stage,' Harrison
explains. 'I had lots of good contacts inside the club telling
me what was going on, the players and staff weren't getting

paid. One day I ran a story, that somebody gave me, that the Bhattis had suddenly arrived at the club one day with a suitcase stuffed with cash to pay the wages. I ran the story and the police called me the next day, saying, "Do you mind not running that kind of story again because we're going to have all the bloody hoods in Wolverhampton hanging around there." That was fairly early on in the takeover.'

A tour to Sweden in the summer of 1983 also stands out in Harrison's memory. The tour took in games against lowly opposition Vargarna, Nykoping, Krylbo, Ludvika and Vateras.

'I was covering the team for the *Express and Star*,' Harrison continues. 'We were playing a lot of little friendly games in the outback of Sweden. Most of them were just on parks pitches. There had been a few injuries and I had previously played for the Wolves Old Boys team with Graham and Jim. We got to this pitch one day and Graham said, "You're on the bench today, we're a bit short."'

'We turned up for one game and there was a mix-up over the strips. Wolves didn't take a change strip to Sweden, and there was a colour clash. The home team said they could borrow their change strip, which was green and white hoops. When they brought it out, Andy Gray [a Rangers fan] looked at it and said, "I'm not wearing that." So in the end Wolves played in their own kit and the Swedish team played in their change kit.'

Wolves were never likely to avoid relegation when they were back in the top division for the 1983/84 season. With the promise of money, Hawkins had identified targets including centre-half Mick McCarthy from Manchester City, midfielder Paul Bracewell from Sunderland, Coventry City midfielders Ashley Grimes and Micky Gynn, striker Gary Lineker from Leicester City and goalkeeper David Seaman from Peterborough United.

Hawkins told Harrison, 'I went to a board meeting that summer and said it would take between £750,000 and

£1million to get Seaman, Grimes, Bracewell, McCarthy, Gynn and Lineker. That was the quality we needed to move forward but the money was never there. Then I went on my family holiday to Greece and while I was away I found out we had signed a winger, Tony Towner, from Rotherham for around £100,000. He would have been about number 45 on my list of targets.'

Towner made 25 league appearances as Wolves finished bottom of the First Division. A 3-1 win in the Black Country derby at rivals West Bromwich Albion and a shock 1-0 victory against soon-to-be-crowned league and European champions Liverpool were rare highlights in a terrible season. Nineteen-year-old Steve Mardenborough's winner at Anfield was his only goal in just 11 appearances for the club before he was moved out to Cambridge United on loan. In an era long before squad rotation, an astonishing 32 players were used for the league campaign, as various youngsters and journeymen came and went.

'They weren't equipped for the First Division, as it was known then, just because of the lack of established players and the ability of the ones there,' says Harrison. 'Graham did a fantastic job still, but then he got the sack and it just plummeted. They appointed Tommy Docherty for the Second Division, which was good for stories, but he was a cavalier character. He didn't get on with Dougan. I think Dougan was persuaded by other board members, they thought it would generate some interest with Tommy being here. In his first press conference, Dougan said, "He could do for this football club what JFK did for American politics." And Tommy answered, "But he got shot didn't he?"'

Stories emerged of coaching staff who lived outside of Wolverhampton sleeping in the boardroom on some nights if they had stayed working late. The club could not afford to put them up in hotels. Docherty also told Harrison of an incident down at the training ground during pre-season which sent a chill down the spine:

'By then the rot had really set in,' Harrison explains. 'There was a young player called Neville Hamilton, who had a heart murmur and collapsed up at the training ground. That was at the Castlecroft training ground, which was falling apart, it was riddled with asbestos. They were carting him off and putting him in an ambulance when Tommy's number two, Greg Fellows, went over and started taking his football boots off. Tommy asked him what he was doing and Greg replied, "Gaffer, we've only got 14 pairs of boots in the whole club, and we can't afford to lose these."'

Hamilton recovered from the incident, but the heart condition forced him to retire from playing and he moved into a career in coaching. Players would regularly train in their own gear, given the shortage of any official kit. Dougan cut an increasingly forlorn figure during the 1984/85 campaign, eventually resigning under pressure from other board members in January.

'The memory of The Doog as a player meant he was up there as a hero, he was one of my heroes,' Harrison adds. 'He was tainted by the Bhatti brothers and I think he saw in the end that it was going to affect his legacy as a Wolves legend.'

The Bhattis were nowhere to be seen. Under Docherty, a second successive relegation for the club was inevitable. A 4-0 home defeat to Fulham, with four games remaining, condemned Wolves to their fate. They finished rock bottom of the Second Division, seven points adrift of safety.

After relegation was confirmed, the *Express and Star* spoke with the club's decorated captain during that glorious 50s era, Billy Wright. 'I am terribly upset,' he said. 'It is a tragedy that a club the size of Wolves' stature are in the Third Division. When I and my colleagues put on the gold shirt we did so with pride and affection for a great club but this feeling doesn't seem to exist anymore. Wolves always used to be inseparable from the town and its people but that relationship doesn't seem to exist either, with the current owners in control.'

The following weekend, Wolves were beaten 5-1 at Brighton. 'Wolves loped off into the Third Division, toothless and with their tails between their legs,' wrote Harrison in his match report. 'A club who once roamed the globe terrorising the world's best are now facing the awful task of scratching around for survival in football's backwoods.'

It may have felt like the end of the world for the club and its supporters, but there was far worse to come. Allied Properties were faced with a winding-up order in the High Court, from a Finnish Bank for a £270,000 debt. On 20 May 1985, nine days after the season finished, a team of fire safety officers inspected Molineux in the wake of the stadium fire disaster at Valley Parade, which claimed 56 lives at Bradford City's final game of the season. It would lead to the closures of the Waterloo Road and North Bank stands. With no money for stadium improvements, Wolves could only keep two sides of the ground open.

The following day, Professional Footballers' Association secretary Gordon Taylor revealed that the players had not received their latest wages. The squad was in Malta at the time, on an end-of-season tour. Docherty was dismissed on 8 July. 'You could bring Brian Clough or whoever you consider the best manager in the country to Wolves tomorrow and he would still face the same problems,' he said.

'When Docherty got the sack I had to try to go and interview him about it,' Harrison recalls. 'I went down to the club but they told me he had already left, and he was at Newbridge tennis club. So I went down there and he was holding court buying champagne for everyone in the bar. I think he saw it as a bit of a relief. There were times when I'd be in his manager's office and he'd be on the phone to his bank asking if his wages had gone in.'

Sammy Chapman took the reins on a temporary basis for the beginning of the 1985/86 campaign. Bill McGarry, such a success in his first spell in charge from 1968–74, was tempted back in September and supporters finally had some hope to cling to. But he lasted just 61 days before handing the reins back to Chapman. Wolves finished in 23rd place, second from bottom, and became the first club to drop from First to Fourth Division in successive seasons. Supporters who lived through it view that Third Division season as the hardest one of all during the 1980s. The club had yet to bottom out, and as long as the Bhattis remained at the helm there were no signs of recovery on the horizon.

Before Wolves could kick a ball in anger in the Fourth Division, they had to sort out further problems off the field. In June, for the second time in four years, the club fell into administration, with Lloyds Bank calling in the receivers to bring an end to the Bhattis' regime.

Unlike in 1982, the threat of Wolves' closure was not a long-running front-page story. 'This time there was an inevitability about it, that they were going to the wall again. You kept your head down, you were almost embarrassed to admit you were a Wolves fan,' says Harrison. The receiver did create one major front-page headline early on, though, when he came up with an enterprising plan to preserve the club's future.

The proposal was to allow Wolves to enter the Conference as a part-time team, and hand non-league Enfield their place in the league. In the days before promotion and relegation between the two divisions, the news was met with astonishment. In June, receiver Adam Stanway announced, 'If this is the only way I can keep the club in existence then I shall do it, subject to both leagues being in agreement. The only alternative is if local business and the public come forward and clear the debts to enable a new group to take over in time for the Football League kick-off on 23 August.'

Secretary of the Conference, then known as the GM Vauxhall League, Peter Hunter said, 'If Wolves can turn out 12 players on 16 August, we'll have them.'

Wolves vice-chairman Hope did not approve of the plan: 'I am lost for words but God forbid anything like this happening,' he said. 'It would be like switching off a life support machine for Wolves.'

In July a 200-strong group of supporters travelled to Newcastle-Upon-Tyne to present a 3,000-signature petition to the Football League, who were at a hotel discussing the club's future. Their plea to allow Wolves to take up a place in the Football League the following season, regardless of whether a rescue package was agreed, fell on deaf ears. The Football League set a 31 July deadline to sort out the debts.

Sir Jack Hayward flew back from the Bahamas and announced he was willing to help the club on one condition: 'I am not going to bail out the Bhatti brothers, they have had enough out of Wolves already,' he said. 'I would be willing to help but only to save the club, and the last thing I want to do is put money in the Bhattis' pockets.'

Eventually, but only through club solicitor Michael Cooksey, the Bhattis broke their silence. With the receiver revealing total debts of £2.4million, including £800,000 to Allied Properties, the solicitor's statement claimed the Bhattis were owed £4million. Cooksey said the brothers were propping up 'gigantic debts' amassed by the club over the course of their ownership. 'They are fed up of being the butt of everything. They are misunderstood,' he protested.

The deputy leader of Wolverhampton Council disagreed. 'I think this just demonstrates their attitude,' he said. 'They are jeopardising efforts to save the club. Nobody has been given any chance to validate any of these claims. Let them show proof.'

The Bhattis were eventually forced to cooperate with the receivers when a High Court ruling by Mr Justice Walton ordered them to hand over records of Wolves' financial affairs. Allied Properties lost its grip on the club when a Middle East bank called in the receiver over a £700,000 debt, leading to the seizure and sale of Allied Properties'

London headquarters. The way was now clear for Wolves' receivers to sell off the ground and buildings without the owners' consent.

It was the Labour-run council, led by John Bird, that stepped up to secure Wolves' future with a consortium fronted by Jack Harris and Dick Homden, proposing a property development deal to purchase Molineux and all the club's land. The council struck a £1.1million deal for Molineux and the remaining club property, including the Castlecroft training ground. Asda agreed to pay £1.8million in return for planning permission to build a superstore behind the North Bank, with the Birmingham construction firm J.J. Gallagher, fronted by Harris and Homden, purchasing the club and renting the stadium from the council.

Although Wolves entered the 1986/87 season in the Fourth Division, there was a sense that the club was bottoming out. Brian Little took caretaker charge before being replaced by Graham Turner. There were still a few nasty surprises around the corner, including an FA Cup first-round defeat to non-league Chorley, but the club rallied to finish in the play-off positions, losing out to Aldershot over two legs, before the revival and climb back up the divisions began the following season.

'Graham Turner, I still don't think he gets the credit he deserves for what he did for that football club, and the players,' says Harrison. 'Those people who saw it through the hard times, they did the hard work. Again, it was on a shoestring.'

The Bhattis were consigned to history. Their four-year absentee tenure ran the club into the ground. They left as they arrived, neither seen nor heard. They have still never commented on their time in charge of Wolves. Attempts at correspondence with Mahmud were made at his registered business addresses in north London and Dubai during the writing of this book, but no reply was received.

Questions over their motives still remain unanswered. Had the land behind the North Bank been sold to the Bhattis in 1982, could Wolves' history have taken a different turn? 'It might have been different, you don't know,' says Harrison. 'There was a lot of suspicion about them because of the way things turned out, but whether or not they'd have put money in, I don't know. Graham Hawkins was promised all this money but it never happened. I went down to London with Albert and Muriel Bates [from Wolves Official Supporters' Club] and other fans to knock on the door of their offices but they never answered. The Bhattis were almost mythical figures. You knew they were there but you never met them, saw them or spoke to them.

'Dougan was hoodwinked by them to a large extent. When he first met them it was in a Portakabin up at Manchester Airport. They were wearing robes and convinced him that they were genuinely wealthy, like the current Manchester City owners. Dougan said he went to their offices in London and they had pictures of King Faisal and other Saudi princes all over the wall, and it turns out they were of Pakistani heritage from Manchester.'

For Harrison, his spell as a full-time reporter covering Wolves came to an end shortly after the Bhattis were removed in 1986, but he has continued to report on the club in various roles ever since.

So how does he regard that turbulent period of Wolves history? 'As a journalist it was almost like manna from heaven, but at the same time it was heart-breaking to see the club go through that, going through such a traumatic time when you didn't know if there was going to be a Wolves from one day to the next. It was never dull, put it that way. Every day there would be a story, and sometimes you didn't have to do that much work, they would just fall into your lap.

'I almost had to divorce myself from being a fan. I used to have to write stuff I didn't like writing because it was about my club and the struggles they were going through

– people not getting paid and the ground in decay, the fans deserting them.'

The supporters left in their droves during those dark times. But it can also be argued that the fans did not give up on the club, it was the club that gave up on the fans. 'That's probably true,' Harrison reflects. 'The exact opposite of what we're seeing now. There's such a stark contrast between Allied Properties and Fosun. It's not just the financial clout, it's the quality of the football as well isn't it? You're seeing something off the scale now. Football today is about how much money you spend; you can correlate those top six or seven positions in the table with how much money you spend. But it's not just the money, it is the recruitment and the quality of players we've signed. It's what we've been waiting for all these years.'

Chapter 5

MOMENT OF TRUTH

An unlikely audition for Derek Ryan

ON THE opening day of the 1984/85 season, one of the more colourful scenes in Wolves' history was played out. Three months earlier, in May, the club had suffered the first of three successive relegations, which took Wolves from the top to the bottom division in just over two years. Under the management of former Manchester United boss Tommy Docherty, the hope was that the Second Division team could bounce straight back to the top tier. Sheffield United were the opponents in front of 14,908 spectators at Molineux on 25 August.

Sat next to Docherty in the home dugout was a highly rated Irish teenager named Derek Ryan, who did not even have a professional contract. Next to Ryan was a BBC reporter and his cameraman. As the game progressed, the reporter conducted an interview with the manager and his young hopeful, who had never kicked a ball in professional football.

'It's not normal for an apprentice to go on as a substitute, is it?' asked the reporter.

'You're not a normal player, are you Derek?' Docherty replied, as Ryan smiled self-consciously. 'He's a good player for an apprentice, that's why he's sitting here today.'

After 57 minutes, the 17-year-old replaced Alan Ainscow for his first appearance in senior football. For three months the BBC film crew followed Ryan and Steve Blackwell, a fellow apprentice and Wolves supporter, as they tried to earn a contract at the club. The filming was for a documentary entitled *Moment of Truth*, screened in 1985. The half-hour programme ended with the pair being called into the manager's office to find out if they had earned professional terms.

A dramatic voiceover announced, 'Derek Ryan will sign professional or get the sack,' as he walked down the corridor to Docherty's office. It was a fascinating insight into the state of the club at the time, and the trials and tribulations of players trying to make the grade. It has been uploaded on to YouTube. The contrasts between then and now are stark. It was a scenario that could not be further removed from the current recruitment set-up at the club. There was certainly no Jorge Mendes to call upon, as Wolves looked to pick up untapped talent.

Almost 35 years have passed since that debut, when we meet up to discuss the career path that eventually brought Ryan home. Wolves' 2018/19 season is over. The club have qualified for Europe for the first time in 39 years. It is the day of the Europa League second-round qualifying draw in mid-June. Wolves will face either Faroe Islands side B36 Tórshavn or Northern Ireland's Crusaders. 'Up to the north, hey. They'll get a big crowd for that. There'll be a lot of Wolves fans on this island now,' says Ryan.

There are three parts to Ryan's story. It is one of potential and hope. Then of setbacks and rejection. And finally of, ultimately, fulfilment. Ryan has chosen a scenic spot for a chat, close to his home on the outskirts of north Dublin, where he grew up. Sitting down on the terrace of the Shoreline Hotel in Donabate, overlooking the Irish Sea and the coast down towards Malahide and the Howth cliffs, he starts from the beginning.

'Where we lived, in Coolock, there was an under-12s team. Back in the day you'd start at under-12s, there were no smaller-sided games for younger players then. I was nine and we used to play in the Road Leagues every summer. The Road Leagues were a competition between all the local roads. The manager of the under-12s team was there and all my mates were saying, "You should ask him if you can play." I remember walking round the back of his house one Saturday morning, he was a big guy from Cork, a lovely fella, and I said, "Is it okay if I come and play with the lads today?" And he said, "Yeah, I've seen you play, no problem."

'So we went out that Saturday morning and played a local team from just up the road and we won 12-3, and I scored six goals. Something clicked with me then where I thought, "This is good, I like it, I'm good at this." That's my first-ever competitive game of football that I can remember.

'When I was 12 or 13 my dad got a job at Dublin Airport so we moved to Swords, which was closer. I joined a local team called St Cronan's. I played really well for them, and we won the league. There was a guy at school who played for St Kevin's, which is one of the biggest schoolboy clubs over here, and I started playing for them at under-14s. Once you play for them you've got people watching you. I got selected for the Dublin under-15s team, I started scoring a few goals and you've got different people watching their games too. Eddie Corcoran was the scout here who spotted me, he was Wolves' scout over here back in my day.

'I played one particular game for St Kevin's against Home Farm, and that was a big derby match. We hammered them 5-1 and I had one of those games where it was just brilliant, nothing could go wrong. I scored four and won a penalty. Eddie was there that day. He was a local guy who lived up that neck of the woods and he'd probably seen me a few times. I remember I came home from Mass one Sunday morning and he was sitting in the front room talking to my dad. I didn't even know he was coming round. He told us he was with Wolves and asked if I wanted to go over and have a trial.'

Ryan had become an Ireland schoolboy international by the time of his trials, in 1982, and was well known in football circles in his country. He travelled to the United Kingdom on his own, knowing that his whole future in the game lay ahead.

'It was exciting. From when I started playing and realising you went on a trial if you were any good, it was something that I always wanted to do. I stayed in digs by the Connaught Hotel with Tim Flowers for a week. I would have done that maybe three times during the school holidays in 1982. When I was 16 you were allowed to sign as an apprentice, but I was only 15 when I went on a trial. I was there in October, when Graham Hawkins was manager, and John Jarman was the coach looking after us. He called me into the office and said I'd done well and that they'd like me to come back and sign for them on a two-year apprenticeship when I was old enough. I went back and signed terms the day after my 16th birthday, on 3 January 1983.'

For the duration of his time at Wolves he stayed in digs in Finchfield, with Stan and Joan Probert. 'You're 16 years old and you think you know everything, but you need someone of that maturity and responsibility to keep you in line, but it was good, they were really lovely people.'

Ryan settled in quickly. He got on with his apprenticeship as the first team won promotion from the Second Division in May 1983. The following season, as Wolves struggled in the top flight, the Irishman continued to progress.

'By the start of 1984 I'd been there a year and was starting to play regular reserve-team football, scoring quite a few goals,' Ryan explains. 'Then the following season I came back after the summer break and started well again in pre-season. Doc was manager by now, and he moved me from a striker to a winger. He said he thought I was too small to be a forward. Back then there was a lot of tackling from behind and people looking to hit you, not like it is now, so purely because of my size he moved me out. I was quite technical, good feet and quick rather than being a big lad who was good at heading the ball.'

As well as a new manager, there was a BBC Manchester television crew on the scene, who had been given permission by Docherty to follow the progress of Ryan and Blackwell.

'Doc called me into the office one day and said that they wanted to do a documentary about the club, and about the kids at the club,' Ryan recalls. 'It was all based on a final decision of, "Did you or didn't you make it?" It was me and Blackie, we were next in line as the ones who the decisions had to be made about, so it fitted in with the filming of the programme.

'He said there was a few bob in it for the club and he asked if I was ok with that, and I said it was no problem. I remember them being at pre-season a few times, that game wasn't the first time they showed up. It was nerve-racking being on the camera, I wasn't used to that at all. I was quite a shy kid until I stepped on to the football pitch. Then I was a completely different character, I was quite vocal and wasn't afraid to say what I thought or have a go at referees or other players. But the television cameras were not an area that I was naturally comfortable in, but it wasn't a problem.'

So how did the prospect of being joined on the substitutes' bench go down?

'I was more nervous about the football, wondering whether or not I was going to get on, than bothering about a camera,' Ryan adds. 'I remember the ground back then. There were huge spaces between the pitch and the stands. It wasn't so bad at the goal ends, but on the sides it was ridiculous. I don't remember anything about the game, though, it's all just from watching the documentary clips back.'

Docherty had turned up at Molineux on a one-year contract, as the wise-cracking, larger-than-life manager looking to reinvigorate the players. 'We pay weekly here, very weakly,' was one of the gags he tried out in front of the cameras when addressing a young apprentice. His often abrasive character could rub people up the wrong way. He did not get on with chief executive Derek Dougan, but Ryan warmed to the Scot.

'I liked Doc, he was funny. I remembered seeing him on the television when he was Manchester United manager in the 70s. Back then he had that aura about him. I know there were plenty of stories about him over the years, but at the time I thought he was great. He was playing me, I was enjoying my football and I was playing with some big name players who had been playing in the First Division the year before, so it was all good.'

A second story emerged from *Moment of Truth*, involving the youth-team coach Frank Upton, who had been appointed by Graham Hawkins. Upton had been overseeing the development of Ryan and Blackwell, but was sacked towards the end of the filming.

'Did you have any inkling this was going to happen?' asks the BBC reporter during an interview at his home the day the news breaks. 'None whatsoever,' Upton replies, visibly upset. A couple of the apprentices appear on camera to say how sorry they are about his dismissal. Docherty replaced Upton with one of his former Manchester United players, Greg Fellows.

'Frank was a great guy, a really traditional, old-fashioned coach,' Ryan remembers. 'He would regularly tell us about how we could be working down the mines. "This isn't a real job lads," that sort of thing, and he was dead right. He used to drive around in a club car, with a tape of *You'll Never Walk Alone* playing, and he'd just be singing his heart out in the car, a great guy.'

Throughout the documentary, Ryan is referred to as 'Dodger' by his coaches and team-mates. 'I got a reputation for not doing all the jobs that you were supposed to do, which was completely unwarranted,' he adds. 'They called me the Artful Dodger, so Dodger stuck. Totally unwarranted, a very hard-working man, I was!'

It is at this point Ryan reveals there was some artistic licence at play when the moment of truth came to pass, when the cameras followed him into the manager's office in November as he prepared to find out whether or not there was a contract for him.

'Doc told me beforehand, he called me in a while before. That part was all for the cameras, I knew what was happening. Because I was doing well and had played a couple of games, as I was leaving the room he said, "Listen, don't worry about this other thing with the cameras. I'm going to sign you pro. Do you want a two- or three-year contract?" That's exactly what he said to me. I got the rest of that season and another two years. Eventually, after I had played six or seven games, he said I'd done well but needed to go back to the reserves and regroup, I was too young to be playing regularly.'

Blackwell shook on a deal with Docherty for the cameras and made it on to the pitch as a substitute in late April. But when the 1984/85 season finished he left the club, returning to the terraces to follow the club he supported. Ryan was the much better prospect. On awarding him a contract, Docherty said, 'There's no reason why you shouldn't go on and play for your country.'

'I was still dreaming about achieving that, absolutely,' says Ryan. 'I played schoolboys at under-15s and under-18s. I remember one game we drew 3-3 with Wimbledon, I played on the right wing and made a couple of goals. I was up against Nigel Winterburn and skinned him alive, I did well that day.'

However, for the club, the season ended in relegation from the Second Division. There was turmoil off the pitch too, as the Bhatti brothers' failing regime saw the club lurching from one financial crisis to another. Ryan, still only 18, found himself working with two more managers during the 1985/86 season in the Third Division. Wolves made a dreadful start under the caretaker management of Sammy Chapman. But when Bill McGarry returned for a second spell in charge at the club in September, there was renewed optimism. McGarry restored Ryan to the side as a striker. It immediately paid off when, in late October, he played arguably his best game for the club. Wolves travelled to face Reading, who were top of the table on 39 points after winning all their opening 13 matches. Wolves were second from bottom, above only Darlington, on eight points. Ryan scored twice to secure a 2-2 draw, and it looked as if he had made the breakthrough.

'I thought we had a decent enough team,' he adds. 'Things were starting to come round a bit with McGarry. We used to train down at the racecourse, and I remember he came down one Friday morning, out of the blue, and called us in and said that he was gone, back to South Africa or wherever it was. I did really well under him. Then Sammy Chapman came back in and he kept playing me, and there was a point where I should have been left out of the team, because there was about seven or eight weeks when I was being picked when I was really struggling.

'Of the 15 starts I had that season, six or seven of those games I shouldn't have played in. I was too young. I wasn't able to do it physically. We were going through the motions, it probably didn't help that we were getting beaten as well. My memory of that season was that I played for too long. If everything was being run correctly with a proper squad and a development process then I should have gone back to the reserves before they had a look at me again. Eventually I was dropped. The club wasn't in the proper state where anyone could be developed correctly. I'm not using that as an excuse, by any means, but when you see the way things are done now it's totally different. Even going over as an apprentice, flying over on my own as a kid, that doesn't happen now.

There was a time when I should have been rested and given a chance to recharge the batteries.'

So was there a sense of being on board a sinking ship?

'With all due respect to Sammy Chapman, he obviously didn't have the clout of Bill McGarry. I think he might have been a little out of his depth, we were probably all out of our bloody depth in that situation.'

It was a chaotic season, with 34 different players used in the league. Only two, David Barnes and Jon Purdie, started more than 30 games. Eleven players made only eight starts or fewer. Gates had plummeted to a record low, with four league attendances at Molineux dropping below 3,000. It was no surprise when Wolves were relegated for the third successive season. Off the pitch, the club was lurching to a second administration in just four years.

'You knew there was no money there, there was nothing, but at that age I didn't know how it was supposed to be run properly,' Ryan says. 'There was no proper training gear, you just grabbed what you could. I was only on 30 quid a week when I started, and living in digs, but I always got paid, I don't remember any issues with being paid. Maybe in other areas of the club things would be cut. I vaguely remember noticing the guy who made the tea had gone one day and he was never replaced. He'd have been doing it for virtually nothing anyway. Then there were times when one or two of the office staff left.'

There were other moments that reveal the frustrations being experienced by supporters. Ryan laughs as he tells the story, but the first-team squad was involved in a very serious motorway incident on the way back from a defeat in the north of England.

'We were coming back on the coach from a game somewhere up north one night, I don't know who we were playing, it was quite early on in my time there. I remember Jim Barron was still involved with the team, but it was when things were starting to go a bit pear-shaped. We'd obviously had a bad result because there was a fan on the way back from the match too, and he copped the bus going down the motorway and started driving in front of the coach and then slamming the brakes on forcing the coach to stop. This went on for ten or 15 minutes, it got quite bad. Jim was up at the front, shouting, "Get his fucking licence number, get the police!" It actually went to court, and the man was done for dangerous driving. God love him, some poor fan who'd gone up and watched us getting trounced, and it was his way of letting his frustration out. "Let's kill the lot of them!" he must have been thinking.'

Ryan was one of many youngsters thrown in at the deep end. Several of his old team-mates still turn out in the gold and black today. The Wolves All Stars, a former players' team that takes part in charity fundraisers, are growing in strength each year. Under the long-time management of Mel Eves, scorer of Wolves' last goal in Europe prior to the exploits of Nuno Espírito Santo's side, they are building a strong following as they tour the Midlands playing in various charity games.

One of the best-supported fixtures of their 2018/19 season took place at the Tally-Ho Sports Ground, in the shadow of Birmingham's Test cricket venue, Edgbaston, when they faced their counterparts from Birmingham City. The Wolves All Stars starting XI contained three men who played in front of the lowest league crowd ever to walk through the gates of Molineux. Purdie, Micky Holmes and Dean Edwards all played in the 1-1 draw with Bury on 18 March 1986 that drew a gate of just 2,205. A fourth, Neil Edwards, would also have been in the line-up that infamous day, had he not been out injured.

'I'm a local lad, I was a supporter, I stood on the North Bank terrace and then when I played for them it was great, because I'd be playing and half my mates were there watching,' says Dean, who made his debut midway through the Third Division relegation season. 'It was just an honour to play and they are still good memories. We didn't have a bad side: Tim Flowers was in goal and Geoff Palmer was still playing. We weren't losing just 1-0, we were losing 5-3. We were 3-0 up at Wigan Athletic in one game and came out for the second half and let in five. We were just letting in too many goals.'

Dean partnered Andy Mutch at Wigan that afternoon, the penultimate game of the season, and the pair both got on the scoresheet.

'At that age you don't really take into account what is going on behind the scenes, I just wanted to play for Wolves, I'd have done it for nothing,' Dean continues. 'It's difficult, I got in a consortium at Torquay years later and when you see it from the other side of the fence you understand more about the way football is run. It's a money industry. I'm still good friends with Greg Fellows, who was on the coaching staff at the time, and he's got some great stories.

'We were playing Grimsby away in the reserves and the coach turned up outside Molineux. The driver said to Derek Dougan that he wasn't going to take them anywhere until they paid for the last three match trips. They didn't pay so the driver just took the coach away. Tommy Docherty, the manager, said to Greg that he'd have to take the minibus, which was a clapped-out old thing. It was only a 12-seater so they could only take 12 people up. Greg had to be the driver and substitute, they couldn't take any more.

'We beat them 2-1. On the way back Greg stopped off to buy all the players fish and chips. He went into the office the next morning to see Keith Pearson, the secretary, to give him the chitty for the chips, and he wouldn't give Greg his money back. To this day he says the club owes him for 12 portions of fish and chips. The stories you could tell about those days are phenomenal. What annoys me is that we had five or six thousand watching us and now they get 30-odd thousand. Those fans who stuck with us, you've got to give them credit because they stuck with Wolves through thick and thin.'

Neil Edwards was a quick and nimble teenage striker with great promise. He was plucked from non-league outfit Oldswinford by Chapman and thrown straight into the starting line-up, bursting on to the scene in the 1985/86 season with seven goals in the opening 11 games. But an injury at home to Walsall in October was the beginning of the end.

'I did my cruciate, medial ligament and cartilage at the same time,' he explains. 'It was a twist against a guy who tackled me, he wasn't a dirty player or anything, but funnily enough I ended up playing with him at Kettering years later. It was just one of those things. I did it 35 years ago so to still turn out now and be playing for the All Stars is ok.'

After a 14-month lay-off, he returned in December 1986 with Wolves now a Fourth Division club, but six weeks later broke his leg during a 5-2 win against Burnley and never played for the club again. Despite the personal setbacks, Neil never talks down his time at Molineux.

'We formed a really good bond as players. We were quite a close-knit team. It was just with everything else going on – the Bhatti brothers owned it then so there wasn't a lot of money knocking about – it just made it difficult. But we knew we had that camaraderie that gets you so far. I loved every minute of it.'

Purdie came through the youth ranks as a promising attacking midfielder at Arsenal, lining up in the same Gunners junior side as Tony Adams, Martin Keown, Michael Thomas, David Rocastle and Niall Quinn before signing for Wolves in 1985. He made over 100 appearances during his three-year stay, before moving to Oxford United and later going part-time in order to pursue another career. He is back in the country for a few weeks in between his coaching job in Thailand on the tropical island of Koh Samui.

'I've been working in a community academy over there, where the parents pay for their kids to be coached,' he reveals. 'There's a mixture of Thais, Russians, Australians, French, English and more, from five to 16 years old. There are a lot of different nationalities, but I've learnt so much in the last year about all the different cultures. We've got six coaches and we train after school in the week and then in the daytime on Saturday and Sunday. It's enjoyable, but I do miss the banter over here. It's great to catch up with Micky, Dean and Neil today. Obviously the club didn't have the money that it's got now and we didn't enjoy the riches the players enjoy now but we had a great social time.

'The Bhattis were in charge when I first signed and the place was literally falling down, so it's great to see the club having grown and reinvigorated itself. I was 18 years old when I first signed so it was a matter of an opportunity to play first-team football and put yourself on the map. I was aware that things were not great, you couldn't not be, you read about it and you knew, but it was about personal ambition and enjoying it as well, getting paid to play football. It's every kid's dream, isn't it? Football is a tough old ambition, it's not all glamour that it seems on the outside. In those days the money wasn't great but we built up good friendships at the time because we all stuck together, we were a close team.'

The 1986/87 season was a watershed one for the club, and for Ryan. The receivers had been called in to bring an end to the Bhattis' ownership, with the club coming into the hands of a new owner, construction firm J.J. Gallagher. For the first time in the decade, there was a stable environment off the pitch. But the new broom, with Graham Turner installed as manager, swept Ryan out.

'Straight away I didn't get a sniff, and I don't know why,' Ryan says. 'Graham took me up to that famous cup match at Chorley, and he brought me on two minutes from the end when we were losing 3-0 to cup-tie me. My take on it is that Steve Bull was the man coming in. He probably looked at it and saw I had been playing centre-forward and knew that he was bringing Bully in, that's the only explanation I can think of, but I didn't get a sniff.

'I stayed for the entire season, which was a mistake. I look back on it now with a bit of maturity, but at the time I thought as I had a year left on my contract I'll stay and see it out. I should have got out straight away. After Christmas I went on loan for a month to Shelbourne. There was also a time when we played Bournemouth in December, and a couple of months later Graham told me that the Bournemouth manager Harry Redknapp had asked why I wasn't playing. So in around February time I rang Harry and asked him if he was interested in me coming down, but nothing ever came of it. I didn't pursue it any further. There was no agent or anything like that, no one to offer advice. I don't remember having a conversation with anyone. All the guys I was mates with at Wolves had gone by then as well. I think I was one of the longest-serving players, which was crazy as I was 19 years old, and only turned 20 that season.'

The new-look Wolves was starting to take shape, with Bull, Mark Kendall, Andy Thompson, Robbie Dennison and Ally Robertson becoming mainstays of the subsequent promotions. Ryan's contract expired in the summer of 1987, but with age on his side and a long playing career still the most likely option, he took a completely different career path.

'When I came back here to play for Shelbourne in February and March that's when the whole Australia thing came into my head,' Ryan continues. 'A lot of people from Ireland were going over to Australia on working visas, it was the done thing at the time. There weren't a huge amount of jobs about for anyone really, but especially people like myself who didn't have that much of an education who had left school early.

'There had been nearly a full year of not playing, being in the reserves. So by the end of the season I wasn't even playing for the reserves, I was back with the youth lads where I'd been three years earlier. I got a bit demoralised with it all, I just knew my face didn't fit in that scenario. There were some guys who were writing to other clubs to try and get fixed up somewhere, but I never did that. I don't know why, I knew I wasn't going to make a career out of it, so I wasn't going over to Australia to play professional football, it was a clean break.

'I went on my own but a couple of mates followed me over. We stayed in Sydney for a year and a half and loved it. I worked in a sports shop selling trainers, football boots, stuff like that. I played football at the weekends part-time, trained three nights a week and played on a Sunday. I just found a club when I went over. They were called North Shore United. We lived in a place not far from Chatsworth, and we used to get the ferry over to Manly.'

Ryan had put some distance between himself and Wolves. The time spent working and socialising away from football proved to be valuable, particularly for his own state of mind.

'Put it like this, the year and a half over there was the best thing I ever did, because if there were any lingering issues with the football, it put them to bed,' he explains. 'I knew when I finished at Wolves that that was it, whether that was right or wrong, I knew I wasn't going back. I got a call just before I left from the ex-Ireland international Jimmy Holmes, who was manager of Nuneaton at the time, and he wanted me to go down to them the following season. But I had come over to England to be a professional footballer with a decent club, no disrespect to anyone who plays for Nuneaton, but I didn't go over to do that.

'That wasn't going to work for me. I wasn't going to go down and play in the lower levels of the league and spend the next ten years going around from club to club. I didn't want to end up in my 30s, married with a couple of kids and then be out of work because my football career was over. I didn't want to be that guy. No disrespect at all to anyone who does that, I take my hat off to them, because that's what they want to do, they've lived their dream, they've had a real football career compared to what I've had, but that wasn't for me. I was thinking, "Let's get out of here." In that year and a half away in Australia I didn't come home so there was no one saying, "Oh you're back, what's the story? You didn't make it?" I had a great time over there.

'By the time I did come back I had been six years away from home and then I had to decide what the next step was after that. If I had come back I may have gone to a League of Ireland team, played part-time and still not really sorted out my career. How long do you pursue the football? It was good to get away from it all.'

At the age of 22, Ryan began to build a new career for himself after getting a break back home.

'I came back to Swords and I had been home about a month when a friend of my uncle's rang, who worked in the Voluntary Health Insurance (VHI), which is a private health insurance company in Dublin. He asked if I'd like to go in for three months and work there during the summer. All the insurance companies and banks in Dublin used to have this soccer competition in the summer, where you'd play matches every Tuesday night and there'd be a final at the end of the summer. It was a bit of a big deal for part-time footballers, but you had to work for the company to play.

'So he said, "I'll get you in but I can't get you a full-time job because you don't have your Leaving Cert." That's the exams you do at 18, the equivalent of 'A' Levels. Because I'd left school at 16 I hadn't done them, I had just done the equivalent of 'O' Levels, and then I moved to Wolves. I went in there for three months, working in the post room, which is the place everybody goes when they start at a big company, playing football on Tuesday nights.'

Ryan moved from the post room to a job in the security department, before the opportunity to work full-time presented itself in a conversation with a member of the human resources department. The company saw Ryan's potential, but in order to progress he needed to do his Leaving Cert.

'At the time there was a culture at the company of people studying for better qualifications at night on various courses, it was encouraged and paid for by the company,' he explains. 'So that's what I did, while I did the exams I stayed on working with the promise of a full-time job at the end of it. I did five exams, which meant I passed my Leaving Cert. It took two years. When that two years was up I was made permanent and then I was entitled to go for other jobs. Because I had got used to studying at night, I decided to go to Trinity College and study for a degree in IT. So I spent seven years studying at nights for the degree. Half-way through that an opportunity came up for a position in the IT department in the telecoms area and I got into that. And that was about 20 years ago. I'm still with the company now.'

The only football Ryan got involved in back in Ireland was strictly on a part-time basis for the love of playing. There was never a moment when he thought about attempting to get back into the professional ranks.

'When I first joined VHI, I started dabbling a bit in the League of Ireland, training with Drogheda and playing a couple of games with them,' he adds. 'Then years later we used to have a team that played in the amateur leagues over here, and I played until about the age of 33, but eventually we ran out of players and had to pull the team. That was when I stopped playing.'

So does it feel like 35 years have passed since that Molineux debut in front of the watching BBC documentary crew?

'No, absolutely not! The first three years there I loved it, it was all good. You can sort of nit-pick at different parts of the period when things weren't going well, but in general everything was great at that age. It was just the last nine months that things went pear-shaped. But other than that I look back on it very fondly.

'I suppose, with hindsight, I couldn't have picked a worse time in the sense of what was happening around the club. If I'd been there earlier there may have been a chance to get some stability, or if I'd come in later then I might have come out of the other side, but being there then was right in the middle of it all as we went down through the divisions.'

Ryan has two sons now, with his wife Eva. Fifteen-year-old Daniel and six-year-old Josh are keen football fans, but their dad's exploits have largely been consigned to history.

'It doesn't mean much to them because it was so long ago. They've seen a few photographs and they've watched the documentary. None of my goals were filmed though. There was actually a television strike on at the time of many of them. That Reading game, when they were top and I scored both goals, it might normally have had a camera there, but the blackout went on for quite a long time, so as far as I know none of my goals were ever filmed.'

But since Wolves' elevation to the Premier League under Fosun's ownership, Ryan's previous career has become a conversation topic again.

'The funny thing is, there's guys who've been at the company as long as I have, big football fans of clubs like Arsenal and Liverpool,' he reveals. 'And it's only in the last 12 months they have pulled me up and mentioned they were thinking of me when they saw Wolves playing on television against these big teams. "Oh that's who Derek used to play for," without realising there's quite a contrast between the team I used to play for and what's going on there now. Some of these people have been here 30 years and they've never said anything before, but now Wolves are becoming such a big club again, qualifying for Europe, people are bringing it up again.'

Ryan is proud of representing Wolves. It may have been the most turbulent era in the club's history, but he recognises that he played his small part. As a schoolboy boarding the plane to England, he set out on the journey with childhood dreams. Those dreams were already over by the time his teens came to an end, but the life Ryan has built since is one to be proud of. Every now and then his thoughts return to Molineux, and the supporters who watched him play for a club in chaos.

'Sometimes I think, "I hope those 2,000 people are still going now," and not being ripped off with a 70 quid ticket. Do you know what I mean? I just hope they can afford to go. It was more than football for those fans watching back then, with what was going on, especially at those away games.'

Chapter 6

BULLY

A working-class hero

THE ENTRANCE hall and bar of the Oakengates Theatre in Telford are packed with Wolves supporters. Tickets were snapped up months in advance. They are here to see their hero, the man who is responsible for the rebirth of the modern-day club, a man who led Wolves out of the most shambolic and embarrassing period in its entire history. Through a double door to the auditorium, along a walkway to the right of the stalls and down some steps to the side of the stage, is the theatre's makeshift green room, where the stage stars wait before their performances.

Steve Bull is sat at a dressing room table signing autographs. A steady stream of paraphernalia is being ferried from the bar by his daughter Gracie. 'Can you sign that one "Best wishes to Tony" please, Dad?' she asks, placing a replica football in front of him. There is a knock on the dressing room door. A pair of audience members have backstage passes. The couple are in their 50s but have the excitable disposition of wide-eyed teenagers as they are welcomed into the small room for a chat with Bull. The man who so many fans still idolise has never quite understood it all. His unassuming manner and the matter-of-fact way he went about his job for so many years is at odds with the way he is perceived by others.

It is two decades since the club's record-breaking striker last kicked a ball for the club, and another ten years on top of that since his goalscoring heyday at Molineux. Yet, for the generation old enough to have witnessed him in his pomp, he will always be box office.

Bull is a hero like no other. His own career is a rags-to-riches fairy tale that stands as an incredible story of its own. But that barely tells the half of it. Bull's achievements transcended the field of play. He changed the fabric of the club beyond recognition. He joined a Wolves going through an existential crisis, playing at a crumbling Molineux in England's basement division, and left it proudly rebuilt and fit for the Premier League.

He is ingrained on the psyche of every supporter who can remember a Wolves before Bull. Supporting Wolves, as they slumped from the First Division to the Fourth Division between 1984 and 1986, was an undignified experience. A glance at attendance figures for the 1985/86 season, in Division Three, reveals the grip of the demise. On four occasions the league gate at Molineux dipped below 3,000, as Wolves limped to their third relegation in a row on the pitch. When hope is lost, there is little else to cling to. Supporters saw no way out of the situation.

Around the same time as the Bhatti brothers took control of the club, Bull was taking his first steps into working life. Raised on a council estate in Tipton, in the heart of the Black Country, he was the youngest of six children to parents George and Joan. Still too young to vote, he left school with few qualifications and needed to find work.

'I was 16 years old. What do you do in Tipton? You have to go and earn your crust,' Bull explains. 'I had three jobs before I played football. The first one was in a bed factory called Vono in Dudley. It was through an agency and I was on £27.50 a week. I used to have to give my mum the pay packet at the end of the week, and she'd give me the pocket money back. That was just the way it was in those days. All they said to me at the factory was, "Glue the ends of the beds and screw the screws in, and you'll be alright." Well, some of the screws wouldn't go in so I used to hammer them in. So, if you had a bed in 1982 and it bust, I do apologise.'

From there, Bull moved on to a builders' yard in Tipton with a company called Willner Building Supplies. Again, it was manual labour, driving the forklift trucks around, loading and unloading building materials. The job came to a swift end when he was caught loading up vans in the yard with stock that hadn't been paid for. 'It's an 'orrible word to say but, in Tipton, they call it fiddling.' Bull smiles, but looks slightly sheepish. 'When you're on £27.50 a week, it's not enough.'

His third job was at a warehouse in Sandwell for a company called Dom Holdings, packing fasteners in readiness for distribution. 'I was doing 12 hours a day then. I was on my bike at six o'clock in the morning, cycling along the canal cut and not coming back until six or seven in the evening. I was playing for three football teams back then. I was turning out for the Red Lion pub on Saturday morning, Tipton Town in the West Midlands League later on a Saturday afternoon, and then for Newey Goodman in the Holts Sandwell League on Sunday morning.

'I just wanted to play football all the time. I remember having to work extra to save up for a pair of football boots.'

But that simple wish took a blow when Bull was diagnosed with a serious knee injury. 'I had to have an operation when I was 17. I had a floating body in my knee, a piece of bone that had broken off. They sent me to get it out and initially they said I'd be okay to carry on playing for Tipton Town. I had a job too so I was alright, but when I went in for the operation the anaesthetist said I'd never be able to play professional football.'

The condition, known as osteochondritis, could have caused Bull's knee to break had it not been operated on. His surgeon at Wordsley Hospital, Harold Bowie, was in no doubt that the injury was serious enough to prevent Bull ever stepping on a pitch again.

'It would have been quite logical to say he wouldn't play football again,' Bowie recalled some years later. 'His was a similar injury to the one that ended Denis Compton's career. I had doubts at the time about how the operation would turn out, because there were a lot of loose bodies within the knee.'

Following a period of rehabilitation after the operation, Bull continued playing for his Saturday and Sunday teams with little concern for trying to make it as a professional. Most players had already been spotted by his age, and would have been taken under the wing of professional clubs as Youth Training Scheme (YTS) players. He was coming to the end of his teenage years, happy to play at amateur level, work in the week and spend his evenings in the pub.

But a few years earlier, without realising as much, Bull had been spotted. It was whilst playing for Willingsworth School team that a scout called Sid Day, who ran the Tipton Town youth team, saw the potential in Bull. He invited the 15-year-old to join the club. 'He was nothing to look at, no physique. He was skinny but he could hit a ball hard,' Day recalled several years later. Bull joined his youth team and began playing in the Sandwell Sunday League Division Five. As the striker progressed through the ranks to join the senior team, Day kept an eye on his progress.

'Sid used to come along and watch with his little Jack Russell,' Bull continues. 'He knew Johnny Giles [manager] and Nobby Stiles [youth-team coach] at West Brom. He went in to Nobby one day and told him that he'd seen a player who could probably score a few goals, "If you could get him off his work." So Nobby asked him to bring me along to train on Tuesday and Thursday nights after work had finished.

'I'd do the six-to-six shift, then get on the number 401 bus from Tipton to West Bromwich and walk the rest of the way to Spring Road [where Albion trained]. I remember going into my first training session as a 19-year-old and thinking, "What is this?" They were all about 14 years old, and they were all dribbling around me. I did it for several months, progressed through the intermediates, then the reserves. And Nobby came up to me one day, said they believed in me, and I got taken on.'

It was an unexpected rise. Bull handed in his notice at the warehouse and signed a one-year contract with West Bromwich Albion at the age of 20. Meanwhile, in less than the time it had taken Bull to progress from pub football to the ranks of the professional game, Wolves had dropped from the top to the bottom division. They began life in the Fourth Division in August 1986 with Brian Little as caretaker-manager. Off the pitch, a rescue package had been put together which finally saw the back of the Bhatti brothers.

When the new board replaced Little with Graham Turner on 7 October, supporters, relieved that the threat of going out of existence no longer hung over the club, felt that a backward step had been taken. Turner had struggled during his time as manager of First Division Aston Villa.

One of his first decisions on arriving at Molineux was to persuade directors Dick Homden and Jack Harris to part with £54,000 to bring Bull to the club from their near neighbours. 'It is a big investment,' Turner said at the time. 'But the club will get a long-term reward.'

He also signed Andy Thompson from Albion on the same day. Turner agreed with the advice of his chief scout, Ron Jukes, that Bull had the potential to thrive in the Fourth Division.

The unrefined striker had broken into Albion's first team, managing three goals in the Second Division, but by now Ron Saunders was in charge. Saunders did not rate the striker, going on record to suggest his touch was not refined enough for the level Albion were competing at.

Bull made his Wolves debut in a 3-0 home defeat to Wrexham on Saturday, 22 November. Two days later he travelled up with Thompson – both were ineligible to play – to watch a second replay of an FA Cup first-round tie against Lancashire part-timers Chorley, who had finished 20th in the Northern Premier League the previous season. Wolves lost 3-0. The following Saturday, Bull was back in the side for the trip to Lincoln City. He was booked and, for the third successive game, Wolves lost 3-0.

'We just got on with it,' Bull says, reflecting on a truly dreadful beginning to the duo's time at the club. 'In truth, we just wanted to play football. We didn't really understand the league. We had blinkers on really. We just put our boots on and went out there. If I'd understood then what I do now then there was no way I'd have gone down there.'

The club's fortunes improved, as he began to form an effective partnership with Andy Mutch. Bull scored 19 goals that season as Wolves improved to finish fourth in the table. They would lose a two-leg play-off final to Aldershot, missing out on an immediate return to the Third Division.

Saturday, 15 August 1987 is an infamous date in Wolves' history. It was the opening day of the club's second season in the Fourth Division. The fixture was away at Scarborough, the home club's first-ever match as a Football League club after being promoted from the Conference under manager Neil Warnock. The Wolves support had a hardcore hooligan contingent at the time who had caused trouble in the previous couple of seasons. There was crowd disorder at the end of a fixture at Blackpool in April 1986, further trouble in November away at Torquay, and a pitch invasion following a defeat to Southend in April 1987. The supporters involved were targeting seaside towns.

The local paper, the *Express and Star*, sent their Wolves correspondent David Instone up to Scarborough on the

Friday night in case any trouble began in the town on the eve of the game. 'The office asked me to keep an eye on it, let them know if anything happened,' Instone remembers. 'There was no problem on the Friday night, but the Saturday was a horrible, horrible day. Wolves had a crowd-control problem at the time and that was one of the games that told us why. It should have been Scarborough's proud day. It was crazy that the Football League sent Wolves there on the first day of the season. It was a stupid decision of theirs.'

The match was not all-ticket; 3,000 Wolves fans turned up, including the element that Instone had been sent to watch. 'Hundreds of those fans went, the disruptive fans,' Bull recalls. 'They were all on a mission to either fight or watch football. This fan was up on the roof of the stand, jumping up and down, and he just fell through it. We didn't see it happen but when we heard about it they said he actually bounced when he landed.'

The supporter fell through the roof of the Hinderwell Road Stand, where trouble had been taking place between rival sets of supporters, and was stretchered off by St John's Ambulance staff. Wolves fans were causing havoc elsewhere inside the ground. A newly refurbished refreshment kiosk was smashed up and stock taken, metal fences were pulled down, toilets ripped up, cisterns pulled off the wall and seats thrown on to the pitch. The kick-off to the second half was delayed for ten minutes, whilst manager Turner pleaded with fans to restore order and helped clear the pitch. In total, 56 supporters were arrested, including 40 from the Wolverhampton area.

Scarborough chairman Terry Wood gave an impromptu press briefing on the pitch after the game ended. 'I think they're a set of animals,' he said of the visiting supporters. 'I would urge Fourth Division clubs to ban all Wolves fans this season. Ken Bates [then Chelsea chairman] had the right idea in wanting electric fences. If farmers can use electric fences to get their animals in check, football clubs should be allowed them to halt soccer violence.'

Incredibly, the supporter who fell through the roof checked himself out of hospital and returned to the ground. 'We got the game over with, and we got back on board the coach afterwards,' Bull recalls. 'All of a sudden, as we are about to leave, a bloke gets on at the front with a sling on, asking for a lift. "I fell off the roof, I've been in hospital and my mates have left me. Can I come and sit at the back?" It was unbelievable. The gaffer actually gave him some money to get himself home.'

The fall-out from the trouble was significant. Wolves supporters were banned from attending six away games, with the club adding a further two-match sanction of their own. The West Midlands police launched operation G.R.O.W.T.H. [Get Rid of Wolverhampton's Troublesome Hooligans].

Divisional Commander David Ibbs held a press conference to highlight the work being done to rid the club of hooligans. He said, 'They'd meet at certain public houses and as visiting fans came into Wolverhampton they'd be waylaid and attacked. And there were many instances of quite dreadful violence being perpetrated. Inside the ground they'd act as a team, they'd leave before the end of the game to create ambushes. The whole scenario was a disgrace.'

Hooligan 'firms' had calling cards printed such as 'Bridge Boys on Tour, WWFC 1987/88'. One of the trouble causers called up a local radio station, Beacon Radio, in the aftermath of the Scarborough match. Speaking on condition of anonymity, he admitted, 'The football team aren't doing anything so the hooligans have to. Wolves haven't been in the papers, except for when we went down to Scarborough and battered them.'

It was warped logic but it revealed the state of mind that had taken root amidst a significant minority of the club's support. The decline of the previous years had stripped some fans of their status. Causing disorder was a means of regaining it. Whilst the majority of those attending games had no interest in trouble, it highlighted the deeper malaise. Wolves, a club that had been competing in the UEFA Cup just seven years earlier, were now a million miles from making headlines for anything they did on the pitch. Only the hooligans were interested in violence. But all of the supporters felt the pain of watching their club in the Football League's basement.

Bull scored on that opening day at Scarborough. And then he scored another 51 goals over the course of a season that ended with the club winning the Fourth Division title and lifting the Sherpa Van Trophy at Wembley. In Mutch, he found the perfect strike partner.

'Mutchy is the unsung hero, he's top drawer,' Bull says. 'I owe everything to him for my career at Wolves. We had a real combination, on the field we knew where we were. We linked really well. If you look through the archives of what we did together, we complemented each other, we were a great pairing.'

As supporters returned after the ban, the atmosphere began to change too. A team winning on the pitch shifted the focus. There was something to pin their colours to. There was someone to pin their colours to.

The 1988/89 season brought more of the same. Bull continued to excel on the pitch. He was becoming more prolific. Over a six-game spell between November and December he scored 14 goals, including three hat-tricks and two games when he scored four.

As supporters went on their travels, back at the old haunts of Blackpool and Southend, a repetitive chant grew stronger and stronger, following the club wherever they played. 'Ooh Bully Bully. Ooh Bully Bully.' The trouble never completely disappeared, but the usual calling card was now a goal or more from Bull.

He became a lower-division icon. A star of Ceefax's football pages on television. Fourth Division latest scores. Page three hundred and twenty something. Team names in blue letters and, underneath in white, the scorers. Wolves 1-0. Bull. Fifty times that season he scored for his club, adding to the 52 of the previous campaign. His half-century of goals in 1988/89 helped Wolves complete consecutive promotions, this time as Third Division champions.

The camaraderie amongst the players was unique. Many of the younger ones had been rejected at other clubs and had found validation under Turner. Others of a more senior age were enjoying an Indian summer. It was encapsulated by the introduction of car park training on a Friday, behind the disused North Bank stand at Molineux.

'Graham started it off,' Bull explains. 'On a Friday morning, wherever you were playing next day, we had to train on the car park. There was grit and gravel, bricks, cars, everything on the ground. We had to shift the cars out of the way before we started, and sometimes the alarms would start going off. All we did was put two cones at either end to make the pitch.

'We made it fun. We had the yellow jersey. The gaffer would mark on the chalk board who was the worst player over the week and they'd have to wear it on a Friday. In the end we got an Albion top instead. Everyone was flying into tackles, falling and rolling over, it was serious. But we never had any injuries at all. You'd just end up with a bit of grit in your hands.

'The fans used to stand down the sides and they'd help us with the cars as well. Over the weeks the cars were getting sparser and sparser because we kept hitting them. At the end of the training session we'd see other people coming back looking for their cars, they'd be 20 yards away.'

When the players left for a promotion celebration in Spain at the end of the season in late May, Bull found himself catapulted into the national spotlight. He joined his clubmate Mutch on an England B tour of Europe, taking in games against Switzerland, Iceland and Norway. It was a successful trip. Bull scored against Iceland on 19 May and then again against Norway three days later.

Meanwhile, the full England team were involved in a round-robin friendly tournament, the Rous Cup, with Chile and Scotland, which began on 23 May. England manager Bobby Robson had been unable to call upon any players from either Liverpool or Arsenal as the two clubs were involved in an extraordinary league title decider at Anfield three days after England's opening match against Chile. The fixture was one of two Liverpool matches re-arranged after the season's scheduled finish, in the aftermath of the Hillsborough disaster. John Barnes, Peter Beardsley and Alan Smith were consequently ruled out. With Gary Lineker's Barcelona side also involved in a late season finish in Spain, Robson was down to the bare bones.

The England manager handed debuts to John Fashanu and Nigel Clough at Wembley, as England laboured to a 0-0 draw against Chile. The following Saturday, 27 May, England faced Scotland at Hampden Park. With Fashanu a doubt after receiving a knock in the Chile match, Robson put a call in to Dave Sexton, who was managing the B team, to find out how Bull had been performing. He decided to take a chance on the player, who had only just arrived back in England after the B tour. Wolves secretary Keith Pearson made the telephone call to inform him, and Bull was on the next flight up to Scotland, where he was transferred by car to the senior team's hotel in Troon.

'I arrived and the only kit I had was my Quaser boots,' Bull recalls. 'It was like Christmas at the hotel, though – in your room you've got boots, trainers, tracksuits, the lot. I slept for a couple of hours, got up and then Bobby introduced me to all the players the next day. I was so nervous. It was such a step up from the under-21s and B team. You get to the senior squad and you're wondering what you're doing there. I didn't know what to think.'

Bull was a Third Division player mixing with established stars like Peter Shilton, Bryan Robson, Chris Waddle, Stuart Pearce and Terry Butcher. With almost 65,000 inside Hampden Park, Bull could not quite believe the situation he found himself in as he took his seat amongst the substitutes.

'I looked up at the corner where our fans were and I could see a load of Wolves fans, I couldn't believe they'd come to see me,' he says. Thirty years on, there is still a tone of incredulity in Bull's voice as he recounts the events of that sunny May afternoon in Glasgow. 'The game's going on and then, quite early on, John Fashanu goes down. Bobby tells me to warm up, but I'm still not thinking I'll be going on. Ten minutes later Fashanu goes down again, and I'm back out for another warm-up.

'Then Bobby shouts for me. I'm coming on. Fashanu walks off the pitch towards me, we smack hands and he wishes me all the best. Then about ten minutes from the end, it was Gary Stevens at right-back, he launches the ball forward, I go up for it and it bounces off my back, and the ball drops down for me. I just hit it. Bang. I'd scored. It was unbelievable. I started running, but I didn't know what to do, and I ran towards the Jocks! What was I doing? It was amazing, I couldn't understand it.'

Bull's goal made the rest of the country sit up and take note. In an era when only a handful of games were shown live on television each year, millions had tuned in for the Rous Cup decider that afternoon. Football fans across the country had been given a taste of what Wolves supporters had been enjoying for the past two seasons. 'I don't want to go overboard,' said Robson after the match. 'But Bull is the most refreshing player to hit the scene for a long time.'

No player is bigger than a club. But for a time it appeared that Bull was as big as Wolves. The immediate success of the team from the moment he pulled on a Wolves shirt – because he pulled on a Wolves shirt – meant that the player's fortunes were intertwined with the club's. Bull symbolised the shift from bankruptcy to respectability. His achievements became part of the identity of supporting the team.

The lines became blurred at times. Was it Wolves or Bull that the fans were cheering on from the terraces as the team progressed through the leagues? A fanzine named *A Load of Bull* sprung up from the terraces. When supporters made their vocal presence felt at matches, as many songs were devoted to the working-class hero as they were to the club itself. When Bull made the short journey across the Black Country on that cold and dark November day in 1986 there was no belief on the South Bank. Supporters had lost hope. Bull, with his phenomenal goalscoring feats, changed all that. The impossible became possible.

He became a frame of reference for supporters of other clubs all across the land and beyond. 'Who do you support, mate?' 'Wolves.' 'Oh yeah, Steve Bull.' Three decades on, similar exchanges still take place.

As Wolves embarked on the 1989/90 season in the Second Division, supporters were just as excited about Bull's international prospects. The second part of the season was in a World Cup year. Was it possible that he could be called upon to play on such a grand stage? There were two games that proved pivotal for the player that season. The first was the New Year's Day Second Division match at Newcastle. His four goals in Wolves' 4-1 win were watched by Robson. From that moment onwards, Bull stole a march on Smith as the preferred back-up striker to the established England forwards Lineker and Beardsley.

The game that changed his name from pencil to ink on Robson's World Cup squad list took place at Wembley on 26 April 1990. It was against Czechoslovakia, the penultimate friendly before Robson named his squad of 22.

Bull lined up in attack alongside Lineker. Just 21,342 were inside Wembley stadium to see Bull's two goals that evening as England ran out 4-2 winners. His first was a powerful shot from the edge of the area after he chested down a fine ball from Gascoigne, the second was a clinical header from another Gascoigne pass.

As the only England player operating outside the top division of the country he was playing in, Bull stood out. 'I was the wildcard,' he says. 'I asked Bobby Robson once why he took me, and he said that none of the other countries knew much about me, they hadn't really seen me play.'

As the 25-year-old headed off to the World Cup in Italy to join the biggest names of world football, it was hard to imagine that just five years earlier he had been a non-league footballer at Tipton Town. 'It was excitement and disbelief,' Bull reflects. 'I was thinking back to being 17 and not even thinking about being a professional footballer. I was very lucky to be there.'

Bull scored in England's final warm-up game, a last-minute equaliser against Tunisia in Tunis, before the squad headed on to Sardinia where they were based for the group games. He was given a few minutes off the bench towards the end of the opening match, a 1-1 draw against Republic of Ireland, where he was marked by future Wolves manager Mick McCarthy. Then, in the second match, against European champions Holland, he was given just over half an hour up front alongside Lineker. This time he came up against the Dutch centre-back pairing of Ronald Koeman and Frank Rijkaard.

'Bully found himself in a match out of all proportion to anything he's ever been in in his life,' the England manager said afterwards. 'In all his life.'

Despite the game finishing goalless, Bull impressed with the way he unsettled the two illustrious figures at the back for Holland. Back home, the clamour for his selection from the start had been gaining impetus. Jimmy Greaves appeared on ITV's *Saint & Greavsie* wearing a t-shirt with 'LET THE BULL LOOSE' printed across the front. Another television programme ran a poll asking who England fans would like to see up front alongside Lineker. Of over 25,000 respondents, 64 per cent opted for Bull. The *Express and Star* sent their reporter out to the England camp in Sardinia with two sacks full of good luck letters from Wolves supporters back home.

'I was aware of the clamour, the *Saint & Greavsie* stuff, it was all over the place,' Bull says. It is hard for him now, almost 30 years on, to recall much of what happened on the pitch in Italy. Robson gave him a start against Egypt, a game England won 1-0 with a late Mark Wright header. Then another substitute appearance in the dramatic second-round victory against Belgium, won by David Platt's volley with virtually the last kick of extra time. Bull never got on the pitch again, though. He was an unused substitute in the quarter-final win over Cameroon, and remained on the bench throughout the epic semi-final against West Germany in Turin.

His last hope of getting on the pitch disappeared when Lineker equalised to make it 1-1 late on in the semi-final to send the game into extra time. 'I'd been warming up for a few minutes, and the gaffer had said I was going to get on,' says Bull. 'But when Lineker scored he told me to sit back down again. I'd have done anything to get on in that game. I'd have given it everything, just a few minutes to try to do something.'

Despite the tournament ending in such a heart-breaking manner, with defeat in a penalty shoot-out, Bull has nothing but fond recollections of his time away with England. It was a surreal time for the player, with memorable moments that encapsulated the leading characters of the time.

'I remember to keep us busy we had a race night, organised by Lineker and Shilton,' he says, smiling. 'They'd put on this video of some horse racing from a different country, and we'd have a few bets. Lineker and Shilton were the bookies, we're all sat watching the races. First race, everybody loses. Shilton is rubbing his hands together. Five races went on, hardly anybody won. Shilts and Lineker have got all the money lined up.

'The sixth race comes on, and there's a horse called Paul's Destiny running at 16/1. Gazza is telling us all to lump on. We're all saying, "No way Gazza, we're not doing that," but in the end we all bet on it. The race starts and this Paul's Destiny rears up at the back. It's five yards off the pack from the start. We all start jumping on Gazza, shouting and swearing at him. But then this horse starts closing in on the pack and coming through them. It just gets up to win the race on the nose, it was unbelievable.

'Lineker and Shilton are distraught – we've all won so much they have to go and get more money to pay us. Then the next morning, we're eating breakfast, all smiling. Lineker and Shilts have a table for two on their own. Then Gazza stands up and says, "Howay lads, you've got to give them the money back. I watched the video the day before." We had to give it all back. Scandalous, but that's Gazza for you.'

And that was the World Cup for Bull. Six weeks away with the best players in the country and a place in history. No player from outside the top division has ever represented England on the pitch at a World Cup since. There would be a couple more caps under new manager Graham Taylor, but Bull's time as an England player came to an end shortly afterwards, as England entered an era of decline which culminated in a failure to qualify for the 1994 World Cup.

Bull returned home to a place that had changed forever. At the end of the 1989/90 season, with Wolves now established as a Second Division side, the Gallaghers sold the club to lifelong fan Sir Jack Hayward. The Bahamas-based businessman set about rebuilding the dilapidated Molineux. The vast South Bank was the only part of it that Wolves fans had any remaining affection for. The huge terrace could still produce an inspiring atmosphere, despite it being able to accommodate only a fraction of the 30,000 supporters it could hold in its heyday, but the remaining parts of the ground were either unloved or unopen.

The John Ireland Stand had been completed in 1979. It was a smart two-tier structure with some of the country's very first executive boxes, back then. But it had been built over 50 yards from the pitch in anticipation of a ground redevelopment on all four sides. The project was shelved in 1981, owing to rising debts, leaving the stand cut adrift from the rest of the ground.

It was, at least, able to accommodate supporters. The North Bank terrace and Waterloo Road stands were closed in the wake of improved safety regulations after the Bradford City stadium fire in 1985. The North Bank's only function was to house a small club shop and the tiny office of the supporters' club, run by the devoted Albert and Muriel Bates. The Waterloo Road stand was home to the dressing rooms and administration offices, but closed off to everyone else.

Sir Jack's money paid for three new structures, built closer to the John Ireland Stand. By the end of 1993 the new Molineux was completed. A nostalgic floodlit friendly against those prestigious opponents of the 50s, Honved, marked the stadium's official opening on 7 December. Bull finally had a stage his feats merited.

Yet, it was this second phase of his career that was to be characterised by frustration. The forward had almost single-handedly lifted the club to a position of respectability. He had brought ambition back to a Wolves that had lost its way. Yet it was this renewed hope that gradually became poisonous during a decade that turned out to be a sustained and futile period of under-achievement. The fairy tale part of Bull's career was over. Following the 1990 World Cup, his days would be defined by a series of deflating near misses.

After the amazing rise through the lower divisions under Turner's stewardship in the late 80s, the club stabilised for a couple of seasons in the Second Division. There was no meaningful progress, though. They finished the 1992/93 season in the renamed First Division – following the birth of the Premier League – in 11th place for a second successive occasion, with a record of won 16, drew 13, lost 17.

When supporters stood on the South Bank for one final time during the penultimate game of the campaign against Millwall on 1 May 1993, they were not just saying goodbye to the famous old terrace but they were waving off another season of obscurity with promotion no closer than it had been during their first season back at that level three years previously.

The squad was littered with hard-working players who could easily hold their own at that level, but they lacked the calibre to mount a serious promotion challenge. It was Bull and Mutch's last season together as a strike partnership. Robbie Dennison and Keith Downing had also survived from the Fourth Division days. But newer arrivals like Paul Blades, Paul Edwards, Mark Burke, Mark Rankine and an ageing Derek Mountfield did not quite cut the mustard, despite their work ethic.

Wolves had been bargain-basement shoppers for years. In addition to Blades and Edwards, the only other two signings made ahead of the 1992/93 season were Lee Mills, for £20,000 from Stocksbridge Park Steels, and Darren Simkin, for £10,000 from Blakenhall Town.

That all changed during the summer of 1993. Sir Jack released significant transfer funds for a squad overhaul. The headline-grabbing arrival was Geoff Thomas. An England international at the top of his game – who had been the subject of a bid from Arsenal the previous season and was being chased by Manchester City – was secured for £800,000. It was a signing that changed the landscape. In came Republic of Ireland international David Kelly from Newcastle United for £750,000 to partner Bull, followed by winger Kevin Keen from West Ham United for £600,000.

These were Premier League players coming down to Wolves. Even the free transfer of veteran striker Cyrille Regis from Aston Villa brought a touch of star quality. Four days into the season, defender Peter Shirtliff would come in from Sheffield Wednesday to complete an eye-catching set of summer acquisitions.

Supporters bounced into Molineux with great anticipation on a sunny August afternoon for the opening match of the 1993/94 season. There were changes to the kit, as players wore a traditional gold and black strip with the town's crest now replacing the wolf head, harking back to the era when Wolves won trophies.

It was not just a new-look team that excited supporters. Molineux's structural transformation really took shape during those summer months. The Stan Cullis Stand had replaced the North Bank the previous season, and with the South Bank now demolished, the majestic Billy Wright Stand rose from the ashes of the old Waterloo Road Stand.

Bristol City were beaten 3-1 in front of a sold-out Molineux. Two goals from Bull, including a vintage strike from outside the penalty area set up by Keen, and one from Mountfield sent fans home with the belief that his was the season they would complete the rise back to the top flight.

But an early season injury to Bull severely weakened the attack before a September afternoon at Roker Park delivered the biggest setback of all. Thomas was proving to be the talisman in midfield and had just scored a remarkable solo goal, collecting the ball ten yards outside his own box to run through the entire Sunderland defence to put Wolves 2-0 up. Then the Wearsiders defender Lee Howey exacted a brutal revenge. His over-the-top challenge put the England man out for the rest of the season.

Turner's men did not win any of their next five games and by November fans were calling for his head. A Bull hat-trick at Derby County helped keep his boss in a job, but by March, with the season seemingly meandering to another mid-table finish, a 3-0 defeat at Portsmouth spelt the end for the long-serving manager.

'When the money started coming to the club he lost it,' Bull admits. 'The money was overpowering the manager. We played Portsmouth away that night, then Jonathan Hayward [the chairman] came on to the bus after the game and had a right go at Graham in front of the players. He was gone after that.'

Bull had lost the manager who believed in him at a time when few others did. 'He had to twist Jack Harris's and Dick Homden's arms just to find £54,000 to sign me,' says Bull. 'He was under so much pressure then, the debtors were on his back, the chairman was on his back. He was top drawer, a superb man-manager. One of the best friends and best managers I've ever played under. We do stupid things as players, sometimes. Back in those early days the gaffer cut us some slack off the pitch. He used to give us some rope and say, "Go and hang yourself. Don't be any trouble, just come back with a result." I loved Graham Turner for that.'

With Turner gone, the Wolves board aimed high. Former England manager Taylor was brought in for his first role back in club football. Taylor had been hounded out of the England job by a blood-hungry tabloid media after a horrendous spell in charge of the national team. It was not a universally popular appointment at the time, with many supporters unconvinced by a man whose reputation was in tatters after failing to qualify England for the 1994 World Cup finals. He was also responsible for curtailing Bull's own England career prematurely.

The 1994/95 season saw further investment, with England winger Tony Daley and England under-21 international winger Steve Froggatt prised from Aston Villa during the summer, and Mark Walters and Paul Stewart brought in on loan from Liverpool. Taylor was unlucky with injuries too. Daley made just one substitute appearance all season, whilst Froggatt picked up an injury in December that brought a premature end to his campaign. Midway through the season, Taylor returned to his old club Villa to sign Gordon Cowans, whilst also adding Don Goodman from Sunderland and Dutch defender John De Wolf from Feyenoord.

Bull missed a third of the campaign with injury, but scored 16 league goals as Wolves qualified for the end-of-season play-offs. A 2-1 first-leg semi-final victory over Bolton Wanderers, with Bull on target, set up a nail-biting return leg at Bolton's old Burnden Park. But the night of 17 May 1995 turned out to be one of the most dispiriting of his entire career, as Wolves crashed out with a 2-0 defeat in extra time. Bull sank to the rain-sodden turf at full time as Bolton's players celebrated their triumph.

'We really thought we were going to do it that year,' Bull recalls. 'We battered them in that first leg but Peter Shilton [by then aged 45] had an absolute blinder for them, saving all sorts of shots. We still thought we had enough, but then it just never happened for us at Bolton. John McGinlay [who scored both goals in the second leg] should have been sent off after he smacked David Kelly. There was a massive brawl but the referee didn't see it. It was a horrible night.'

Bull almost left Wolves ahead of the 1995/96 season, to the consternation of supporters. The club accepted an offer from Premier League Coventry City for the striker. Bull met with Sky Blues manager Ron Atkinson on four occasions before deciding to stay on at Wolves. Supporters blamed Taylor at the time. 'It wasn't Graham Taylor, it was them upstairs,' Bull insists. 'It was Jonathan who wanted to get a bit of money back.'

The season began poorly, with just two wins from the opening ten league games. Fan unrest quickly grew, and after a 0-0 draw at home to Charlton Athletic Taylor was sacked in mid-November. Wolves head-hunted Mark McGhee from Leicester City. For the third time in as many years, another rebuilding job began. Millions of pounds were spent on Simon Osborn, Steve Corica, Iwan Roberts, Keith Curle and Adrian Williams. Wolves began the 1996/97 season as promotion favourites.

Bull, now aged 31, rose to the challenge. His 23 league goals saw him finish behind only his old foe McGinlay in the division's scoring chart. Bolton ran away with the title, but Wolves fell short of automatic promotion, pipped by outsiders Barnsley. They had to settle for the play-offs once more. This time, their hopes were ended after a 3-1 first-leg defeat to Crystal Palace. Despite a spirited 2-1 victory in the return leg, once again Bull had to face up to another season outside the top flight.

Owner Sir Jack's patience had snapped. 'They think the Golden Tit – me – will go on forever. It's blackmail. There has been too much sloppiness and disregard for money,' he said of his son Jonathan and manager McGhee a few days after the season ended.

'Sir Jack was top drawer,' remembers Bull. 'He was a very good friend of mine. He was absolutely brilliant, like a dad in a way. Kind and generous, gave anything to charity. He did a lot for the Albrighton Trust [a local charity supporting the disabled]. He was getting old, he had to let go of things. He gave enough to this club in terms of money. Wolves cost him a lot. When Graham Taylor came in they gave him the money, when Mark McGhee came in they gave him the money.'

Bull would never come close to achieving his Premier League dreams again. The following season saw the emergence of Robbie Keane, plucked from the youth team at the age of just 17. His two goals during an explosive debut outing on the opening day of the 1997/98 season, against Norwich City, served notice of his talents. Bull managed only half a season as injuries began to penetrate deeper. An FA Cup semi-final appearance off the bench against Arsenal left supporters furious with McGhee, who entrusted recent short-term signing Steve Claridge with their hero's place in the starting XI.

The 1998/99 season turned out to be Bull's last. It ended with a game at Molineux that epitomised the frustration of the decade. Players and supporters watched on as Bradford City won a five-goal thriller to secure automatic promotion, leaving Wolves one place outside the First Division play-offs. As Bantams manager Paul Jewell danced across the pitch in celebration, Bull exited the stage with little fanfare.

It was a cruel way to end a career that had turned the fortunes of Wolves around. His 306 goals will never be surpassed at the club. It was some tally for a player who only ever took one penalty – scored, of course – during his Wolves career. Bull announced his retirement on 13 July 1999, on medical advice, after persistent problems with his left knee. The team the 34-year-old left behind looked a long way from ever achieving promotion. His iconic number-nine shirt was inherited by a journeyman Norwegian forward named Havard Flo, who scored just ten goals during his two and a half years at the club.

But the seeds of change had been sown, with youngsters like Lee Naylor and Matt Murray having already broken into the first-team squad alongside Bull, and Joleon Lescott in wait in the youth team ranks. All three would be key players in the side that eventually secured promotion to the Premier League four years later.

Two and a half hours of reflections and nostalgia at the Oakengates Theatre ends with a question and answer session. The night has over-run by an hour but nobody is leaving early. 'What would you be doing if it had not been for the football, Bully?' asks one supporter.

'I'd probably still be in a warehouse,' he replies. 'It's weird, when I was turfed out by Albion, I still had a job to go back to. And I would have done it. I didn't mind getting off my arse for a bit of graft.'

Instead, 13 years of toil on football pitches up and down the country, wearing the gold and black, cemented a legacy that is all around Molineux today. In 2003 the John Ireland

Stand was renamed in his honour. It is a deserved, but not entirely fitting, tribute to his achievements. That is the only stand that remains from the day he walked in to the club. It is the other three stands that are the real structural testament to Bull's impact here. He ensured the club never slipped back down to the depths he discovered on arriving in Wolverhampton. In doing so he secured its future.

For a generation of Wolves fans he means so much more. Something changed when Bull stepped into the team. He altered the psyche of Wolves supporters. Disaffection and embarrassment turned into excitement and pride. He will never truly comprehend it, but Bull gave supporters their club back.

Chapter 7

A DIFFERENT
WEMBLEY DAY

The Sherpa Van Trophy Men

IT IS the first week of July. The Mander Centre in the heart of Wolverhampton's shopping district is playing host to the keenly awaited kit launch ahead of the 2018/19 season. This slick corporate event has all the commercial fanfare you would expect from a club about to enter the Premier League for the first time since Chinese owners Fosun International took control.

Rúben Neves and Diogo Jota, the stand-out Portuguese stars of the previous season, are modelling the new home and away strips in front of an adoring public. Representatives from Adidas, the global sportswear giant whose logo will adorn the shirts, are present. WW88, another of the online gaming shirt sponsors that have proliferated in the sport in recent times, have their logo emblazoned across the new strip. All the components of the modern-day top flight that will so excite supporters over the coming season. Matt Murray, hero of the 2003 First Division play-off final in Cardiff, is on stage speaking to head coach Nuno Espírito Santo about the season ahead. It is a campaign that will culminate in the club's highest league position for 39 years, qualification for Europe and an appearance at Wembley in the FA Cup semi-final.

Less than a mile away, back at Molineux, another former player is on stage recalling a very different time in the history of this illustrious club. Jackie Gallagher is explaining how he and his team-mate Floyd Streete ended up in a Spanish jail cell just a week and a half before Wolves' last appearance at Wembley in a cup competition.

There are tears of laughter in supporters' eyes as they sit at their dinner tables in the Sir Jack Hayward Suite, on the first floor of the Billy Wright Stand, listening to the former striker try to explain away the spot of bother that occurred in Majorca back in May 1988. Wolves had travelled to the Spanish island to prepare for a match against Burnley in the Sherpa Van Trophy Final, the Football League knockout tournament for teams from the bottom two divisions in English football.

For a club of Wolves' stature, to be entered into such a competition highlighted the fall from grace that had occurred in the preceding years. Yet, far from being a blot on the landscape, the final is regarded by supporters as one of the most uplifting and symbolic moments in the club's history – an occasion that symbolised the rebirth of a football club.

It was the culmination of the 1987/88 season that presented a chance to complete a memorable lower division double. The match, between two Fourth Division clubs, was attended by 80,841 spectators. To this day it remains the largest-ever attendance recorded for a fixture between two teams from the bottom tier of English football. The Wolves side which completed this double is held in the highest regard. Assembled at a similar cost to one week's wages of the club's highest earners today, the team of 30 years ago restored the club's dignity.

Graham Turner's side had just won the Fourth Division title, and the trip to Wembley was the last hurrah of a season that confirmed the club was on its way back. Turner has been joined on stage at this 30th anniversary dinner by former players Steve Bull, Andy Mutch, Ally Robertson, Robbie Dennison, Andy Thompson, Micky Holmes and Gallagher. The seven men are seated at the top table in front of screens replaying the Wembley final. It quickly becomes apparent that the jaunt to Majorca almost derailed the second part of that famous lower division double.

'The preparation was great for the final. We'd finished the season and just won the league, so it was suggested we go away for a little break, a training camp,' Thompson recalls. The dependable full-back, who famously arrived with Bull from arch rivals West Bromwich Albion in November 1986, is a popular figure around Molineux and still watches Wolves in his role as matchday summariser for the club's in-house commentary. 'I don't think we ever saw a ball. The warm-ups were interesting. Everyone had red eyes, falling over on the beach, saying we had hay fever – in a place with no plants! Ally was in charge of everything to do socially. That's why Jackie said he was best friends with him.'

The Wolves players had been given the night off on the condition that they reported for training at eight o'clock the following morning. Whilst hitting the town, they bumped into the Burnley players, who were also on the island enjoying a break ahead of the final. A drinking game ensued and the night took a hazy turn of events. After what could best be described as a minor brush with some locals, two of Wolves' squad found themselves in trouble.

'The Spanish police just appeared. Me and Floyd were in the cells, a week and a half before the cup final,' Gallagher says, remembering the moment when the raucous night on the town came to an abrupt halt after the local constabulary stepped in. 'They wanted the equivalent of 150 pounds from us. Floyd would not pay. He said, "We'll fight the police!" I had to take them back to the hotel with me, and I gave them

100 quid. I think Graham knew about it but that was it, we were out of prison. I do apologise, Graham!'

Gallagher was always on the fringes during his time at Molineux. As understudy to star strikers Bull and Mutch, he had no chance of making an impact but he weighed in with a few goals that season when called upon. 'He's fat, he's round, he's worth a million pounds,' was a popular terrace refrain at the time, which the player took in good humour.

The anniversary dinner is an opportunity for supporters to show their appreciation of the men who helped shape the future here. Behind the Sir Jack Hayward suite, out in the expanse of the stadium, work is going on all around. The pitch has been re-laid, the dugouts are being widened, the camera gantry hanging from the roof of the Billy Wright Stand is being extended and the temporary seating structure of the Graham Hughes Stand in one corner is being prepared for its re-opening to raise the capacity further. Even the floodlights are being upgraded to provide enough light for the Premier League broadcasters' ultra HD cameras.

The bowels of the stadium are being ripped out and redesigned too. The dressing rooms and tunnel area have been completely remodelled in compliance with the Premier League's regulations. Most of the changes in this part of the stadium are being done to satisfy the broadcast rights holders who have invested their billions in the league. The new state of the art media suite is being built along the first-floor corridor. A new boardroom and manager's suite are also being constructed. Everything is being done on a grand scale. The pace of change at Molineux and down at the Compton Park training ground is astonishing. It is the industry equivalent of three years' worth of construction taking place over three months, to ensure the club has never been fitter for the Premier League.

Yet none of this would be here were it not for the feats of the side that Turner built after his arrival in the early stages of the 1986/87 campaign. Robertson, the veteran captain, had arrived from West Bromwich Albion during acting manager Brian Little's brief tenure at the beginning of that season. His first game was a 1-0 home defeat to Burnley in the Fourth Division. A crowd of 5,786 turned up to watch. It was a significant improvement on the record low of 2,205 who had attended the Molineux fixture against Bury in March of the same year, but the shoots of recovery had not yet sprung.

'I'll be honest, when I joined I thought, 'What the bloody hell have I done?" says the Scot. 'We were down at the bottom of the Fourth Division and the whole club was in disarray and I couldn't believe how bad the squad of players was.' The situation was so desperate that there was not enough training kit at the club to give Robertson his own set. Instead, he returned to The Hawthorns and sought out Albion kitman Dave Matthews, who furnished him with a set of gear from Albion's supplies. Robertson took the Albion crest off the clothing in case anyone spotted the identity of the kit he was training in.

The decision of directors Dick Homden and Jack Harris to replace Little with Turner on 7 October was not popular. Turner had struggled during his time as manager of First Division Aston Villa. After a poor start to Villa's 1986/87 campaign, a 6-0 thumping at Nottingham Forest in September proved to be the final straw. He arrived at Molineux under no illusions about the task in front of him.

'I remember it very well and the least popular place was in the dressing room. I used to throw my hat in first before walking in,' Turner recalls. 'It wasn't too pleasant walking through the door here. Everybody knows the state that the club was in but nobody knew the state of the dressing room. There were probably 12 or 14 players who were not good enough to have been here. Some of them had been from the top division to the bottom half of the bottom division and they started telling me how we should play and that was a mystery.'

Mutch, Streete and Holmes were three of those who survived the cull. Bull and Thompson arrived in November. Others such as Dennison, Mark Kendall, Phil Robinson, Keith Downing and Gary Bellamy entered in the months that followed.

'The club was in a mess for different reasons, whatever they were, and I suppose we were very fortunate we were given an opportunity,' Mutch adds. 'Because maybe if we were at another club we might not have been good enough to get in the side. So he [Turner] gave us chances and the lads that are here tonight, and others from our era, took those opportunities.'

Dennison, a stylish winger also signed from neighbouring West Bromwich Albion, who seemed to drift effortlessly along the flanks with the ball tied to his feet, agrees with that sentiment: 'The first three or four years when we joined and got things moving again under Graham was a vital time for the club, but it was also a fantastic time for the players. Everybody says it was a difficult time to join the club but I think it's the best time of the lot to join really, because they were struggling and there was only one way to get them back to where they belonged. It was great to be a part of it.

'Ally Robertson was the only one who had done anything in the game. All the rest of us were trying to make our way, trying to do something right. We just wanted to play football and try and get on the ladder of making a career for ourselves.'

Dennison was 23 years old when he signed for Wolves. He knew this was his last chance. Two years earlier he had been playing semi-professionally for Glenavon, just nine miles from his home in Banbridge in Northern Ireland, in an altogether different climate.

'I turned semi-pro when I was 16, getting lumps kicked out of me by full-backs who were men, and who were involved in the paramilitaries,' he reveals. 'That's what it was like. I played there until I had various trials at clubs, but it didn't look like I was ever going to get the chance to come across here. And then finally I got a break to come across to the Albion.'

It is apparent as the night wears on that the camaraderie of the side played an important part in the success. The drinking culture was not encouraged but neither was it clamped down upon.

'The socialising, the togetherness, the ability to have a laugh at each other, seeing people doing well, like Bully scoring for England, you're happy because he's part of your club,' Dennison continues. 'That was why we were successful at that time. There were characters along the way and the first three or four years were the best years of my football career, and it's great to see the boys today.'

'We wouldn't have had the success if we hadn't done it right,' Turner is quick to point out. 'We were aware of players going out. Tuesday morning the lads used to run their socks off around here – up and down the terracing at the ground or out in the hills. Then Ally would take them to a wine bar in town. I'd get a phone call … "The lads are in town again." … "Are they alright, have they behaved?" … "Yeah, no problems, but they're drinking plenty!"

'And I'd say, "Well, let me know if there's any problems, keep an eye on them." And that's how it went, but we wouldn't have had the success if we hadn't had the serious side. You've got to remember at that time there was a drinking culture in football, and these were Premier League players at that.

'It was part and parcel of the whole package. The club was run down, there were rats in the dressing rooms, the place was falling apart and the training kit was atrocious. Players had to come into this. Part of the whole thing was the laughter, you made up for things. We went and trained on the car park, we had to lift cars out of the way at times. You'd get 12 or 14 players around a car and we'd bounce it off the little pitch that we played on. That's how bad it was. It was almost a defence mechanism – the humour – it was brilliant at times. I was the brunt of it, that's obvious now. I had no idea what Jackie got up to, that's news to me. If I can get hold of Floyd Streete he's going to be fined!'

A pivotal moment of Turner's first season came with midfielder Holmes's post-war record scoring sequence of seven goals in seven games. Wolves were struggling in mid-table when Holmes came off the bench to score the first of his run in a 3-2 home defeat to Crewe Alexandra in January. But Wolves won four and drew two of the next six he scored in, to kick-start a run to the play-offs.

Holmes is sat next to Gallagher on stage and it is clear the pair have been enjoying the hospitality on offer by the time it is his turn to recall the part he played in the club's recovery.

'It was great, Graham was struggling and then he put me in the team and then I banged them in. He was under pressure, Hednesford Town had enquired about his availability, and I stepped up. Boom, boom, boom – seven in seven!'

The audience is enjoying Holmes's recollections, and he is revelling in a light-hearted cameo amongst the more household names on stage, deliberately hamming up his part. His club record came under threat during the 2017/18 Championship-winning campaign when Brazilian striker Leo Bonatini scored in six successive games.

'I didn't know it was a record until the commentator mentioned it during a televised game. It was when Bonatini got six in six, and he was aiming to equal my record. The following game I was down in London with my wife when I heard Wolves had won 3-0 and I thought, 'Oh my God, has he scored?' But he didn't. So, yes, the main man has still got seven in seven!'

There is a nice side story to Holmes's record. In November 2017, when Bonatini had scored for a sixth successive game, Holmes was contacted for an interview about his own scoring feats. He revealed that he had never watched any of the seven goals back on camera. 'I've tried everything and it appears not one of them was filmed,' he said at the time. 'It would have been nice to show my son, but I've looked everywhere and can't find anything. I'd have loved to watch any of those goals back.'

After the feature appeared in the local *Express and Star* newspaper, a reader got in touch to answer Holmes's plea for a copy of one of his goals. Fay Sherrington, a university director in Lancashire, contacted the paper with news that she had some valuable footage. Her husband James was an 11-year-old mascot at the time of the 2-2 draw with Preston North End at Deepdale in February 1987. And for the last 30 years he had kept a VHS of the entire match that he was given by the club on the day. The couple were only too happy to help out, copying the footage on to DVD and sending it on to Holmes so that he was finally able to show his family a little part of his own playing history.

The 1986/87 season would end in play-off heartache with defeat in a two-leg final to Aldershot, who had finished nine points behind fourth-placed Wolves. But there was to be no let-down the following season as Turner's side stormed to the Fourth Division title.

Wolves actually made two appearances at Wembley during that successful season. The first came in a bizarre tournament called the Mercantile Credit Football Festival, which was held over two days over a weekend in April 1988. It was a Football League centenary celebration involving 16 teams across all four divisions.

Qualification had been over a short period early in 1988 when the teams with the best record in their respective divisions were selected to play in the tournament. The knockout matches were just 20 minutes each way in duration. Wolves drew the country's reigning league champions, Everton, in the first round, losing only on penalties after a tremendous Dennison strike from over 30 yards out had secured a 1-1 draw.

'The big thing about that tournament was that we got a little taste of Wembley so that when we went back in the Sherpa Van Trophy it wasn't strange to the players,' Turner explains. 'They'd been in the dressing room, they'd been on the turf, they had played there. So it stood us in good stead for the Sherpa Van Trophy Final and I think it helped us enormously.'

So does Dennison remember his goal against Everton after all these years? 'Vaguely, yeah.'

'He's been talking about it all night,' Thompson interrupts.

'They were just great memories really, the two Wembley things we did, that was all part of it,' Dennison continues. 'Twenty minutes each way, was it? We should have played more but Mutchy missed a penalty and we lost the game. That's all part of it; you win together, you lose together. Mutchy, do you know what I mean?'

'He's supposed to be my best friend,' Mutch replies, as the gentle ribbing on stage continues. Mutch played second fiddle to striker partner Bull for the duration of his time at Molineux, but nobody in the room is in any doubt about the importance of his weighty contribution. Signed from non-league Southport for just £5,000, the Liverpudlian scored over 100 goals of his own during the club's ascent.

'We all had to muck in and from that we built a team and started winning a few games of football,' he adds. 'Then from that a few people started getting a bit of recognition. The most important thing was that after the club had been in a bad state and had lost its identity, we slowly started to bring that identity back and I think that's probably why we're remembered today in great heart by everybody. We all appreciate that, it's nice to be here tonight and it's nice to see all the lads again.'

So how did the Wembley preparations that began with a marathon squad drinking session, and a spell in the cells for a couple of players, end with a trophy lift little over a week later?

'Believe it or not, with the trip to Majorca, we had a week out there and when we came back it was the best we'd looked since I came to the club,' Turner explains. 'The training was absolutely brilliant and you knew then that we were going to Wembley to win it. I'd never seen us looking so sharp, so ready for a big occasion.'

'In the build-up everybody was excited for it, they were desperate for tickets. Half the village where I lived were asking for tickets,' remembers Thompson. 'People were turning up at the door with carrier bags of money. It was unbelievable. It felt like everybody in Wolverhampton went. We were fortunate enough to get the amount of tickets that we did. The actual town at the time was alive. It was the best time of my life when I went to Wembley and the best game I've been involved in, just because the fans made it for us. Coming into the ground with the streets lined with gold and black and then coming out of the tunnel the roar was unbelievable, you'll never forget it.'

The day itself was sun-baked and sweltering hot. For Mutch, a dyed-in-the-wool Liverpool fan, it was the opportunity to experience the occasion from the other side of the fence. 'As a young kid I did go to watch Liverpool at Wembley many times. And I couldn't believe it, going down Wembley Way on the coach and seeing gold and black everywhere. It was absolutely amazing for the players. I think Burnley played their part as well because they brought the best part of 30,000 to make an 80,000 crowd.'

His opening first-half goal put Wolves in charge before one of Dennison's trademark free kicks in the second half secured a 2-0 victory and a memorable lower league double. But it didn't end well for every player that famous day, as Holmes is quick to remind everyone.

'It wasn't a great day for me because I broke my ankle. The next day, while they were having an open-top bus tour, David Instone [Wolves' *Express and Star* reporter] told me in hospital that I'd been given a free transfer.' It was a sign of the times that there was no duty of care from the club for a player who had played such an important part in the revival. Holmes, though, would make a happy return to Wembley, scoring a penalty to help Torquay United overcome Blackpool in a shoot-out in the Fourth Division play-off final of 1991.

For Wolves there was to be one more promotion under Turner, as Third Division champions in the 1988/89 season. Bull's prolific partnership with Mutch was unstoppable. The pair scored an astounding 148 goals in all competitions in the two successive promotion seasons. The club left behind the most tumultuous decade in its history with fresh optimism and heads held high.

Dennison pays tribute to the man who oversaw it all: 'It starts with the manager to put the principles in place – to organise the club and organise the players around you, to have the best players at that level to win things. You saw that last year with Wolves in the Championship. The players were good enough to win the Championship comfortably.'

'With the exception of Ally and Floyd, most of the players were very young, very fit and free from injury. It was a very good squad of players,' Turner adds. 'We certainly had the talent way above the standard of the old Fourth and Third Division. We had super quality in the club, and as the crowds started to come back and the supporters started to get behind the team we became almost unbeatable.

'When I left it was with a great deal of pride, having gone from the bottom half of the Fourth Division to getting on the fringes of the play-offs in what is now the Championship. You cannot take those years away from me, and the lads have all said the same. Despite what they've said, they did work tremendously hard other than just drinking. It laid the foundations for what is happening at the club now and that is something we should all be proud of.

'The whole period where we climbed through the divisions, bringing the club back to respectability, was a great time. Robbie said it was the best part of his career, it certainly was the best part of my career as well, terrific.'

'I was sad in a way that I couldn't have stayed for two or three more years – that I wasn't two or three more years younger,' a wistful Robertson adds. 'We could have got back to the First Division. From 3,000 crowds, then we started to see 20,000 crowds to turn it around. The Sherpa Van Trophy Final, in a way, meant nothing to most people, but to see 50,000 Wolves fans there it was absolutely out of this world. When I was ready to walk out I remember saying to the lads, "This is for those supporters out there. We have got to win today." And of course, what a fantastic day.

'I started laughing the other week because when Wolves got promotion back to the Premier League and the bus was going around Wolverhampton, well that was us 30 years ago. The turnout for us that Sunday when we returned with the trophy was incredible, and it just shows you what it means to the fans. Absolutely brilliant and we were so lucky to be part of it.'

Chapter 8

AIRWOLF 90

The greatest away day in Wolves' history

'CHAOS IS a very good word,' says Albert Bates. The chairman of the Wolverhampton Wanderers Official Supporters' Club (WWOSC) is in his late 70s now. He is sitting in his living room, alongside his wife Muriel, the secretary and treasurer of the organisation. It is a place that was once the fulcrum of the most ambitious away day ever attempted in this country. A time when almost 1,000 supporters were airlifted to a football match, and witnessed their hero run amok. 'Chaos, because we didn't anticipate anything going so manic. We thought it was wishful thinking, to jump on a plane.'

Christmas-time fixtures remain the most popular matches of the season. The Premier League fixtures in 2018/19 bestowed two trips to London on Nuno Espírito's side. A 1-1 draw at Fulham was followed by a memorable 3-1 win over Tottenham Hotspur at Wembley. It made the hassles of away travel worth it for the 3,000 or so Wolves supporters who took in both games. The festive period often brings families and friends together, but it is also a time when travelling to the match can be difficult, with public transport regularly shut down. On New Year's Day 1990, Wolves fans embarked on the most ambitious day of travel ever undertaken by a group of supporters in this country. This is their story.

The WWOSC was formed in 1984. Its early years were spent battling against the regime of the Bhatti brothers as Wolves lurched from one crisis to the next, eventually going into receivership as a Fourth Division club. By the 1989/90 season the club was riding the crest of a wave. Graham Turner's team, fuelled by the astonishing scoring feats of striker Steve Bull, had just won back-to-back promotions as Fourth and Third Division title winners. Wolves were now holding their own in the Second Division and, whilst never likely to challenge for a third automatic promotion in a division of big hitters like Leeds United, Newcastle United, West Ham United and Sunderland, they were pulling off some decent results.

Wolves had been taking a healthy away following to matches for the past two seasons. A trip to Newcastle on 1 January was an exciting prospect, but for many supporters the prospect of a long drive or coach journey to Tyneside the morning after the New Year's Eve festivities was deeply unappealing.

George Dawidow was 38 at the time, and running a successful business as a bedding manufacturer. A home and away diehard, he was determined not to miss the trip, so got together with some friends, months in advance of the fixture, to plot a course to the North East. 'A five and a half hour journey on a coach? That was a bit too much for us with all the alcohol so we thought about a plane,' he explains. Crucial to their plans was Albert, then working as a technical sales engineer for Dana Spicer.

'I had contacts within the air industry, not directly with aircraft, but with support equipment at the airports,' says Albert. 'They naturally assumed I might know somebody who'd give them the opportunity of flying to Newcastle.

That's how it kicked off, three or four businessmen asking if I could organise something for them because they didn't fancy a five- or six-hour drive having been on the pop the night before.'

Albert made some enquiries and came back with a cost well in excess of £300. For a while the idea seemed to have stalled, but days later the businessmen returned and said there were a few more people interested in flying. When Albert made some more enquiries, the cost came down again, but still there did not seem to be enough people involved to make it a commercially viable prospect.

It was at this point Albert received an unexpected phone call at his home. 'It was from an ex-pilot called "Rick", whom we didn't know. He rang here completely out of the blue, there was no intermediary, unless someone within the airline industry said there's an opportunity to charter an aircraft and gave him our number. He said he had heard we were looking for a plane.

'At that time we said we weren't really, but he said not to turn people away, if the word gets out and we get enough people then logic says the price will tumble and we might find ourselves being able to put the aircraft on.'

'Rick' was Ian Rixon, a former Dan Air pilot who had set up his own business, Farnborough Executive Aviation, as a charter broker.

'So we put an advertisement in the Wolves programme as the official supporters' club, so that people would know this wasn't some kind of crank or anything like that, because quite frankly that's the way we looked at it. It went manic, just jumping – 30 people, 40, 50 and so on. I was getting rather concerned because we kept ringing this guy "Rick",' Albert continues.

'He kept reassuring us that, however many it was, he would match the number of fans with the plane. And I took him at his word, because he knew his business. When it got to 80 he said, "I can get you a Boeing 737 airliner for that number of people," and the price came down again. The plane, as it turned out, was based at Birmingham so it was only taking into account the price of the seats from there and the landing fees and so forth. Then it spiralled beyond that, the grapevine became enormous when people knew that there was a jet airliner going. Another lot came on and the numbers grew very quickly.'

The numbers kept on growing. One plane became two, then three, then four and so on. Eventually enough supporters had signed up for the trip to fill six planes. Rixon had chartered the Boeings from Monarch Airlines. Suspicions had been raised at the top of the company.

'The doorbell went here one day and it turned out to be two directors from Monarch Airlines who had come to see us,' Albert says. 'They were well dressed and presentable, and asked if they could have a word with us. They said that on average they might get around 300 enquiries a day to charter an airliner, and if two of them come off they've had a good day. They said, "Then Mr Bloggs walks in off the street and charters the entire fleet, none of us believed that was possible."'

The Bates's home in Penn had become a hive of activity. Supporters were turning up at the door at all times of the day trying to pay for a seat on the trip.

'I was dressed in my nightie and dressing gown and all I was doing was opening my door to men,' remembers Muriel. 'There were men coming in and men going out, cars pulling in and cars pulling out. They wore my carpet out, literally. I wrote them all receipts with their names and addresses and phone numbers so it took a lot of time to do things, and they'd just be waiting in our living room.'

'At one point, when we checked, we had around £75,000 in cash,' Bates reveals. 'A lot of it we didn't know who it belonged to, we must have had envelopes all stuffed with money. We were getting phone calls day and night saying, "Have you had my money?" We were trying to match people to postcodes. It spiralled to a stupid level where we couldn't keep the money here any longer, it had got out of control from our point of view.

'We'd get calls from people all over the country wanting to join up with various relatives and friends. Monarch sent us all the tickets and asked us to do the manifest for each aircraft because we knew who the people were; all the families and who mixed with who. We were writing out manifests trying to colour code families to bring them together on the bloody aeroplanes because they were joining up late. It was a nightmare trying to bring the people together and move them around to balance everything out.'

As for the money, depositing it securely was not going to be straightforward. 'I stuffed it in a Tesco carrier bag and we went up town on the bus with all this money,' Albert continues. 'We got to the bank and to my shock there was a very large queue waiting to get to the windows. I couldn't stand there with a big bag of money so I ran to one of the windows, tapped on it and said, "Would you be kind enough to take this money?"

'The manager came across then and they opened the window and glanced down into the bag. The girl at the counter was shocked. She said, "Oh my God, we've got to count it!" We had to prove the money was genuine and where we had got it from. The whole thing was staggering, there is no other word for it.'

Albert and Muriel were essentially doing the job of a travel agent, without all the insurance and protection that the industry demanded. The couple had to re-mortgage their house as a guarantee that they would not default on the trip.

'From an operational point of view, it went crazy,' Albert recalls. 'Birmingham Airport asked me to go and see them as they had concerns. I'd asked for ten-minute departure slots to get each plane away. They said the departure lounge could only hold 300 people and we had over 900 people coming and they couldn't really accommodate them. They said that people travelling on New Year's Day were concerned that they were going to be mixing with football fans. I said, "Do you think these people are a bunch of loonies? They're going to a football match to enjoy it.'"

'We had to organise coaches at this end and that end to get the fans to the airport and back from the ground, so that caused a lot of problems,' Muriel adds. 'Twenty-six coaches we took to Birmingham and we had to organise another 26 coaches at the other end in Newcastle.'

Despite all these considerable obstacles, 'Airwolf 90' – as it became known – took place amid huge publicity. What started off as a half-hearted enquiry from a handful of fans who didn't fancy a long drive with a hangover, turned into the most spectacular day of travel in the history of English football. Eight planes took off from Birmingham Airport on the morning of New Year's Day – 928 supporters travelled on six Monarch Airlines Boeing 737s and 757s organised by the WWOSC, along with a propeller plane chartered by independent supporters' group Hatherton Wolves and a private jet that took the owners, the Gallagher brothers, and their family and friends.

Television news crews from BBC Midlands and Central Television also joined the trip, with their filming making national and international news reports later that day. Amongst the first fans who appeared on the reports were a couple stood in the check-in hall at Birmingham Airport dressed as Sylvester The Cat and Tweetie Pie – it was George and his wife, Anne Dawidow, who died some years later.

'We thought we'd stay in and have a quiet night and see the new year in,' George recalls. 'Famous last words! About half past 12 the next-door neighbour came round. He worked for a big brewery. He turned up with three cases of vintage this, that and the other. So then it's quarter to five in the morning and we're totally green, both of us! We had a taxi booked for half past seven. We got to the ground at a quarter to eight, arrived at the North Bank car park and there was nobody in fancy dress besides us pair.

'So there's me – the prat dressed as a cat – and Tweetie Pie. The idea was that I was in black and white like the Geordies and she was in gold like the Wolves. Everybody is taking the mickey. We were absolutely green. The coach journey to Birmingham Airport was an event just to try and keep ourselves straight.'

They need not have feared. On arrival at the airport there was an assorted collection of fancy dress reindeer, snowmen, tigers, bears, chickens and a pink panther. As fans congregated on the tarmac before climbing the steps to board the plane, they were vox-popped by the television reporters. One of those was Johnny Martin, a 23-year-old carpenter who caused much amusement on the day when he told his inquisitor, 'I've never flown before and I'm frightened to death. My girlfriend bought me this ticket and I didn't know anything about it!'

Well, 29 years on, he has a confession to make. There may have been some artistic licence at play for the cameras. 'I've got to put my hands up, there was no girlfriend, to be fair. My mum had helped me pay for the ticket,' Johnny reveals. 'Don't tell my dad that either! There wasn't a girlfriend, and I had a bit of a tan too as I'd just come back from holiday.'

For Johnny and his friends, getting on the trip was at the forefront of their minds as soon as they heard about the flights.

'Going up to the Wolves week in week out, somebody said there was a plane going so we thought about how we could get on it. We were all in our early 20s so there was a question of whether or not we could afford it. I was an apprentice in a joinery shop earning 30-odd quid a week. We were like, "It doesn't matter. It's the Wolves. We're going out for a party."'

There was one supporter who stole the show that afternoon. Kevin Round was a 29-year-old holiday rep who had been working in Tenerife. He arrived at Birmingham Airport in a Santa Claus outfit and was immediately targeted by the television crews. He gave what turned out to be a prescient interview for BBC Midlands just before boarding the plane.

'Over Christmas I talked to a lot of managers – Kenny Dalglish, Alex Ferguson – and they all wanted the same thing for Christmas. They all wanted Stevie Bull. And I'm very, very sorry, but Santa is a Wolves fan and there is no way they're getting him. And I think a hat-trick today would go down very nicely,' he said at the time. 'Santa is a Wolves fan' was quickly adopted as the anthem of the day amongst the travelling hordes.

'It all started the night before, in actual fact,' says Kevin, looking back today, 'at a New Year's Eve party with my mates. We all ended up getting very drunk and woke up in the morning with little time to prepare. I was already dressed as Santa so it seemed the appropriate thing to go in.'

Kevin was relieved when he walked into the airport and saw, amongst others, Sylvester and Tweetie Pie. 'I felt at home! It was a great crack. The amount of people that went was unbelievable. We were very proud to be part of it. We got up so late we missed the coaches from the Wolves ground to the airport so we had to get somebody else to take us. We weren't doing very well altogether at that stage. The airport staff and the stewards were really good, they got into the spirit of it. I think we behaved impeccably. We drank a lot, we enjoyed ourselves and had a great day and we were a credit to the town, the way we behaved.'

George, Johnny, Kevin and several other supporters who made the trip almost 29 years ago have gathered at The Lych Gate Tavern ahead of a Wolves home game. They were contacted with the help of other fans after messages were put out on social media seeking to track them down for this story. Another supporter who got in touch was Ron Westwood. He saw an image of his dad in the appeal, which came from the Central News piece at the time.

'I went with my dad, bless him, he's no longer with us now,' says Ron, who was a 34-year-old Royal Mail manager at the time. 'So the memories are bittersweet really. My old man was with me and we had a great time, so to do it together was special. We'd go all over the country watching Wolves but nothing would cap that. Just the uniqueness of it. I vividly remember on the plane, at take-off, all the Wolves fans singing "Going up, going up, going up!" You just couldn't bottle the atmosphere that day. I wish I could, I'd have made a fortune by now.'

'When the plane took off, all the stewardesses were really nervous about all these football hooligans on board,' George adds. 'But within 20 minutes they're singing and dancing up and down the aisles, joining in the fun. The pilot came out and congratulated us; he said he might become a Wolves fan himself. We got to the airport at Newcastle and the planes were offloading, Santa was doing his routine, and I must praise the Geordie copper in charge of the day up in Newcastle. He was a lovely character, made us all feel welcome, treated us like royalty. We had a cavalcade down to the ground and got there about one o'clock, in good time.'

Another who arrived early at St James' Park was Kevin Walters. He was nine years old at the time and was the Wolves mascot for the day. 'I remember getting there and being given a tour of the ground, the trophy room and then meeting the players as they started to arrive,' he says. 'When you're meeting Steve Bull, who you were watching week in and week out at the time banging all the goals in, it was amazing just to go and shake his hand. Andy Mutch and Paul Cook were another two of my favourites at the time. It was fantastic.'

The players, unlike the supporters, had taken a more conventional journey to Newcastle, arriving by coach early the day before. Crucial to their hopes was Bull. He had made his England debut the previous May, as a Third Division player, and scored his country's second goal in a 2-0 win over Scotland at Hampden Park. This was a World Cup season, with Bull firmly in England manager Bobby Robson's thoughts for a place at Italia 90. The 24-year-old forward had scored ten goals in 20 games during that Second Division season, but had only scored one in his last four going into the trip to Newcastle.

Wolves occupied tenth place in the table at the time, five points behind Newcastle who sat in the last play-off position. What had been a routine day of preparation, took an eventful turn as the night wore on.

'We had our pasta and all our carbs to get ready for the next day, and come eight o'clock we were playing cards,' Bull explains. 'The gaffer [Graham Turner] got up and said, "Oi, I want you in bed by five past 12. Ring the missus and wish her a Happy New Year, five past 12," and he walks off. We were sitting there thinking about playing cards for four hours and then he turned around and said, "You can have a couple of halves."

'So what did we do? A couple of halves of what? A few halves later I'm ringing the missus at 12 o'clock, half cut, wishing her a happy New Year, and she's saying, "What are you doing, have you had a drink? Get to bed." There was a handful of us. I can't name names, but Cookie [Paul Cook] was in there, Mutchy was in there and Thommo was in there!'

Andy Thompson remembers having to convince Bull to stay within the confines of the hotel. 'Bully ordered a taxi from reception to go out in Newcastle,' he reveals. 'I had to tell him to cancel it. It was alright having a couple of drinks in the hotel but to go out in Newcastle itself was something else. I wouldn't say he was the ringleader, but he did get carried away and he just wanted to go out.'

'We were there in our Wolves tracksuits and I said to Thommo, "Are we going clubbing?" He was saying we couldn't but I was feeling bulletproof by now,' Bull adds. 'In the end we finished off another bottle of wine and went up to bed. We woke up the next morning thinking, "What have we done?" It was just one of those spur-of-the-moment things. That was the last time we ever did it and, to be fair, it paid off.'

So were the guilty players struggling to conceal their late night?

'We were a little bit sheepish because we'd had more than we should have had, but the manager never said anything to us,' Thompson recalls.

'Yeah, yeah, blurry eyed, checking the breath,' Bull continues. 'When the gaffer got up and said we had to go for a walk to get some fresh air, then come back and go through some set plays on the board, that was when reality kicked in and we thought about the 3,000 fans coming up here to watch us. "What have we done?" But then we got out there in the freezing cold, looked over to the fans and your inner self comes out and we just got on with it.'

The highlight of a drab goalless first half was a penalty save from Wolves keeper Mark Kendall. Half-time proved more entertaining as Kevin, still in his Santa outfit, managed to get on to the pitch to rally the Wolves support.

'I just got on and everyone thought I was part of it. I wasn't being a hooligan,' he recalls. 'I walked around, shook a few hands, patted a few divots down and got involved. There was no bother at all. I did a little bit of singing, I had some help up on to one of the barriers to do a bit of singing. It was nice that all the fans were singing "Santa is a Wolves fan", which was great, it was just absolutely tremendous.'

The second half unfolded in a way no Wolves fan could have expected. Bull completed a nine-minute hat-trick to put Wolves three up with less than an hour played. Newcastle pulled one back before Bull added a fourth. All in front of the watching England manager.

'It was unreal, and one of the big factors was that we were playing towards our own fans,' Bull says. 'It was like something drawing us towards the goal. I think there were two left footers in that lot you know, that's my standing foot! I couldn't believe it. People ask me which was the best goal out of the lot of them and I always say the third one, the hat-trick goal. I didn't find out until after the game that he [Robson] was there so it was a good job I put in a good second-half performance.'

For Bull, the display put him at the forefront of the England manager's thinking. Five months later, in the final World Cup squad selection reckoning, it came down to a choice between the Wolves man and Arsenal's Alan Smith, a league title winner just 12 months earlier.

'I think it did a lot for me that day because Newcastle were high-flying then and one of the top teams in that league,' Bull explains. 'Bobby actually said to me, because I couldn't understand why he took me, that he picked me as a "wild card" because nobody knew who I was and which division I'd come from. Most players play in their top division.'

Kevin's optimistic prediction in front of the television cameras had come true. For fans of his generation, Bull was the best hero a supporter could wish for.

'He came and saved us really. When you've gone to Chorley and lost you know you're in trouble. When he arrived he turned the whole ship around and we started going in the right direction. That's why we've got a stand named after him and he's still involved with the club today. He's an absolute legend. He just did everything for us. He had the club heart. Numerous times he could have gone somewhere else and furthered his career, but he stayed with Wolves.'

'An absolute legend,' Johnny agrees. 'We'd meet with our mates in The Goalpost pub opposite Molineux, have a pint, and the players would come in afterwards. On an away game, say we were up in Manchester, we'd rush to get back to The Goalpost because the Wolves coach would drop the lads off and they'd come in. Bully would be in there with them and you'd have a game of pool with the lads. It was like a dream.

'He was just sent to us – from the Albion of all places. Week in and week out, he was the heart and soul. For us, at our age, we were watching the boys on a Saturday and then playing football on a Sunday morning ourselves. That's what we lived for. They were exactly the same as us. The players were there trying their hardest. They were just normal lads. Now you see them earning hundreds of thousands of pounds, but Bully was there just having a game of pool and going for a pint. You grew up with them, it was the best time of my life. My wife won't mind me saying that because she knows it was the best time of my life.'

The New Year's Day hangovers of players and supporters had long been forgotten by the final whistle at St James' Park. Whilst the players had to endure another long coach journey home, many of the fans on the terraces were looking forward to continuing the party on the return flight home. 'At the end of the game this policeman got up on the barriers with a megaphone,' George recalls. 'We're all going mental, and he just got up and said, "You've had a fantastic day but I'm going to have to keep you in while we clear the roads outside, but we'll get you back to the airport. And, by the way, who's this Stevie Bull?" And the place just erupted. It was brilliant, never to be forgotten. But Muriel and Albert, the work they did for that, was absolutely awesome.'

Despite the achievement of taking over 900 fans to the game without a hitch, Albert has one regret about the day. 'When we got to Birmingham Airport there must have been 50 people or more standing outside hoping that somebody wouldn't turn up or that kind of thing,' he explains. 'There was just no way, but I went in and approached staff and believe it or not we actually got another aircraft. We got a plane to take those who were there, but they couldn't get a bloody crew together. It was so sad for them, they were there and we had a plane but we couldn't get them to the Newcastle game. That hurt.'

George sums up the feelings of the lucky ones. Almost three decades on, the day is still at the forefront of his memory. 'It will always be the best away match of my life. I've been on this planet 66 years and nothing will ever match that. I've been to Wembley three times and we've won on each occasion. Cardiff for the play-off final was a great day, but Airwolf 90 was really special.'

Bull remains grateful to the supporters for making his day so memorable too. 'After Christmas and New Year's Eve they've got no money left, but they forked out of their pockets and said, "Go on, we'll go on the plane." Six planes! That is unbelievable and it astounded us, every single one of the players and the manager.'

Bull was the star of the show on the pitch, but there was one man who ensured the day captured the imagination beyond the local news and sports pages. For Kevin Round, the Tenerife club rep, wearing that Santa Claus outfit is something he will never regret. He has kept it to this day, and it will always be associated with English football's greatest-ever away day. 'I didn't know how mad it was,' he remembers, 'until my mate from New Zealand phoned me afterwards and said, "I've just seen you on the telly!"'

Chapter 9

TAYLOR MADE

The season of what might have been

WHAT IF? All football fans deal in that familiar currency. Wolves supporters' big 'what if' of 2018/19 came during added time of their FA Cup semi-final against Watford in April. The concession of a last-gasp penalty, when Leander Dendoncker tripped Troy Deeney, gifted Watford an equaliser. Hopes of playing in a first major cup final for 39 years disintegrated, snatched away in agonising fashion at Wembley. Watford won the match in extra time.

That was just one moment in one game, though. Wolves recovered from the setback, and although the tantalising prospect of a trophy was taken away they rallied over the remaining month of the campaign to finish seventh in the Premier League, qualifying for Europe. With Watford losing 6-0 in the FA Cup Final to an all-conquering Manchester City team, maybe the course of history did not change too much with Dendoncker's unfortunate intervention.

Ahead of the 1994/95 season it felt as if Wolves were about to change course forever when, as a mid-table second-tier club, they appointed the man who had just left the job of England manager. It put the club in the national spotlight and, initially, on a path that appeared to be heading to the Premier League. At the end of that particular chapter of Wolves' history, supporters' hopes had been shattered and they were left wondering, what if? Nobody personifies that sense of what might have been more than Steve Froggatt.

Catching up at his Staffordshire home, less than 15 miles from Wolverhampton, one of the club's headline signings of the 90s reflects on a time that captured the imagination, not just of those who followed the club but also a wider football audience.

Froggatt was born and raised in Lincoln. A promising schoolboy footballer, he was on the radar of several clubs before signing for Aston Villa on schoolboy forms. They were managed by Graham Taylor at the time, himself a highly rated coach. Taylor had made a name for himself at Lincoln City, when he became the youngest manager in the Football League on his appointment in 1972, at the age of 28. He guided the Imps to the Fourth Division title in 1976, and a year later he moved to Watford. He took the Hertfordshire club from Fourth to First Division in just five years, leading them to a second-place finish behind Liverpool in the 1982/83 season. A year later his side finished runners-up in the FA Cup Final.

Taylor's success continued on his arrival in Birmingham in 1987. Aston Villa won promotion from the Second Division in his first season in charge, and in just his third season he guided the team to league runners-up, behind Liverpool once more. One of his last acts at Villa Park, before leaving to become the England manager in 1990, was to sign Froggatt as a professional. The following season, under Ron Atkinson, Froggatt made his debut away at champions-elect Arsenal.

Villa were a formidable force under 'Big Ron'. In the 1992/93 season they pushed Alex Ferguson's Manchester United all the way for the title. A year later they beat United 3-1 to win the League Cup at Wembley.

Taylor had kept an eye on Froggatt's progress, bringing him in to the England under-21 squad in 1992 for the first of two caps at that level. But Taylor's own career was about to take a downward turn. After England were eliminated in the group stages of the 1992 European Championships in Sweden, they then failed to qualify for the 1994 World Cup, missing out on the finals for the first time since 1978. The manager was pilloried by the national press during and after his time in charge, which came to an end in November 1993. A Channel 4 fly-on-the-wall documentary, *An Impossible Job*, chronicled the qualification failure in painful detail, leading to further opprobrium being heaped on Taylor.

It was huge news, then, when just four months later he was announced as Wolves manager on 29 March 1994. The club sat 13th in the second tier of English football. Over 300 supporters assembled at the front of the Billy Wright Stand ahead of his unveiling. They were not all there to cheer the new man. There had been considerable opposition to his appointment amongst the fan base at the time.

Inside the stand, a huge gathering of media had assembled in the Hayward Suite for the much-anticipated press conference. 'Some clubs approached me immediately after I left the England job, but I didn't feel the time was right,' Taylor said. 'I needed to recuperate. There were only a handful of clubs I'd have come back for and, though I flew in from Spain for Wolves, I'd have walked back if necessary.'

After fulfilling his press commitments he walked out of the main reception and spoke directly to the fans, managing to turn any jeers into cheers. Despite an immediate bounce in results, Wolves could not improve enough to finish in a play-off position, but Taylor knew the real job began that summer. Meanwhile, Froggatt's career at Villa was not progressing as he would have liked. He appeared in only nine league games in the 1993/94 season, so when the opportunity came for a transfer, even one that involved a move down a division, there was little persuading to be done.

'People said, "Why did you move?" There were no doubts, none whatsoever,' Froggatt says. 'Part of it was because, as a young kid coming through the ranks, you don't get a fair crack of the whip. There are things that went on that I can't really tell you about that were the reasons I had to get out of Villa.

'And Graham being at Wolves was a big part of it, we struck it off straight away. Graham was from my part of the world, I'm from Lincoln and he was from Worksop. He managed Lincoln City, who were the team I used to watch on the terraces at Sincil Bank when I was very young. The connections were unbelievable all the way through. Two of the Lincoln side I used to watch went on to coach me, Dennis Booth at Aston Villa and then John Ward at Wolves. Graham was a father figure to me in the end. When he became England manager he took me into the under-21s at Villa, so all the way through my career he was a massive influence on me.

'And also some of my best mates in the game had left Villa to join Wolves too. Paul Birch had been there a while and then Tony Daley joined, so they talked me into coming down. It was a massive club. But it was really Graham who was the main reason I went because I totally trusted him. I knew the plans he had and the sort of manager he was and I fully expected him to do big things for Wolves. I'd shaken hands on a deal with Graham and then literally a week later I got a call from Liverpool to go up and see them, as they were interested. I couldn't because I'd already promised Graham and I wasn't going to dump on him at the last minute. Also, when I went to Wolves, the whole history was a massive thing for me. When I look back at the 50s and 60s, players like Billy Wright, it was the sleeping giant. Everyone could see that.'

When Froggatt arrived at Molineux he found a manager who had gone through some harrowing experiences in the four years since they were together at Villa.

'He came back with a bee in his bonnet, I think it had changed him,' Froggatt explains. 'The England experience made him a different person to the one I knew before. He was less trusting. He had this burning desire to prove that he was a good manager again. But everyone knew he was, after what he'd achieved at Lincoln, Watford and Aston Villa. Everyone knew what a good manager he was, but like every other England manager he just didn't have the players. He had bad luck with injuries to certain players at the time as well. He got so unfairly ridiculed in the England job. It was a different Graham who came back, he meant business and he had huge plans for the football club.'

Froggatt and England winger Tony Daley were the marquee summer signings, with Neil Emblen also joining the club from Millwall. Wolves went into the 1994/95 First Division, a season when only the champions went up automatically, as one of the promotion favourites.

'I remember playing my first game at Molineux, and it was a full house, 28,000 people. And I think virtually every game that year seemed to be a full house. Clearly it was a huge club that just needed reawakening.' Froggatt scored in that opening game, against Mark McGhee's Reading, who went on to finish second that season. 'A tap-in from a yard, I didn't get many tap-ins in my career so I was happy with that one.'

A derby win over rivals West Bromwich Albion in the third game added to the uplifting mood around Molineux. Taylor appeared to be building something special. In an emotional week in September, Wolves put in a performance that seemed to characterise the togetherness and positivity amongst players and supporters. Arguably the club's greatest player, Billy Wright, had died earlier that month. The former England captain led Wolves to all of their three league titles in the 1950s. His funeral on 12 September was attended by the country's greats: Sir Bobby Charlton, Sir Stanley Matthews and Sir Tom Finney. The funeral cortege began its journey at Molineux.

The following evening Taylor's team, who had attended the funeral together, took to the field against Southend United and put in their best display of the season. A 5-0 victory could have been doubled, such was the number of chances created.

'There was a vast amount of experience in the squad and at times it felt like it was men against boys. We were just battering teams,' Froggatt recalls. 'It was like an irresistible force pushing us on to promotion. We were a really powerful side. That Southend game, when we thrashed them at home, that's when people started to say, "These boys are the real deal."'

Wolves went top of the division for the first time in two years. When asked after the match about the start he had made to life at the club, Taylor said, 'The Wolverhampton people have been brilliant. I could not have asked for a warmer reception from day one, they've been excellent. They are very, very warm-hearted and they call a spade a spade. They like to see their team working and hopefully we're going along the lines that they like watching.'

It had not been a trouble-free start to the season, though. Injury problems built up almost immediately. Talisman Steve Bull had been missing for the opening six games and Daley, the club's most expensive recruit, suffered a cruciate ligament injury that restricted him to just one substitute appearance all season.

'I played with Tony at Villa, I knew how devastating we could be as a pair,' Froggatt adds. 'I knew we would be a real force down the flanks. His career at Wolves just never got started. I don't think I ever started a game with Tony while I was at Wolves. He had horrific injury problems and that was a massive blow for the club as he was still at his peak. He had lots to offer, he was still lightning quick. I still say to people, had Tony been fit that first season, we would have won the league by about 20 points.'

Froggatt succumbed to a season-ending injury of his own in December, when he was on the receiving end of a late and nasty challenge from Reading's Scott Taylor in a defeat at Elm Park. The winger was treated for five minutes on the pitch before being stretchered off.

'It was a bad tackle but we didn't think it was a serious injury, it was only when I tried to make a comeback in training that I just fell apart and they realised I'd absolutely knackered my ankle. I had to go through an ankle ligament reconstruction. That was me out for the rest of the season. As a winger you always watched out for yourself in those days, because the full-back would have two or three whacks at you before the referee stepped in. It would almost have to be an assault to get a yellow card. Unfortunately, I was one of those players who didn't pull out of a tackle. I didn't help myself going for challenges that were maybe 70/30 against me and I ended up getting done. In a way, it's my own fault that the injuries happened.'

The injury pile-up prompted Taylor to go on a further round of spending in December, bringing in striker Don Goodman from Sunderland, young midfielder Jermaine Wright from Millwall, defender Brian Law – a free agent at the time – and veteran midfielder Gordon Cowans from Aston Villa.

'He was right at the end of his career then, but Gordon will always stand out as one of the best players I ever played with,' Froggatt insists. 'I always remember when I was a youth-team player at Aston Villa and he was playing in the reserves. He used to hit the ball 70 yards right on to my left toenail.

'So after playing with him I was really disappointed if a player hit a pass ten yards in front of me, with the idea that I had to run and chase it. He'd won everything in the game, including a European Cup, that experience was really important. Graham realised that, because of the crowd and the intensity of the supporters, especially if things weren't going well, we needed strong characters in the dressing room and we had plenty of them.'

But the stand-out capture was veteran Dutch international defender John De Wolf from Feyenoord. Aside from being a Wolves headline writer's dream, De Wolf had played a key role in the Netherlands' 2-0 victory over England in Rotterdam, just over a year earlier. It was a defeat that virtually ended Taylor's hopes of taking England to the World Cup finals. The match was also the centre-piece of the Channel 4 documentary that came to define the most difficult part of Taylor's career. The signing raised Wolves' profile higher. Some of the Dutch press came over to Molineux for his photo call and followed his progress throughout the remainder of the campaign.

'I remember Wolfie,' says Froggatt. 'He was a six foot four Adonis-looking figure. He wasn't very quick but he was very commanding in the air, decent on the ball and the fans took to him straight away. He had that commanding presence and he became a real cult favourite.'

After an inconsistent run of results during December and January, De Wolf's first career hat-trick on a quagmire of a pitch at Port Vale in late February took Wolves back into the play-off places. The month began with an FA Cup tie that, a quarter of a century later, remains one of the greatest nights the redeveloped stadium has ever hosted.

Taylor's men were drawn away at top-flight Sheffield Wednesday in round four. After a goalless game at Hillsborough, the teams returned to Molineux for a replay. Owls boss Trevor Francis's side was full of internationals, including England quartet Chris Waddle, Des Walker, Andy Sinton and Mark Bright. The match finished 1-1 after extra time, with goals from David Kelly and Bright. The Wednesday goalscorer was also responsible for squandering an incredible chance in front of goal with less than 30 seconds of extra time remaining.

Billy Wright and Ferenc Puskas lead their teams out at Molineux ahead of Wolves' floodlit friendly against Hungarian champions Honved in December 1954

Billy Wright and Joy Beverley hold new-born daughter Vicky in April 1959, with support from Joy's sisters Babs and Teddie

Graham Hughes prepares the first team kit whilst a workman attends to the home dressing room during the 1992/93 season

Graham Hughes helps the Molineux groundstaff mow the pitch during the 2018/19 season

Kenny Hibbitt addresses the ball during a round of golf at Cotswold Edge Golf Club

Hibbitt goes down under that infamous challenge from Glenn Hoddle during the 1981 FA Cup semi-final against Tottenham Hotspur at Hillsborough

Dave Harrison's front page story for the Express and Star *in July 1982, after the Bhatti brothers' consortium, fronted by Derek Dougan, rescue Wolves from administration*

A teenage Derek Ryan at Wolves in 1984

Derek at his home in Donabate, on Ireland's east coast

Tommy Docherty in the dugout alongside substitute Jim Melrose and assistant Jim Barron during the 1984/85 season

Albert and Muriel Bates lead supporters' protests against the Bhatti brothers during the mid-80s Express & Star

The Bhatti brothers leave the High Court in 1986

Steve Bull held aloft by his team-mates in front of the South Bank, after Wolves secure the Fourth Division title in May 1988

*Albert and Muriel Bates with one of the sweaters they printed for the 'Airwolf 90'
trip to Newcastle on New Year's Day 1990*

*A ticket and boarding pass for the Monarch Airlines flight from Birmingham to
Newcastle on New Year's Day 1990*

Graham Turner watches his team from Molineux's disused Waterloo Road Stand in March 1990

Steve Bull receives instructions from manager Bobby Robson as he prepares to come on as a substitute during England's match against Holland at the 1990 World Cup finals

Graham Taylor reads from his resignation statement at a hastily-convened press conference at Molineux in November 1995

The ensuing penalty shoot-out is still talked about today. When Wednesday keeper Kevin Pressman belted an unstoppable spot kick into the top corner – arguably the greatest penalty ever taken – it put his side 3-0 ahead after misses from the usually dependable Andy Thompson and Robbie Dennison. But Wolves scored their last three spot kicks and the South Yorkshire side missed their next two. Chris Waddle, taking his first penalty since his miss in the 1990 World Cup semi-final shoot-out against West Germany, saw his sudden-death effort saved by keeper Paul Jones. It was left to Goodman to secure a remarkable Wolves win.

'At 3-0 down you're not really expecting to go through in a shoot-out, but you've just got to keep your nerve and you never know, it just takes one thing to change it all,' said Taylor, with some sympathy for the opposing players. 'It's amazing what goes through players' minds, or people's minds. That's what players are, they're human beings and once they miss that one penalty, all of a sudden doubt comes in.'

What is sometimes forgotten when that dramatic shoot-out is recalled, is the penalty save made by Jones from Chris Bart-Williams in the dying minutes of the first game in South Yorkshire. Without that, none of the Molineux drama would have taken place.

The FA Cup was one of three knockout competitions Wolves were involved in that season. Interest in the League Cup came to an end after a thrilling 3-2 defeat at home to Frank Clark's Nottingham Forest, who went on to finish third in the Premier League. It was one of many compelling evening fixtures played under the Molineux floodlights that season. There were also four Anglo-Italian Cup ties, a competition for second-tier teams from England and Italy. In all, Wolves played 13 cup matches that season.

After a late Bull winner away at Southend on 1 April, Taylor's men sat six points behind leaders Middlesbrough with two games in hand, and nine games remaining. But the injuries and intensive fixture programme was starting to take its toll. With only one team earning automatic promotion, Taylor knew his team had to go for it in the remaining fixtures, only three of which were at home.

Throwing caution to the wind, Wolves' approach produced some captivating contests. There were three 3-3 draws away from home – to Luton Town, Derby County and Sheffield United. At both Luton and Derby, Wolves came from 3-1 down, scoring added-time equalisers. But at Bramall Lane, Wolves were on the receiving end of a last-gasp goal, when Jostein Flo headed the Blades' equaliser in the fourth minute of injury time.

Taylor was involved in an ugly incident as he headed for the tunnel at the end of the Sheffield United fixture. A home fan stepped forward from the stands and spat in his face. It was a horrible reminder of the baggage that still followed the former England manager at the time, much of it caused by the treatment he suffered at the hands of the tabloids. Taylor was incensed and climbed into the stand to confront the supporter, attempting to make a citizen's arrest, leading to a scuffle involving stewards and police.

At Derby, Dean Richards's two late goals earned a point. The defender arrived on loan from Second Division Bradford City in the last week of March. After signing permanently, he enjoyed a successful career at Molineux before moving on to Southampton and Tottenham Hotspur. In March 2005, at the age of 30, he was forced to retire from the game after seeking medical advice when suffering from dizzy spells and headaches. He died less than six years later.

'As a person, he was one of the nicest lads you'd ever wish to meet, such a lovely lad,' Froggatt remembers. 'But what a talent, and he obviously proved himself when he went to Spurs. He was just a top-class footballer. He was great on the ball, commanding in the air and quick. The boy had absolutely everything. If you look at the current England squad right now, Deano would have been perfect for the way we play, playing it from the back. He was one of the new generation of centre-halves who was gifted on the ball.' Wolves finished the season in fourth place, level on points with Tranmere Rovers. With 77 goals, they were the division's top scorers, with ten more than champions Middlesbrough. But it was at the back they struggled, with 61 in the goals-against column, the most for any team in the top half of the table. It set up a semi-final play-off against third-placed Bolton Wanderers, with the first leg at home. Bolton were without their first-choice keeper, Keith Branagan. Manager Bruce Rioch took a gamble, and instead of turning to second-choice Aidan Davison he called up recent emergency signing Peter Shilton for his first start in over a year and a half. The former England keeper was 45 years old, but he made a series of saves to keep a struggling Bolton side in the tie, with dominant Wolves winning the first leg 2-1.

'We are going into a 90-minute game with a one-goal lead, when does that ever happen?' Taylor said in the tunnel, after the match. 'It's great news, isn't it? I'd pick any game to have a one-goal lead before we kick a ball and that's what we've got.'

The tables turned in the second leg. Bolton were rampant at Burnden Park. Wolves supporters' pantomime villain was John McGinlay. The Scottish forward scored both goals in a 2-0 victory to take Bolton through 3-2 on aggregate after extra time. At 1-0, McGinlay and Kelly were involved in an altercation that led to the Bolton player punching the Wolves forward to the floor, after Kelly had initially pushed McGinlay in the face.

'He's got to go, the referee has no choice. McGinlay has got to go,' yelled Jimmy Greaves, commentating for ITV that evening. Referee Steve Dunn, who was only a couple of yards away from the incident, produced yellow cards for both players after they shook hands with each other. 'That's a cop out,' was Greaves's verdict.

'Maybe I was fortunate enough to stay on, but thankfully the ref saw it as just a wee push,' said a smiling McGinlay in his post-match interview.

'I was sat watching from afar feeling helpless really, and couldn't do anything about it,' Froggatt recalls. 'That season just ended in enormous disappointment because we were absolutely flying. I think the only criticism we could put on that situation was that with the amount of injuries we had we didn't replace anybody. I think at the time we thought we'd be back fairly quickly, yet it turned out that a lot of us had major injuries. Tony, Geoff Thomas and I were out for a long time, so instead of going out and buying one or two extra to cover the situation, they didn't. I think the lack of depth in the squad, perhaps, did for us. We still should have come first or second that year.'

It was, in fact, a larger squad than most clubs possessed in the division. Twenty-seven outfield players were used in the league that season. But Froggatt is right, to a certain extent. Many of the players appeared in just a handful of games, with several loan signings making up the numbers. Only four outfield players managed 30 or more league appearances all season.

'We were fighting on a lot of fronts, I think that was the big issue,' he continues. 'If we had four or five key players missing it would really hurt us. It took its toll on the team. The two main signings of the summer were out, Tony missed the entire season and I missed half of it. If Graham had kicked a black cat a hundred times he wouldn't have had any more bad luck than he had that year. Everyone could see at the start of that season what a good team we were. Sometimes injuries are the difference between success and failure. To have four or five players go down, not just with a little hamstring injury or something like that, we're on about cruciate knee injuries and ankle ligaments, massive injuries that kept players out for a long time. You couldn't have predicted that.'

A subdued summer followed. Wolves had squandered their best chance of promotion since returning to the second tier. The permanent signing of Richards, for a club record £1.85million, was the only incoming transfer. But it was Richards's partner at the back, Brian Law, who made the biggest headlines. A highly rated defender from Merthyr Tydfil, Law had played just a handful of games for Queens Park Rangers when he was called up to the Wales senior squad in 1990, when Rangers coach Peter Shreeves recommended him to Wales manager Terry Yorath. But a year later, aged only 21, his career was cut short by a tendon injury in his foot.

Forced to retire, he used the insurance pay-out to fund a backpacking trip around the world. It was while travelling that he noticed the injury had begun to heal naturally. He returned to England and secured a trial with Wolves, where Taylor was sufficiently impressed to sign the player. Wolves settled his £34,000 insurance pay-out and paid a small fee of around £100,000 to Queens Park Rangers, who still held his registration.

'He was a very bright lad, and more the old-fashioned type of centre-half,' Froggatt recalls.

In July 1995 the players returned to training after the summer break. They quickly organised a team bonding night out.

'We were all out together and then when the night closed, we were all staying in different places,' Froggatt adds. 'I lived in Sutton Coldfield at the time so got a taxi back, but the Wolverhampton-based lads carried on and maybe carried on a bit too much. Brian was not a drinker, and he probably had one or two too many and just lost the plot.'

Law, his brother and two other friends partied long into the night. By the time they made their way home on Sunday morning the roads were empty. Wandering past

Wolverhampton bus station, the four of them entered the premises and stole an empty bus, the 510 to Perton. Law assumed the role of driver and the four of them set off, before their journey came to a juddering halt when the bus crashed into some railings on the Stafford Street ring road. The four men panicked and ran off, but were soon caught hiding in some nearby bushes.

'He got nicknamed "Blakey" from *On The Buses*, he never got rid of that name,' Froggatt says, chuckling at the recollection of the incident. 'He was really devastated by it because he was a really good lad, he just had a single moment of madness. I don't think he ever drank again, he certainly didn't when I was at the football club.'

It was an incident that could have had far more serious consequences. Nobody was hurt in the alcohol-fuelled caper, but Law faced an uncertain few months not knowing his fate before the case came to court. Ten years after the incident he spoke to the *Birmingham Evening Mail* about how the incident transformed his life:

'You live and learn,' he admitted. 'I was a stupid kid messing around and, although it's still a source of amusement, everyone I meet is really good about it. I embarrassed the club and embarrassed the city – they could have fobbed me off but Graham [Taylor] actually returned after he'd been sacked to speak up for me in court. But what happened with the bus reawakened my spiritual side.'

Law received a fine and a community service order for his role in the bus incident. He had become a Christian while travelling, before signing for Wolves, and decided he wanted to put something back into the community. Since leaving the game he has worked with a number of Christian organisations, helping coach and teach under-privileged children all over the country.

Aside from Law's moment of madness, there was more headline news when the club accepted a £1.5million bid for Bull. It was a decision that caused much anger amongst the fan base. At the time, Taylor was held responsible for agreeing to the sale, but Bull has since gone on record to say it was a decision made by the board. Nevertheless, there was less goodwill going in to the 1995/96 season. The first signs of impatience were emanating from the stands. Wolves did not win any of their opening three games, and were on the back foot from then on. A humiliating 4-1 defeat at home to Stoke City in October highlighted the lack of confidence in a team playing with the burden of fans' hopes.

On a cold Sunday afternoon at home to Charlton Athletic on 12 November, with Bull dropped to the substitutes' bench, matters came to a head.

Alan Curbishley's side were familiar opponents. The two teams had met twice in the League Cup third round, with Taylor's men progressing to the next stage of the competition after winning a replay at The Valley in extra time, just four days prior to this league clash.

The match at Molineux was an incredibly tense affair. A large section of the support had lost faith in the manager, and patience was in short supply. Goalkeeper Paul Jones kept Wolves level with an outstanding early second-half save, before the home side laid siege to the Charlton goal as the game progressed. The fine margins of success and failure were on display. A Goodman header deep into added time cannoned back off the crossbar. The visitors from south London escaped with a point.

A vocal set of fans gathered outside the Billy Wright Stand after the match, singing 'We want Taylor out'. The following day, they got their wish.

'It is with much regret that I have tendered my resignation as manager of the Wolves,' said Taylor, at a hastily arranged press conference. 'I am sad, because this is as much to do with matters off the pitch as those on it. Obviously the team has not been playing well but, only 13 weeks into the season, we are still in all competitions. Our recent run of only two defeats in 12 games is not as bad as our sterner critics claim. A return of confidence to the players who, last season, enabled Wolves to have their best season in over a decade is, of course, of prime importance. If this confidence does return I see no reason why promotion cannot be gained this season. However, the team cannot gain confidence if the board of directors and a section of fans do not have confidence in their manager. I would now hope that the privacy of my family and myself will be respected.'

'In my entire career, it's my biggest regret,' says Froggatt, looking back at Taylor's departure. 'I was actually lying in hospital. I had a blood clot problem as a result of my ankle operation, and I was listening to the Charlton game in Wolverhampton on the radio, and I heard all the boos. Then the next day Graham got sacked, and I knew it was the worst decision the club could have made because there were still quite a lot of us missing. The boys that had come back from injury weren't match fit at the start of that season. All the players at the club knew we would turn it around, but unfortunately for Graham it didn't work out. I was devastated, it was probably one of the lowest points of my career. I was on the sidelines watching the team not get promoted and then the following season Graham gets sacked.'

Froggatt believes one person in particular lost his nerve at a time when the noises off the pitch were louder than those on it.

'From my point of view I thought it was the inexperience of the chairman [Jonathan Hayward]. I think he buckled far too easily. Graham went on to do really good things after he left Wolves, as well. To give him just one season was never enough. Jonathan was such a lovely, lovely man but not a football man, not a clue about football. I don't mean that disrespectfully, but he was a farmer. I think if you'd had a proper football man in place, Graham would not have been sacked. They'd have given him more time to try turning it around. You know what it's like in the Championship, it's a long, long season, you can't be guided by the first few games. The amount of teams you see tear it up in the second half of the season, get in the play-offs and get promoted. It was a huge lack of experience, I think.'

Wolves turned to Mark McGhee next, who by then was managing Leicester City. He joined the club in December, after an acrimonious departure from Filbert Street, and oversaw a 1-0 home defeat to Port Vale in his first game. He quickly strengthened the squad, signing Simon Osborn from Queens Park Rangers and Steve Corica from Leicester City, both for fees in excess of £1million. But Wolves' form dipped even further during the second half of the campaign. The club finished the season 20th in the table, just three points above the relegation places.

Iwan Roberts, Keith Curle and Adrian Williams were signed in the summer as Sir Jack Hayward made more money available for transfers ahead of the 1996/97 season. Froggatt started 27 league games that season, mainly in a wing-back role as McGhee employed a three-man central defence. But, again, Wolves came up just short. Finishing third in the First Division, behind Bolton and Barnsley, it was into the play-offs once more. This time a semi-final defeat to sixth-placed Crystal Palace ended any hopes of promotion.

The 1997/98 season is remembered for Wolves' progress in the FA Cup. With McGhee's side never genuinely in the hunt for promotion, their cup run kept supporters interested. It took them all the way to the semi-final, where they lost 1-0 to double-chasing Arsenal at Villa Park.

'It was the first time I'd returned to Villa Park since I left Villa,' Froggatt says. 'I always remember walking out and it was spine-tingling to hear the noise. The Wolves fans were so vocal and totally out-sung Arsenal for the entire 90 minutes. When you look back, it was just a shame that we were playing one of the best teams in Premier League history. They were just amazing. But for the last ten minutes of the match, when we almost gave them a bit of a fright, they were always in control of the game. They had Emmanuel Petit and Patrick Vieira in the middle of the park so it was always going to be difficult to dominate in any shape or form.

'We didn't get the ball high enough up the pitch and a lot of Wolves fans moan at the team selection. Bully and Robbie Keane didn't play; to this day they feel we might have had a better chance if Bully or Robbie played. My honest opinion, in hindsight, was that because Steve Claridge [a recent stop-gap signing, who never scored for Wolves] had done it in big games, I think the gaffer just had a hunch, as lots of managers do, and went with him. Stevie scored in cup finals, he was a big-game player, but it backfired as it didn't work. In all honesty, do I think we would have beaten Arsenal? I don't think they got out of second gear if truth be known. They were that unbelievably good that, had we scored a goal, I think they would have gone up another two gears and scored another one.'

Early on, there was good reason to believe the 1998/99 season could be a successful one for Wolves. With Bull and Keane forming a formidable partnership up front, Wolves won their opening four games of the season. Froggatt, now aged 25, was in good form having recovered from his injury problems. But then, in October, Wolves accepted a £1.9million offer from Coventry City for the winger. His four-year stay at Molineux was over.

'The season I left, we started off like a house on fire,' he adds. 'The first few weeks of the season we were well in contention. We had a strong, powerful side. I thought that was a promotion-winning team in waiting. Then Mark pulled me aside and told me that a few clubs were looking at me. I was out of contract the following summer so could have gone on a free transfer. Mark knew Gordon Strachan at Coventry because he was Gordon's best man at his wedding. I said, "I don't want to leave, I want a new contract." Mark said he would go and ask the chairman [Sir Jack, who had taken over from his son]. Mark was quite pleased that I wasn't going to walk away, but he came back to me and said the chairman wouldn't give me a contract. That first few weeks was some of the best football I'd ever played at Wolves so it came as a big shock.

'But I also got wind that Robbie wasn't going to be far after me. I thought that if they were going to sell me at 25 and then Robbie, who was one of the best players in the club's history, where was the club going? What was going on? Obviously Sir Jack had spent far too much money and he was looking to rein it in. The one thing I loved about Sir Jack was that he was totally honest with me. There was no beating around the bush, it was plain and simple that they wanted to cash in. I totally respected Sir Jack for that. He was a really good man who did so much good in Wolverhampton. But I still felt my time was cut short.'

Froggatt held down a first-team place for the duration of his time at Highfield Road. His form earned him a call-up to the England squad in November 1999, when he appeared as an unused substitute in the first leg of the Euro 2000 qualification play-off against Scotland at Hampden Park.

But his career was ended by a bad tackle from Nicky Summerbee during a Premier League fixture against Sunderland in February 2000. Despite playing a handful more games, he never recovered and missed the entire 2000/01 season before announcing his retirement. Froggatt was only 27 when he played his final game. Despite such an injury-ravaged career, he looks back fondly on the time he spent with all three Midlands clubs.

'It's like choosing your favourite child if you've got three kids,' he explains. 'I had a brilliant time at Villa, runners-up in the Premier League and winning the League Cup Final, amazing times. At Wolves I had four of the best years of my life. I had the best time ever there, just tainted by the fact we didn't have the success we should have had. Then I got back in the Premier League with Coventry City and was called into the England squad.

'When I look back now over a prolonged period of time, I think I played my best football at Wolves. I love everything about the club. I've still got loads of great friends there today, I love going back and watching them now. I'm hugely fond of them. Outside of football, David Kelly is my best mate, we have had businesses together for the last 20 years. I've worked in the media for years with Don Goodman. Tony Daley was best man at my wedding. Iwan Roberts and Simon Osborn are other great mates. I would say most of my best friends in football are from my time at Wolves.'

Alongside appearing as a radio pundit for many years, Froggatt has built a successful career away from the game.

'When I first retired I went into financial services,' he explains. 'I took a load of financial services exams and got on with it. I had passed all the exams by the time I was 28 or 29. They were tough, difficult exams to do and they change all the time, but I just knew I wanted to do something. Mortgage brokering is my full-time job, for a firm in Solihull, I really enjoy it. It's such a drastic change of lifestyle.'

He continues to watch Wolves, and admits that playing in Nuno Espírito Santo's side would have been very appealing.

'Oh, I would have loved to have played wing-back in this side. If you play wing-back with Conor Coady and the other centre-backs, with those diagonal balls to Matt Doherty and Jonny, they are almost like wingers that come back occasionally. I don't see either of the wing-backs having to do too much defending. The back three are so good and they trust them so much to do the defending. It's a perfect set-up because they've got the right players to play it.'

For Graham Taylor there was redemption back in the manager's seat at Watford. He won two successive promotions between 1997 and 1999, guiding them from the Second Division to the Premier League. A short spell at Aston Villa followed before his retirement from management in 2003. Taylor was made an honorary life president at Watford in recognition of his achievements during two spells at Vicarage Road. He died on 12 January 2017 at the age of 72. By coincidence, Wolves and Aston Villa met at Molineux two days later, with many former players of both clubs in attendance to pay their respects during a pre-match tribute.

After that eventful 1994/95 season it was never the same at Molineux. The home crowd earned a reputation for venting their frustrations when matters were not going as planned on the pitch. As if scarred by the way that season finished, patience was in short supply thereafter. Visiting teams relished the opportunity to turn the mood of the Wolves support. There was only one further promotion challenge during the 90s. It was a decade of dispiriting under-achievement, spent entirely in the second tier. The 1994/95 season could have been the start of something special. There were many highlights in a season when Wolves seemed to live on the edge. But instead, it is remembered only for what might have been.

'Every now and then we have a little reunion with the Wolves boys,' Froggatt concludes. 'And every time we say, "How the fuck did we not get promoted that year?" Everyone says it.'

Chapter 10

THE SECRETARY

Working with Wolves

RICHARD SKIRROW is enjoying the early years of his retirement. The day before meeting up to talk through the highs and lows of two decades as Wolves' club secretary, he travelled from his home in Stafford to go walking with a group of friends in the Cheshire countryside. It is something he tries to do most weeks. Making the time to enjoy such regular days of getting away from it all was never really possible in a role that, at times, became all-consuming. There are certain jobs where the employee is effectively on call 24/7. The secretary of a professional football club at the upper levels of English football is almost always on call. Such as on Friday, 29 July 2016.

'I'm part of a fantasy football league with a group of friends, whereby each player can only be bought by one person so you have to get together for an auction every year, and it's a chance for a catch up over a drink,' Skirrow explains. 'I got a phone call from Lin Kennings, chief executive Jez Moxey's PA, at 3pm to say that Kenny Jackett had been dismissed. The new manager is going to be appointed. It's Walter Zenga. Aside from being a great Italian goalkeeper, I could not recall what Walter Zenga had done in management. There was going to be a senior management meeting at a hotel in Wolverhampton at 8pm that night. I wasn't in the Wolverhampton area so that was not an option for me. "Can you liaise with the club's solicitors about his contract?" Lin asks. Well I'd already had two pints, and I was just finishing another.

'I said, "I can't drive, I'm over the limit." So I went out into the car park and stood there going back and forth on the phone with the club's solicitors to draft a contract. Our solicitor was also away, on family business. I couldn't believe that the final draft was needed so urgently. "He's going to want his people to have a look at it. It will take well into next week," I thought. But it didn't, he signed it there and then that night. So I finished off Zenga's contract on the phone in a pub car park. It just seemed bizarre.'

Skirrow completed the detail with the club's head of football development and recruitment, Kevin Thelwell, and the club solicitor, who was finally contacted on the telephone. It was a crazy few hours in the life of a football secretary.

Zenga was one of the more short-lived managerial appointments during Skirrow's time at the club. It was an employment that began during Mark McGhee's tenure in December 1996 and finished at the end of Paul Lambert's period in charge in May 2017.

A key employee at the highest echelons of the company, Skirrow was involved in just about every level of the club's business at some stage or another during his time at Molineux. Born a Yorkshireman, but brought up in Greater Manchester as a keen Manchester United fan, he began his career by qualifying as an accountant at the Manchester-based practice Touche Ross, before moving into industry.

'I was working as a finance director in a fairly bog-standard industry in Denton, in east Manchester. I knew Tom Finn, who was then secretary at Oldham Athletic. We used to play five a side together. Tom moved to West Ham and it was through Tom that I ended up joining West Ham as financial controller in 1992, before moving to Wolves.'

So what exactly is the role of a club secretary?

'There was a pal of mine at West Ham, whom I ended up playing five-a-side with, a bit of an east-end character, who said, "Anyone can book a coach and put the soap out,"' says Skirrow, smiling. 'First and foremost it's player registration, contracts and dealing with the authorities from the league that the team is in, and the Football Association.

'Throughout most of my career at Wolves, Jez Moxey was chief executive there. Jez would be the final arbiter on the terms of the contract, but I'd always draft it. Although there is a standard template, these days there are pages and pages of addenda. The bells and whistles like bonus payments, the uplift after so many games, you're trying to get it as performance-related as you can. Likewise, I would always draft transfer agreements. The role covers contracts, registrations, transfers, work permits. And it's also agreeing club rules for the players and discipline for them with the manager. Club fines would come from the manager. For a clear breach of rules, a sending off or a booking for dissent, if that was enforced by the manager I would draft a letter and often give it to the player. If it's a club fine, it's deducted from their salary at source.

'Sometimes the manager wouldn't put it through the formal system and would just ask for a payment of a hundred pounds or so and it would go in the pot for the end-of-season do or charity. The minor indiscretions for using a mobile phone in the dressing room or canteen, or being late, or not responding to a physio appointment, that small beer fine goes in the pot.

'My role involved a lot of that type of thing, quasi-legal work. Now they have got a qualified legal professional in place. You are the contact with the FA for doping regulations and making sure the players know about the implementation of that. If anything goes wrong, you are the point of contact.

Club secretaries can be from different backgrounds: they can be financial, they can be purely company secretarial or they can be an administrator.'

There is no other role at a football club that covers such a wide brief. The secretary is involved in matters involving players, managers, owners, staff and supporters, and is expected to form working relationships with just about every department of the club. Expect the unexpected, as Skirrow discovered very early on.

'During my first week I was driving home and passed a newsagent which had a wire basket outside with a big front cover of the *Express and Star,*' he recalls. '"WOLFIE IN CANNABIS SHOCK". The guy who was our mascot, Wolfie, obviously not in costume, had been caught with cannabis by the police. That was a good one. He was quickly relieved of his duties so it became a "non-club matter".'

The mid-1990s became one of the most difficult periods for supporters. A combination of raised expectations, through investment in players, and the failure of the team to achieve promotion proved hugely frustrating.

Skirrow joined the club midway through a promotion push under McGhee, a 38-year-old Scottish manager who arrived with a glowing reference from Manchester United's Premier League title-winning manager Alex Ferguson, whom he played for at Aberdeen. McGhee was enticed from Leicester City, walking out on the East Midlands club in acrimonious circumstances, and was given significant funds to invest in the side.

But the promotion challenge of 1996/97 came off the rails and the season ended in disappointment in the First Division play-offs, after unfancied Barnsley pipped Wolves to the second automatic promotion spot behind Bolton Wanderers. McGhee had made few friends in South Yorkshire, with a comment made to the Birmingham *Sports Argus* during the run-in about which club was fit for promotion. 'I would guarantee that most of the Premiership clubs would like it to be Barnsley,' he said. 'They might fancy the prospect that Barnsley would be annihilated next season and thrown to the sharks. They probably think they would go straight back down.' Barnsley's players admitted to pinning a newspaper cutting with the quotes to their dressing room wall to inspire them during the promotion run-in. It was not the first time McGhee had come across as arrogant, having written off Birmingham City as 'a very ordinary team' ahead of a local derby the previous season.

Skirrow paints a different picture of the assured Scot, though. 'Yes, that Birmingham City thing. I think he was still relatively inexperienced in management really and hadn't had any real setbacks. He was the next bright young thing really, one of Sir Alex Ferguson's proteges from Aberdeen. He'd had no setbacks, so if he thought Birmingham were an ordinary team he'd say Birmingham were an ordinary team. And if he thought Wolves were a better bet for promotion than Barnsley and more likely to survive in the Premier League, and of course they should be, then he said so.

'I worked quite closely with Mark and got on very well with him, it was the closest socialising bond I've had with any manager. My wife Jane and I used to go out with Mark and his wife, Jacqui, for meals after games. Mark would bring in music CDs to training. "What do you think of that?" he would ask. He brought in a Hootie and the Blowfish CD once, I'd never heard of them at the time, but it was great, we had similar tastes.

'In his second full season, my first full season, we got to the FA Cup semi-final. It was a time where big ticket sales would often start at 9am and there would be queues around the ground overnight. If the numbers and weather dictated, we opened the Stan Cullis Stand so the supporters could queue inside. I remember Mark and Jacqui turning up at midnight to speak to fans who were queuing for the Leeds United quarter-final. That never got much publicity.'

Skirrow worked with 11 different managers at Wolves. The secretary's office at the club's Compton Park training ground was in close proximity to the manager's, so forming a working relationship was crucial. 'You have to prove you are worthy of trust,' Skirrow explains. 'There was a good example during Mick McCarthy's early days. My office was next door to Mick's and my door would always be open, as would his. I don't think he'd even been there a week, so we hadn't spent a lot of time together. I was on the phone to a friend and used the phrase, "Normal service will be resumed" about the England cricket team's struggles. Mick put two and two together and got five. He thought I was talking about the Wolves team. He stormed in saying, "What are you talking about?" He took a fairly robust stance, but I explained the comment and we got on like a house on fire after that, but there has to be that trust. Managers need to be sure that senior colleagues are with them, and that certainly includes the club secretary.'

McCarthy's reaction revealed the daily pressure that comes with the manager's post. The external hopes and expectations can weigh heavily on a manager's shoulders. Skirrow worked at the heart of the inner sanctum, and witnessed the working pressures that these individuals found themselves subjected to. But, amidst it all, there were always moments that lightened up a room.

'Kenny Jackett's phone went off once in my company, early on during his time here. The ringtone was Kaiser Chiefs' "I Predict A Riot". He just joked, "Oh sorry, that's my Millwall ringtone."'

Music was not always the answer, though. 'One thing Walter Zenga had a habit of doing was coming in and putting Radio 1Xtra on his television. If there is one thing I do not want to listen to in my working day, it is Radio 1Xtra.'

The music stopped when Zenga was replaced with Lambert. 'Paul swore a heck of a lot but in this sometimes Scottish way where it wasn't offensive,' Skirrow adds. 'It seemed to be in every sentence but it wasn't offensive. It was a return, in many ways, to the Mick era. Paul was a more outgoing character than Kenny. He was a very humorous individual and I got on extremely well with him. Paul brought the table tennis back in the players' lounge. So, going from Radio 1Xtra annoying me, I now had the shrieks of the table tennis games going on some afternoons, while the rest of the office was trying to work diligently to the end of the day.'

The most testing times for the secretary inevitably occurred around transfer deadline day. The frantic nature of the business as the clock ticked down to the deadline made for some harrowing moments.

'We had players in the building, often with their agent, who took phone calls and just said, "Cheerio" and that was that,' Skirrow reveals. 'Scott Dann was one that stands out during Mick's time here. I think that was when he went to Birmingham City instead. We had James McCarthy in the building too.'

Irish midfielder McCarthy, then of Hamilton Academical, was so sure that he would be joining up with newly promoted Wolves in the summer of 2009, ahead of the first Premier League season under his namesake, that he left Compton Park after his medical with a copy of the club's commemorative 'Champions 08/09' book to read up on his team-mates, who had just secured the Championship title. The club had a shirt printed with his name and squad number for the obligatory 'new signing' photo call, but the player never returned.

When Wolves tried to sign Georgian international Temuri Ketsbaia from Newcastle for £900,000 in August 2000, the deal was delayed for a few hours.

'I remember having to pick up Temuri from Patshull, on the outskirts of Wolverhampton, and ensure he got to Birmingham Airport,' Skirrow explains. 'At that stage you couldn't get the work permit issued for somebody unless they were out of the country. So he had to fly to Paris, report to the British Embassy, get the relevant stamp, and come straight back in to the UK. He'd come to the club to agree terms and have a medical, and we then had to get him out, back in and eligible as quickly as possible.'

Dealing with overseas agents was often fraught with an extra layer of bureaucracy. In 2003 Belgian international striker Cedric Roussel left the club after an underwhelming two and a half years at Molineux, during which time he scored just two goals.

'One of the most surreal moments, that occurred years later, was attending a court in Antwerp with Jez,' Skirrow continues. 'We sat there listening to proceedings in Flemish, not really knowing what was going on. An agent was claiming a contractual entitlement resulting from Cedric's departure. We won the case, as we knew we should have done, but without ever really knowing what the court proceedings had been decided on. It was a bizarre situation.'

Another strange contract claim, closer to home, was settled without the need for a court case. One of the club's former strikers had, like most players, a relocation fee clause in his contract and tried to use the option in an enterprising manner.

'He wanted to exercise this in the last four weeks of his contract. The relocation was for a house purchase that would have involved him moving further away from the club than where he was living,' Skirrow says, with a sigh, as he recalls having to put the player straight about the matter. 'He said, "I know, bloody Moxey isn't going to give it me is he?" I said, "It's nothing to do with Jez, I haven't even mentioned it to Jez. You're out of contract in a few weeks' time and you are moving further away!"'

For all the despair at certain episodes, Skirrow's duty of care shines through in the conversation. He always wanted the best for the players and was a guiding presence, particularly for some of the younger ones who needed help with lifestyle arrangements, such as sorting out their financial affairs once they broke into the first team. He attended countless youth- and reserve-team games to check up on the progress of the players coming through the ranks. Wolves had built a strong scouting system in Ireland during the 90s, largely thanks to a garage owner named Willie Byrne.

'We had such a conveyor belt of Irish youngsters at one stage, such as Seamus Crowe, Dominic Foley, JJ Melligan and Keith Andrews, although not all of them came through,' Skirrow says. 'Willie would report in to Chris Evans, the academy manager. But part of the secretary's role would be to agree the compensation document with the junior Irish club, which could be interesting. We were able to conclude good deals because we were perceived as a club where the lads would get a chance, which gave you the chance to secure a performance-related agreement. Willie was hugely dedicated and a great watcher of games over in Ireland, and he assessed players very well. He had his own car repair business, which was his primary job. It's a thankless task, scouting. You're watching a lot of pretty ordinary stuff in poor weather for just mileage, hoping to spot a player who might have what it takes.'

The club's greatest academy success during Skirrow's time was an Irish import. There was no shortage of suitors chasing 15-year-old Robbie Keane in 1996. He had been missed by Leeds United a year earlier, even when scoring for one of the Yorkshire club's youth teams in a trial game, but on his return home to Dublin it became clear he was on the radar of some of England's top clubs.

Wolves eventually pipped Liverpool and Nottingham Forest for his signature, and he was taken under the wing of Evans. Keane thrived in the club's junior set-up, scoring 36 goals in his only full season as a youth-team player.

'On the Saturday of home first-team fixtures, the under-18s would have played that morning somewhere,' Skirrow adds. 'Chris would eventually get to the first team game a bit later, before the days of social media and the proliferation of mobile phones, really. We'd ask him the score and then, "Who scored?" The answer was always "Robbie Keane". It got to the stage where we just ended up asking him how many Robbie had scored. He was a phenomenal goalscorer really.'

Keane's professional debut the following season against Norwich City at Carrow Road has gone down in folklore. There was a certain irony that the 17-year-old was thrown into a starting XI full of veterans on that August afternoon in 1997. Keith Curle, Steve Sedgley, Mark Atkins, Steve Froggatt and Don Goodman had been signed for big money in previous years but had been unable to take Wolves into the Premier League. They could only look on and marvel as Keane took Norwich apart with two goals; first with a thumping shot from the edge of the box and then a dance through a crowded penalty area to poke home his second.

When strike partner Steve Bull ran over to celebrate with him, the pair could almost have been mistaken for father and son, such was this Irish kid's fresh-faced appearance. The sprinkling of stardust that Wolves had been unable to find during the lavish spending of the Graham Taylor and McGhee tenures had finally arrived.

'Of course Robbie's debut at Norwich was fantastic,' Skirrow continues. 'Mark had sprung a bit of a surprise taking him on our pre-season tour to Scotland, and he'd done well there. We knew he was going to start at Norwich so we got his family across from Ireland. It was a baking hot day at Carrow Road. I have strong memories of Robbie's dad, six or seven seats away from me, shouting, "That's my boy."'

McGhee, to his credit, trusted Keane from the outset. He made 45 appearances during that 1997/98 season, but supporters never forgave the manager for leaving him and Bull out of the biggest game of the season, the FA Cup semi-final against Arsenal at Villa Park. Instead, recent recruit Steve Claridge was handed a starting place in attack alongside Goodman.

The following campaign started brightly for Keane, with eight goals in the opening 12 matches. But the football under McGhee was regressing. Instead of improving, the team was becoming one-dimensional and ponderous. The aim was for a possession-based dominance but there was so little creativity that supporters quickly became frustrated. With McGhee removed from his post in the autumn, his assistant Colin Lee took over. But Keane never recaptured his early season form. He could only watch on as the final day of the season unfolded with Bradford City sealing promotion to the Premier League with a 3-2 win at Molineux. Wolves missed out on the play-offs. It was a dispiriting and familiar end to the decade.

The club had neglected a growing problem in attack. Dougie Freedman was never allowed to show his finer attributes by McGhee and was shown the door far too early. An ageing Goodman also left in 1998. Bull was by now a spent force, with a knee injury ending his career in the summer of 1999. Keane's strike-partner for that Bradford game was Norwegian journeyman Havard Flo. There was nobody at the club who could offer Keane the support his talents merited. Two full seasons had passed and supporters knew that their prodigy could not be kept at the club for much longer.

The young star only played two seasons of first-team football at Wolves, before the club accepted a £6million bid from Coventry City for his talents. Was there a regret that he never fulfilled his potential at Wolves?

'Yes, there has to be. Robbie must be the best player at the club during my time, although we clearly didn't see the best of him in those early years,' Skirrow reflects. 'Nowhere near the best of him. All we saw was a very good young talent. But we were in the First Division and he was a Premier League talent. Coventry made us an offer and his became the highest transfer fee for a teenager. You regard yourself as every bit as big as Coventry, but they had been an established Premier League team and we weren't, of course. 'But Robbie hadn't really been pulling up any trees just before he went, had he? You also knew it would mainly be reinvested. Ade Akinbiyi was the big buy it funded. To me it just seemed like the inevitable rule of football, that if a player is capable of playing at a higher level, then you are going to have a job hanging on to him.'

The disappointment at what might have been did not end there. At Highfield Road, Keane's potential was finally realised. Amongst team-mates of a superior quality to the players at Molineux, Keane lit up the Premier League during his early days. As if freed from the shackles, his career was quickly back on an upward trajectory. At club level, moves to Inter Milan, Leeds United, Tottenham Hotspur and Liverpool followed for the man who would become Ireland's all-time record scorer. Scoring in three successive games at the 2002 World Cup, including a stunning strike against Germany less than five years after his teenage Wolves debut, was more evidence that he could perform on the highest stage. Keane lived out the stellar playing career he was always destined for. Wolves may have nurtured him as a junior, but the sense of what might have been lingered at Molineux throughout the player's professional years.

Wolves slipped into a period of circumspection as the turn of the century came and went. A final bout of spending under Sir Jack Hayward helped facilitate the 2002/03 promotion under Dave Jones's management. The play-off final win against Sheffield United at Cardiff was a joyous occasion for supporters. 'One of the days of their live's, says Skirrow. But for the club secretary, it also presented one of the greatest challenges.

'The night of the 2003 play-off final, that party in Cardiff was quite something, a totally joyous affair. The whole play-off final experience was one of the highlights at

Wolves,' he admits. 'But being so close to the administration of it, it was difficult to get as much enjoyment from the day as the supporters. There were all sorts of organisational things to do. Dave Jones rightly decided that the players were going to have just one night away pre-match, as would be normal for an away game of that distance, and they were based in the Vale of Glamorgan hotel on the Sunday night. Jez and the board were staying somewhere near the Welsh border. I felt I had to be very near the stadium so I was in the Hilton in Cardiff city centre where, coincidentally, Sheffield United were staying.

'It was only at teatime on Sunday – ahead of the game on Monday afternoon – that we got confirmation of a problem regarding about 170 supporters who didn't have the seats they believed they had booked. We knew their tickets hadn't arrived, but the ticket agency finally admitted that the seats those fans had booked had not been taken off sale and had subsequently been resold. Fortunately, some of the Football League top brass were in the same hotel, so I was able to speak to someone really helpful from the Football League who said that, although it was a lot of tickets, it wasn't totally uncharted territory.

'As it transpired, the Millennium Stadium always held some seats back for, amongst others, catering staff closing kiosks just after kick-off if they wanted to watch the game. The Millennium Stadium staff were brilliant and somehow cobbled together enough tickets to get everyone a seat somewhere in the Wolves section of the stadium. From memory, we only got one complaint. We'd won the game, we'd got promotion, everyone was delirious, and no one else questioned the adequacy of their seat.'

Another highlight came with the club's second promotion to the Premier League under McCarthy.

'Mick was brilliant at bringing everyone together,' Skirrow adds. 'And Ian Evans is the one who doesn't get mentioned as much. Ian came in initially as coach with

Mick, he was number two, and Ian, to my mind, was particularly responsible for bringing in Michael Kightly and George Elokobi. Every club should be trying to get some bargain basement gems and polish them up and we did that with Kightly, Stephen Ward, Matt Jarvis, Andy Keogh and Karl Henry.

'I feel that Mick's time is under-appreciated by the fans. They won the Championship title in style. I think there's almost a re-writing of history in the way the team played, that all they did was put a shift in, run hard, sweat hard and play long ball. Blimey, Kightly in one wing, Jarvis on the other, David Jones in the middle. They also played good football in the Premier League in those first couple of seasons. There was that 24-pass Jones goal on a night game when we beat Spurs at Molineux, completely flying in the face of this kick and run, putting a shift in nonsense.'

When McCarthy's third season in the Premier League came off the rails, one of the criticisms levelled at the club in the wake of his sacking in February 2012, with 12 games remaining, was that nobody experienced enough was lined up to replace him. Assistant manager Terry Connor, who had cleared his desk and thought he would be leaving with McCarthy, was eventually asked to stay on and take the reins, which he did reluctantly. Skirrow sees it differently.

'I feel the club got unfair criticism there, because the criticism at the time was, "How on earth can you sack somebody without having anybody in place to take over?" But to my mind, because I have this Corinthian spirit and want things to be done properly, and people to be treated well, it would have been outrageous if, after everything that Mick had done for the club, something had been done behind his back, and someone had been appointed within 24 hours of Mick leaving. That would have been totally, totally wrong. And, in any case, an impossible scenario as he would not have been sacked had that Albion game been won.'

'Steve Morgan [the chairman] and Jez did a proper recruitment process. Alan Curbishley accepted the job one afternoon at Carden Park [Morgan's Cheshire hotel], drove home and gave his word that he would confirm the next morning. As a regular user of the M6, I can only assume that the journey back to London from Carden Park changed his mind.'

Two more managers came and went the following season. Firstly Stale Solbakken, a left-field appointment who had previously overseen Cologne's relegation from the Bundesliga, and then Dean Saunders combined to take Wolves down to League One.

'It was difficult for Stale, because we had a big thing about keeping most of the backroom staff the same, so that you didn't have a complete clear-out. We had a really good physio, Phil Hayward had just succeeded Steve Kemp, a really good goalkeeping coach, Pat Mountain, and a really good fitness coach, Tony Daley. They should be judged on their merits, not just cleared out because the incoming manager had always worked with the same staff.

'That changed with Nuno. It seems to have been a key part of the success, funnily enough, a complete fresh start with his team. That's not what we did previously and that made it difficult for Stale, in that there was an established backroom team who were very close and knew each other very well. Stale originally only had one guy with him, Johan Lange. Stale, being basically unknown and unproven in the UK, was almost on trial as he was the one trying to gain the respect of everyone else, and show that he is the right person for the job and that his way of doing it is the right way.

'Under Stale, we started well and were third in the Championship at the time of the October international break. It hadn't been very attractive football. The central defenders, Christophe Berra and Roger Johnson, were playing the ball around between them and it wasn't their strength, but we were third. Then we got completely bullied out of it at Huddersfield next game back and you could see it change.

'I think, and this is quite common in my experience of football, there comes a tipping point, where if the squad lose belief that something is achievable it goes into negativity and just drifts away. Once we had stopped challenging at the top end of the table under Stale, it unravelled very quickly. And then Dean, who was doing well with Doncaster, which gets forgotten a bit, well it never happened for him. He finally looked to be turning it around but then Sylvan Ebanks-Blake broke his leg in a victory at Birmingham City over Easter and missed the rest of the season.'

A 15-month spell between February 2012 and May 2013 saw a total of four managers dismissed during one of the most disruptive periods the club experienced since the 1980s.

'You're disappointed to see all of them go,' Skirrow adds. 'And you're also wondering who is going to come in and whether or not you are going to get on with them.' It was Kenny Jackett who came in next, and it was his departure in July 2016 that Skirrow believes was one of the harder ones to take.

'Kenny was a particularly sad one because he had done so well. There was a transformation from the poisonous atmosphere at Brighton away on the last day of the Championship season when the players couldn't give their shirts to the crowd – they were literally getting thrown back at them – when that second relegation was confirmed, to the atmosphere at Preston North End away on the opening day of the League One season three months later. Wolves took 5,000 fans to Preston, full of optimism. The whole atmosphere had amazingly been transformed by Kenny in six weeks of pre-season.'

The 11 managers Skirrow worked with during his 20 years at Wolves is significantly more than the number of owners. There were just two custodians of the club over the same period; two British businessmen with very different backgrounds. He enjoyed a productive working relationship with both Sir Jack Hayward and Steve Morgan, but is pragmatic and honest enough to acknowledge the reality of the progress.

'Wolves were an established second-tier club when I joined and unfortunately we were a second-tier club when I left. It's disappointing that, in my 20 years, we only had four years in the top flight. Whereas I felt I'd been part of a successful, well-run club, you can't puff your chest out too much when you've had only four years out of 20 in the top flight. But that's how difficult getting it right in football, and particularly the Championship, is.'

The club Skirrow arrived at in 1996 was still finding its feet in a changing landscape. The Premier League had been formed four years earlier, and the country's elite clubs were pulling away from Wolves on and off the pitch. Sir Jack lived in the Bahamas and left the day-to-day running of the club to his younger son Jonathan, the chairman. The redevelopment of a dilapidated stadium had been the Haywards' priority. The new Molineux helped reinvigorate the fan base, but behind the scenes the club was still a long way from running entirely successfully.

'One of the first things that struck me when I moved to Wolves was that it was the biggest show in town, whereas West Ham wasn't and never would be,' Skirrow recalls. 'They were a smaller fish in the big pool of London. Coming to Wolves it struck me that this is the biggest show in town, the heartbeat of the town, as it was then.

'The support was great, but it was a very different era. Chief executives hadn't really started to come in to the game, we were just about to appoint John Richards [one of the club's 1970s greats] who would in time be the first appointed to the role of managing director. John is a great guy, very competent, but he came from a local government background, so was understandably inexperienced in the day-to-day running of the club.

'From the two receiverships of the 1980s, to a ground that was only operating on two sides, the stadium redevelopment had to be the initial priority, then it was a case of catching up on the player side. Sir Jack not being in the country didn't help; Jonathan being geographically distant was not ideal.

'He was based near Berwick in the borders and would spend a couple of days a week at the club. Jonathan was a farmer who had had to make some hard-nosed decisions in farming, but he was also a football man. He was on the Football League board at the time. But, with the distances, it's not a great model for running a football club.

'The reason Sir Jack could plough the money into the club was the success of the Bahamas, so he had to keep being there. That's where he lived, that's where the businesses were that were generating the wealth to support the club. So he trusted Jonathan to get it right, and Jonathan worked very hard to do so, but unfortunately they fell out.'

The feud between Sir Jack and his son is the saddest episode of the Hayward years at Wolves. Their relationship began to unravel after the First Division play-off failure in May 1997. Sir Jack took aim at Jonathan and manager McGhee after the expensively assembled squad fell short in the semi-finals against Crystal Palace.

'The Golden Tit' rant, as it became known, was a headline writer's dream, and it highlighted the lack of trust that was starting to emerge at boardroom level.

'It is blackmail. The manager goes to my son, Jonathan, the chairman, and says he must have a player to strengthen the side,' Sir Jack complained, the day after the second leg of the Palace semi-final. 'I ask him why they are so expensive, why are they for sale, why don't they do it for their own clubs, but he asked me if I wanted a team in the Premier League and to win the FA Cup. I also ask why doesn't the player do it for Leicester or Reading, the two clubs we seem to be subsidising.

'Money has been wasted on players who have not come off or performed to their potential. A lot of clubs put the price up three times because it's Wolves and they laugh like a drain when we buy them. I see some players we have bought who do not have the commitment and are overpaid with their sports cars and homes. They have let the fans down.'

'The outburst was just the frustration of spending money and not achieving the objective really,' reflects Skirrow. 'When I was at West Ham, the two clubs you wanted to be on the phone asking about a player were either Blackburn Rovers or Wolves because of Jack Walker or Sir Jack. You just felt they had money. Not that that meant they weren't going to try and negotiate a good deal, but you knew the money was there.'

McGhee admitted that he had 'no relationship whatsoever' with Sir Jack after the remarks had been made. In the autumn of that year Jonathan was demoted to deputy chairman, with Sir Jack taking over as chairman. By May 1998 Jonathan had left the business altogether. The depth of the animosity between the pair only came to public attention in January 1999, when it was revealed that Sir Jack was suing his son over a financial matter at the club.

The Independent newspaper was one of many national dailies that led with the story in its sports pages on Wednesday, 20 January 1999, under the headline 'Football Tycoon Sues Wasteful Son'.

> Sir Jack Hayward, one of Britain's richest men, is suing his son over alleged financial irregularities at the football club on which he once admitted spending his children's inheritance. Lawyers acting for the owner of Wolverhampton Wanderers have filed papers relating to the movement of three sums

of money totalling £237,400 while his son Jonathan was club chairman. The family feud is the latest manifestation of Sir Jack's passion for Wolves. Since 1990, when the multi-millionaire who is listed as Britain's 125th richest man, bought the Midlands club for £2.1m, he has spent £40m on new stands and players in an attempt to fulfil his dream of winning the FA Cup before he dies. Papers filed at the High Court show that Wolverhampton Wanderers Football Club (1986) Ltd, Wolverhampton Wanderers Properties Ltd and WW (1990) Ltd are suing Jonathan Hayward, aged 31, James Nicholas Stones, a solicitor, and his firm, Wiggin and Co. Sir Jack is chairman and president of Wolves.

The writ claims that three resolutions 'purportedly passed' at board meetings in March 1997, May 1995 and August 1995, 'approving the repayment to WW (1990) Ltd of [money], are of no legal effect.' It alleges that the repayments – of £100,000 in March 1997, £37,400 in May 1995 and £100,000 in August 1995 – were made 'without legal authority'. Further, Sir Jack's legal team argue that resolutions at three board meetings relating to the repayments 'are of no legal effect'.

They are demanding that Jonathan accounts for the amounts received and 'for all benefits and profits derived therefrom' and they are seeking damages and compensation for 'breaches of fiduciary duty'.

Jonathan Hayward and James Stones were directors of the club at the time the movements of money were authorised and it is understood they are to contest Sir Jack's claims.

The money was reported to be a form of compensation fee paid to Jonathan for all the time he was spending away from the farm on Wolves business.

'It was really small beer in relation to the overall money spent in that period,' Skirrow explains. 'There was the purchase of a Range Rover that Jonathan was using, that had been funded from the club. Sir Jack then said that he didn't give permission for it. Sir Jack was a great guy, but quirky. He took a black or white view on it, and he thought that was black. There was a big falling out but it was actually sums of money that were before my time. I came into it and was involved in the problems it was creating and providing some documentary evidence but the actual sums of money pre-dated me.

'It was so sad that they fell out. It was never easy getting Jonathan to sign a cheque or approve an invoice. There would always be a thorough process and he certainly wasn't cavalier with spending the club's money. I'm so pleased that, in later years, they reconciled. The father and son bond was very strong in Sir Jack's final years.'

Sir Jack's eccentricities could also be a large part of his charm, although he would often need to be humoured when his worldly views were challenged. He went by the nickname 'Union Jack' owing to his fiercely pro-British outlook. There were paradoxes at play here, too, as he chose to live as a tax exile. His experiences as an RAF pilot during the Second World War had reinforced his belief in the empire.

'I remember when John Richards sanctioned the purchase of a Volkswagen minibus. Blimey, I think John was on the verge of being sacked for buying a German vehicle.'

Having served in the South East Asia Command, Sir Jack had seen the conflict from outside the confines of Europe. His views on Japan's role in the war almost put an end to a trip of a lifetime for Skirrow.

'One of the things I got a chance to do was go to Japan with the Wolves under-12s. This was in 2001 and an area of Japan, Shizuoka, was twinned with areas of other countries rather than a specific town. It was twinned with the West Midlands. The idea was that West Midlands clubs would combine to send this representative team to an under-12 tournament. The Japanese were using it as a dry run for some of the stadiums to be used for the World Cup the following year.

'One by one, all the other West Midlands clubs pulled out so Wolves were the only ones left, so we were going to send a Wolves under-12s team to this international tournament, but unfortunately it was in Japan. So we had to get Sir Jack to sanction it, and he really didn't like the Japanese at all. His recollection of Japan's role in World War Two, well, he was very against this. Ultimately he was persuaded that we should go as we had committed and couldn't back out, but he wanted somebody to go from almost board level so I got nominated to go as a chef de mission for this under-12 tournament.

'Elliott Bennett, who now plays for Blackburn Rovers, was the captain and we won the tournament on penalties. The final was in the stadium that England lost to Brazil in. We were billeted in a country lodge near Mount Fuji. You stepped outside of the lodge and there was Mount Fuji. Being exposed to Japanese culture and food, I would never have gone to Japan, it was incredible. When we got back Jack was fine about it, we'd won the tournament!'

Skirrow recalls many a late-night phone conversation with Sir Jack, discussing all things Wolves.

'I'd get phone calls from him at 10pm or 11pm because he was in the Bahamas in late afternoon. One of the little snippets that still tickles me is when we were talking about players once, it was during the 1998 World Cup, and Sir Jack said, "If we knew where he was, we could get this Davor Suker in." Sir Jack must have thought he was a Croatian sheep farmer who could be plucked from obscurity. "We do know where he is, Sir Jack. He's at Real Madrid!" He wasn't able to follow football as closely as he wanted to.'

One of the main regrets from supporters during Sir Jack's reign was the failure to build on the only promotion to the Premier League during his time as owner. Jones was given just over £4million to invest ahead of the 2003/04 season, and Wolves' ill-equipped squad finished bottom of the table.

'Unfortunately, I think Sir Jack's mindset was almost one of a marathon runner collapsing over the line,' Skirrow adds. 'The promotion was, "Finally, we've done it." Rather than seeing it as the beginning, he seemed to see it more as the end. We didn't invest enough money. He had not given up, but he had already put about £80million into it, when that was a lot of money. People should never forget what he put in and where it was coming from, it was his personal income.'

Sir Jack was approaching his 84th birthday when he eventually sold the club in May 2007, to Liverpool businessman Morgan. The owner of Redrow Homes completed his takeover in August that year.

'It was busy for me, and many others, because I was involved in the due diligence, I was preparing a lot of documents,' explains Skirrow. 'It was a well-run club, Steve was happy at what he was seeing. Steve was a football man, we all knew he had tried to buy Liverpool but, for some reason, was blocked by the Moores family. It was felt that it was probably a good new owner coming in. It had run its course with Sir Jack, especially with regard to his age. He was ready to sell. It needed something new.'

Morgan's legacies off the field include a partially redeveloped ground, after overseeing the construction of a new Stan Cullis Stand, before pulling the plug on the proposed redevelopment of the Steve Bull Stand. There was also an impressive expansion of the Sir Jack Hayward Training Ground, in conjunction with a Redrow Homes development, which led to the Compton Park site being awarded Category One academy status in 2014.

'We had the complicated deal on Compton with the Archdiocese of Birmingham, who owned St Peter's School land, with Saint Edmund's Catholic School on the site moving down to an area that the University of Wolverhampton had vacated, and then putting the academy and indoor arena on the site of the old school. The Redrow housing development made that stack up financially for Steve. Again, I think the fans tend to think Steve pulled a fast one there and managed to get a brilliant deal for Redrow, whereas it was a brilliant deal for the club. The club got more land and Compton has gone from strength to strength.'

Morgan was a key supporter of the club's community arm, Wolves Community Trust, turning it into an official charity, as well as supporting other local charities in the area to the tune of several million pounds. But amongst supporters he was judged for the team's progress on the pitch. Despite three years in the Premier League under McCarthy, the club's double relegation tainted Morgan's ownership. He left behind a team on the pitch that was no stronger than the one he found. The majority of fans were pleased to see Morgan move on in the summer of 2016, when he sold the club to Fosun. So, could he have spent more on the team?

'Yes, he could have done, but it's hugely difficult, isn't it?' Skirrow responds. 'Fosun have invested heavily and are now enjoying the riches of the Premier League. Nuno has been fantastic, because just getting out of the Championship is so difficult? You can look at Leeds United, Nottingham Forest, Derby County and Sheffield Wednesday and how long they have been in there. They have been spending money. Steve was of a view that there would be a correction in player wages, that it couldn't continue, but it has. It's escalated and disappeared over the hill. The amounts of money you need to invest now are huge and, to be fair to them, Fosun have done.'

More often than not it was chief executive Moxey who was the public relations face of the club during Morgan's tenure. Skirrow insists the pair were a force for good, putting the club on a stable and self-sufficient footing. Financially, keeping Wolves in the black was something Fosun benefitted from when they spent heavily to get out of the Championship without fear of falling foul of Financial Fair Play regulations.

'I'd view them very positively,' Skirrow concludes, 'Jez was always prepared to put his head above the parapet and be available for the media to explain something, unfortunately often in a period where we weren't successful on the pitch. Winning changes everything. If you're losing then the pies are awful, the ticket office is poor, everybody is rude and nothing gets answered in time. That's rubbish, really. If you're winning then there are no issues with the same pies, the ticket office and the same staff. I've always been proud of the teamwork and efforts of the staff at Wolves, and the job they did.'

Pies were at the root of Moxey's biggest PR disaster. In January 2007, on police advice, in order to accommodate supporters from arch-rivals West Bromwich Albion for an FA Cup fourth-round tie at Molineux, he moved season-ticket holders out of their much-loved home end, the South Bank, and gave up the entire stand to visiting fans. His decision to compensate the displaced supporters with a free pie and a pint was met with anger. Matters did not improve when Albion ran out 3-0 winners, as their support gleefully sang, 'You sold your seat for a pie and a pint'.

But Skirrow believes Moxey deserves plenty of credit for the day-to-day running of the club during his 16-year spell as chief executive, which incorporated the final seven years of the Hayward regime and all of Morgan's time at Molineux.

'Everything that Jez did was for the benefit of Wolverhampton Wanderers, I've no doubt. He was well-paid but he was very committed, very hard-working, very good at his job and always put the club first. He would always listen to your opinion. He had his strong opinions and would not always be persuaded to a contrary view, but you could always have that robust dialogue with him.'

Skirrow was part of a club that, with its city-centre stadium and a training ground less than two miles away from Molineux, was right at the heart of the community. So what does he miss about a job that spanned nearly a generation?

'The camaraderie is the thing you miss. Being based at the training ground, you're in the football. And if you're a football fan you miss being with the football people. The likes of Terry Connor, Tony Daley and Pat Mountain. I would never forget that I was a "suit". The height of my football career was Sunday morning stuff in Manchester at not a very good level. But they made me feel part of it. Wolves has always had a very good spirit to it, even when the football hasn't been too good.'

But there was more to it than just the camaraderie. For Skirrow, the role of secretary at a club like Wolves brought a sense of something more profound.

'I didn't have any natural affinity for Wolves when I joined,' he continues. 'I'd been to Molineux twice, and the most memorable of those visits was in March 1976, when I was at Birmingham University. It was a cup replay against Manchester United after a 1-1 draw at Old Trafford. United won the replay 3-2. I hadn't got this affinity for Wolves but I had got a real appreciation of Mike Bailey and John Richards. As players of the opposing team, they were the two who always stood out for me.

'And then I ended up working with John when he became chief executive, and playing five-a-side with him. We used to play regular Thursday lunchtime five-a-side at the old Molineux Youth Centre, which is now the commercial car park. To end up playing football with John Richards on a regular basis, well, it was just remarkable. The way he could strike a ball, he was a great player, wasn't he? Then to get to know Mike Bailey was lovely. Both players and their wives became good friends of Jane and I.'

'You are privileged. You get to watch the game in the best seats, you're well looked after home and away. To have had lunch with Nat Lofthouse, Tom Finney and all these other stars was amazing. The reason I got into this industry is that I'm a sports fan – cricket and football, in particular. I caught the tail end of Best, Law and Charlton so I saw the beautiful side of football as a game. Because you're a fan, it's a great thing to work in. The highs when you win a game, it's just fantastic. It was a privilege and an honour to work at such a great club.'

Chapter 11

THE LANDLADY

Surrogate Parents

ANN SCHORAH is standing in her lounge. The television in the corner is on, but she is paying little attention to the daytime offering that the weekday schedules have produced. In front of her is a large ironing board. To her left is a neatly stacked pile of freshly pressed clothing. To her right is a substantially bigger heap that is yet to be done. She has already been on her feet for the best part of an hour. Over the course of the next two hours, as Ann continues to tackle the daunting stack of clothing, she paints a picture of the life of a football landlady.

The surrogate mothers, the child minders, the counsellors, the guardian angels, these are the game's unsung heroes.

Ann lives with her long-time partner Arthur Benton, a devoted Wolves fan, who is out at work on the Stafford Road for OCS Group when we begin to chat. The pair of them have been providing a home for the youngsters of Wolves for over 20 years. Now aged 69, football has been in Ann's life for over 50 years, since she first went to watch her home-town club, Portsmouth. From school, she went to work in the Kenwood factory in Havant, before taking another factory job stitching sanitary products at the Tampax factory in nearby Leigh Park.

Ann moved away for a time with her then husband, a former youth-team player with Everton, who played football for the RAF at Watton in Norfolk, but later returned to the south coast. She raised a son, Darren, who went to work as a lifeguard at a leisure centre in Havant when he left school. Then, in 1994, Ann's world was struck by tragedy when Darren died of leukaemia at the age of only 22. By now she had met Arthur, who persuaded her to make the move to Wolverhampton to start afresh. The couple moved into a new home next to Dunstall Park racecourse in 1996.

A workaholic by nature, Ann was soon throwing herself into employment in the West Midlands. She began working at the Makita power tools factory in Telford, but would use her spare time to ride around on her bike in search of work nearer to their Wolverhampton home. That came to fruition when she found a new job at the Armitage Shanks factory in the city. It was only when she was made redundant there that a new career as a football landlady appeared on the horizon.

It came when Ann took a job sorting the mail in the Wolves ticket office at Molineux. One day, the ticket office manager, Lynne O'Reardon, came into work asking if anyone in the office had any spare accommodation to help out the Wolves academy manager Chris Evans, who had been appointed to the role in 1991.

'He's a tremendous man,' Ann recalls. 'He was a one-man band back then, whereas now they have someone for every different part of the academy. I said that we had a spare room, so a friend in the ticket office phoned Chris and he came over and visited us the next day. He said it would be an ideal place for one of the boys. He remarked at the time, "I've got the next boy who is going to conquer the world." Well, aren't they all?'

A young Irish lad called Gary Mulligan was the first to walk through the door of Ann and Arthur's home. Like most of the youngsters, he never went on to have a career in the game. Since then another 38 hopefuls have occupied digs at the couple's home, in the age range of 14 to 18.

'When they come here they think they've made it,' Ann says, rolling her eyes. 'You're not even on that first ladder yet. I had one recently who was 14 when he came in, a really lovely boy. He's got such a nice way about him. But when he came in he had a chip on his shoulder, he was a bit arrogant. When the chip falls off they're lovely, though, really nice. I remember him sitting here and he thought he'd go straight into the under-23s, but he didn't.'

There is something of the no-nonsense about Ann, pragmatic and ruthlessly efficient in the way she runs the household. Ann and Arthur are kept busy with their latest intake of four young players – Luke Cundle, Dean Pinnington, Faisu Sangare and Jimmy Storer. 'Arthur is one of the funniest men you could meet, he's the friend and I'm the baddie,' she admits. 'I don't mind that, they've all got rules and things to do. There's five of them, Arthur is a child too.'

The club provides breakfast and lunch for the players, with Ann catering for dinner. But food is available at the start of the day too, if the players need something as soon as they get up.

'If their belly rumbles they go out into the kitchen. There's always fruit and cereal out there, yoghurts for calcium and all their proteins, it's all in there. It's a bit different now because the Wolves feed them, it didn't used to be like that. We used to do their breakfasts, then lunch would be Wolves and then they'd come home for an evening meal. We still do the evening meal. I've got four boys now who won't eat a vegetable. Now how healthy is that? But they like pasta and rice which is easy.'

There is, as you would expect, a curfew for the players to observe. 'Years ago they had no rules so we had to put them in place. They've got to be in for ten o'clock but they never go anywhere. As soon as they learn to drive it's a problem. But it's still ten o'clock, that's a rule made by the Wolves so it helps me. No ladies around the house, no girlfriends, nothing!'

The protective side of Ann comes out when the subject of girlfriends is raised. So do the players ever confide in her when their relationships hit trouble? 'Yeah all the time, they don't go to Arthur you know, funny isn't it? You'd think they'd want to talk to a man. Do you know, what bothers me is that when they've got girlfriends their football goes down the pan. There was no welfare when I first started doing it, no one ever thought that the kids wouldn't take to it. I had a boy who got in a bad way. All that was because his girlfriend had dumped him and gone off with his mate. He was living here and we had his mum and dad up, it was horrendous. That went on for about six months.'

Surely even the most delicately balanced relationships are easier to deal with than this mountain of washing, though? 'Yes, I can't dress it up, can I? I still do Kortney's every week, because he is such a lovely lad, I've always done his washing. I've just had a brand-new washing machine put in because my last one went up the stump. I bet I've had four washing machines in ten years, it doesn't sound a lot, but it is really.'

Kortney Hause left Ann's place four and a half years ago. The centre-back signed for Wolves from Wycombe Wanderers on the last day of the mid-season transfer window in January 2014, at the age of 18, and moved straight into digs with Ann and Arthur. He made his Wolves debut in December that year in a 1-0 win against Sheffield Wednesday. He established himself in former manager Kenny Jackett's plans, but under Nuno Espírito Santo his first-team opportunities disappeared. In January, with Wolves riding high in the Premier League, Hause was loaned out to Championship neighbours Aston Villa, where he went on to help them win promotion.

There are several other established professional players who have shared the couple's home, more recently including Dominic Iorfa, Conor Ronan, Wayne Hennessey and Stephen Gleeson. When the time comes for each of them to move on it is an emotional moment.

'Do you know, it's difficult, I knew my two oldest ones last year were going to go and yet it broke my heart when both of them went,' Ann admits. 'I knew they were not going to be kept on, but when the final day came I'd never felt like that. With Dom and Kortney I was really happy for them because they were near and I could still keep in touch. But when they go to places like Scotland, it's heart-breaking.

'I had one boy who left in July, he broke my heart. Jordan Allan, he plays for Cowdenbeath now. He was a lovely footballer. He called us his English family.'

A card on the mantelpiece is testament to how much Allan's family appreciated the work Ann and Arthur put in with their son. 'There are no words we could use to thank you both enough for the love, kindness, care and support you have given Jordan over the past four years of his life,' it reads. It is when their work is validated in this way that it becomes apparent what the true rewards are for the couple. They are remunerated on a material level by the club for their efforts, but the income is a modest one. The dedication required to run a household full of lively, growing lads is immense.

'It's hard when you've got to start again [when players leave] and get the new ones trained up again. Now we're all set up, they know what they've got to do, we know what we've got to do. It is hard, I wouldn't say to someone it is easy money. One night a week they can have a meal of their choice and they can phone a takeaway and it's always pizza, and it's always 50-odd pounds. Fifty pounds for a bit of horrible crust! I do that once a week because it does get monotonous and it gives us a break as well. Some nights you just fancy beans on toast but you can't have that.'

The duty of care does not end when the players take the next step on their journey and leave Ann and Arthur's house for a place of their own. Ann breaks into a wide smile when she recounts a story that will be familiar to many mums and dads up and down the country when their children first move into a place of their own. It involved two players who have since moved on from Wolves.

'They lived up by the canal, down the back of the station in one of those flats,' Ann explains. 'They lived in the Mill House, so they had a great big mill in the front room. Anyway, I went round at seven o'clock one night to take some washing around and they are both sitting in darkness. There's one of them sitting there in just his underpants, because footballers are very proud of their bodies, you know. "The lights have gone off, we've phoned the estate agent, he is going to come around and sort it out," they say.

'Well it's so obvious what it was but we wouldn't have taught the boys that would we? So I asked them where the fusebox was. "What do you mean?" they said, together. "Have you got a cupboard anywhere that you don't go in?" I replied. "Oh that one there," they said. So we opened it and had a look. They were taller than me so I made them sort it. I asked which light bulb had gone out when they turned it on and got them to take it out and they just flicked the switch and the lights came back on. "How did you know that?" they wanted to know.'

As Ann folds a pile of neatly ironed boxer shorts – 'I don't iron socks, that's the only thing I wouldn't iron' – she admits that it is nice to get the house back and enjoy some quiet time on afternoons like these. 'You have to catch up, don't you? To be fair I do have a little sleep sometimes. I have a sandwich about midday, make a coffee and go and have a quick lie down on the bed.'

Any inkling that Ann might be slacking off is quickly dispelled when she reveals that being a landlady is only part of her day job.

'In the mornings, Monday to Wednesday, I work at Woodfield Sports and Social Club over at Penn. It's a bowls, table tennis and tennis club. I'm the bar supervisor, so I go and clean three mornings a week. I'm up at half past five to do that. Then on Wednesday and Thursday evenings, five until midnight, I'm on the bar. It's nice because it's my bit of freedom. Arthur can't understand why I like work, but I've always done it.' There is no let-up at weekends, either. Ann also supervises at the South Bank turnstiles on home matchdays.

But there is no suggestion that the other half of this formidable partnership does not weigh in with his fair share of duties around the house. 'Arthur has got a lot better, he now cooks their dinners, he'll stand and do the ironing too. It took a little bit of moaning and groaning. He's a tea wallah, he drinks about 20 cups of tea a day.'

Right on cue the front door opens and Arthur walks in to the front room after a busy shift at OCS. He immediately heads into the kitchen and puts the kettle on. Arthur's love of Wolves goes beyond providing a home for the young hopefuls. A season-ticket holder, he has been a steward on the official away match coaches for the last 20 years. The boys under his roof are fortunate to have two people so engaged with the club.

'If you love football you've got to enjoy it,' says Arthur. 'Ann is the rock, like. It's 24/7 isn't it? But it's lovely when they make it, like Dom and Kortney. We hope that somewhere along the line we have been able to help them get on.'

'I love it when they make it,' Ann interrupts. 'I don't think there's any one of my boys that I thought, "Wow, I've failed on that one." There's no one more than us wants them to make it. When they walk out on to the pitch you could cry, it's so lovely.'

'Unfortunately, for every one that makes it there are a thousand who don't,' Arthur adds. 'Football is cut-throat and when the time comes around to letting boys go it's terrible. If it was left to us they would all make it, but we'd bankrupt the club pretty quickly!'

Arthur enjoys sitting down at home in front of a football match on the television and listening to the comments that the youngsters make when watching a game.

'Well they're the professionals, aren't they?' he explains. 'So you try and hear what their comments are, and see what they are seeing that you don't see. That's their job. I'd love to have been a footballer but I wasn't good enough, but these lads could be. It is their job at the end of the day so you can learn from them. You never stop learning, do you?'

The afternoon is drawing to a close. Soon, the house will be full once more. Ann and Arthur have clearly made a huge difference to the lives of all the academy players who have stayed at their home. They are not in it to be thanked, but there is an acknowledgement that it is nice to have made a difference.

'We get them through that bad stage of going from a young silly boy to partly a man, do you know what I mean?' says Ann. 'And hopefully we've instilled some good things into them, because we're not bad people.'

It is an understated way of reflecting on the work she has done. Others are more forthcoming when stating the importance of the job. Speaking to Sir Alex Ferguson several years ago, when conducting an interview about one of his own long-serving landladies at Manchester United, Annie Kay, the former Old Trafford boss summed up the role the landladies play in nurturing the teenagers they take on board. 'They're away from home for the first time,' he said. 'Their mothers are worried stiff about them because mothers worry, that's their job. These landladies replace a mother in a big way, there's a good family connection between their real mother and their surrogate mother at that particular time.'

Mark Hughes and David Beckham were two of the players who spent time at the Kay household during their teenage years. The relationships formed have lasted a lifetime. Beckham invited Kay to his wedding in 1999 and Hughes has remained close to the family since he left.

'They were fantastic for me, I was there for seven years and loved every minute of it,' Hughes said. 'You have to be a certain type of person and a certain character to invite complete strangers into your home and make them feel welcome. It's a special talent. Apart from the decision to actually sign for Manchester United, the decision to stay with Annie and her husband Tommy was the best decision I made at that time. I'm still very close to them now, their son David was my best man. If you're lucky enough to have a special person, a special landlady and landlord to look after you in those formative years, then you'll build relationships that will last for the rest of your life.'

'They're not stars, they're ordinary families who are doing us a great service by taking boys in,' Ferguson added. 'They are unsung heroes, but they don't want to be anything else other than unsung heroes.'

Ann stumbled across the role of the football landlady by accident. A chance conversation in the Wolves ticket office led her on a path she still travels along decades later. So how much longer will she be opening her doors to the club's academy players?

'I don't know. I'm 69 now, it keeps me young. It keeps me moving and keeps me going. It's like the house is paying its way. I bought it when I came up from Portsmouth all those years ago. I don't feel 69.'

So has her work felt like a vocation, after she lost her own son all those years ago? 'It was really nice to fill the house up, to be fair. Just because when you both go to work your life is a bit empty. Darren would probably have left home by then anyway, but it was just nice to have the boys around. You look at them all in different ways. No boy is ever going to be like your boy. But it keeps you busy and you haven't got time to think about more things then, have you?'

'I think what sums up what we do is this text from Kortney,' says Arthur. 'He won't mind me showing it you. Before his debut for Aston Villa we texted, "*Good luck for today mate. Me and Ann have always believed in you. Loads of love, Ann and Arthur*". They lost 3-0 to Wigan. He texted back after the game, "*Worst possible start, lost 3-0. Will be back stronger though. Is the washing done?*" That's it, isn't it? It doesn't really matter, because at the end of the day they're like us. They're exactly like us.'

Chapter 12

PLAY-OFF WINNERS

Back at the top after 19 years, 13 days,
22 hours and 20 minutes

'I GOT put up in The Mount Hotel where we are now. Rachael Heyhoe Flint, God rest her soul, met me here and that was my first impression of Wolves.'

Paul Butler is sitting in the Great Hall of the grade-II listed hotel in Tettenhall. It is still used today by the club as a base for players arriving in the city for the first time. Wolves' former captain is appearing at a charity event on this autumn evening, but ahead of the engagement he has agreed to sit down for a catch-up about a short, but hugely eventful, period in the club's history.

That first impression he is talking about came in November 2000, when manager Colin Lee brought him to Molineux to bolster a struggling defence. It was a mutually beneficial arrangement.

'I came down on loan from Sunderland, basically just to get some games as I'd been injured up there,' Butler says. 'I was put up in The Mount then I got brought to the training ground the next morning. It was a tennis club, there was nothing there at all really, just a couple of pitches. But what stuck out straight away to me was the high profile of players, and I won't mention any names, who weren't doing anything.

'They were just happy to be on a joy ride at the place, getting paid big money at the time – big, big money – and they just didn't want to do the work. They were only here for the one thing, which was the money. You could smell that straight away and I remember talking to Colin, saying, "You've got problems in here," and he said, "I know, that's why I've brought you down, to sort it out!"

'After the first couple of games there were issues. With the current team, if anybody is out of the side they're supportive. In that period they weren't and there were a lot of big-name players not playing and they were quite happy not to play, just sit on the medical bench and pull big money. It hurt, because I'd just come from the background of Sunderland – where it was a team of players like Micky Gray, Kevin Phillips, Niall Quinn, Nicky Summerbee, Chris Makin and Steve Bould – into a dressing room where they didn't want to know. You could see Colin had a big issue on his hands.'

Lee's time at the helm is a largely forgotten one. It was sandwiched between two far more interesting periods in the club's history. He was appointed to the role soon after Mark McGhee's departure in November 1998, having served as an assistant to the Scot. The pair fell out spectacularly when Lee accepted the challenge of taking on the Wolves job. He could not have wished for a better start, though, taking charge on a temporary basis initially, with an astonishing 6-1 win away at Bristol City in his first game, which saw the on-loan striker David Connolly score a hat-trick after a 15-game barren run.

The match lives long in the memory for those who attended, not just for the scoreline but for a slapstick mascots' bust-up at half-time. 'Wolfie', representing the visitors, came to blows with the 'Three Little Pigs', who were not Bristol City mascots but representatives of a local double-glazing firm who may have spotted the opportunity for some publicity.

That game was as good as it got for Lee throughout an uninspiring two years. He was never blessed with the same resources as his predecessors. The lavish spending of the Graham Taylor and McGhee eras was over and the club was tightening its belt. After Lee's dismissal in December 2000, Dave Jones accepted the managerial challenge. It was a job that was becoming a poisoned chalice following the promotion failures of the 90s.

His first game was a 1-0 FA Cup third-round win at Nottingham Forest in January 2001, with Adam Proudlock scoring the winner. One of Jones's early decisions was to coax Butler back from Sunderland after his loan spell had finished to sign him on a permanent basis. Wolves stabilised over the remainder of that season to occupy an all-too-familiar mid-table position, finishing 12th in the First Division, as it was then. That summer, the purse strings were loosened once more and Jones was able to put his own stamp on the squad. Seven players left during the close season, with Mark Kennedy and Shaun Newton coming in. As the season progressed, other signings were made. Colin Cameron, Nathan Blake and Alex Rae arrived during the opening two months of the campaign, with Kenny Miller and Dean Sturridge joining them mid-season. Butler identified the new manager's qualities immediately.

'His man-management. His judgment of players. He would go out personally and identify the players,' he explains. 'He had a recruitment team but I can guarantee it was the character of the player that he wanted first. He would identify a player, even in a lower league game he could pick something out in a player that he could see and mould into something. It's how he could get the team to work together. He would bring in characters that should never play with each other really and he got them working with each other. Even in the bad times, where we got beaten in the play-offs and we were losing games, he used to stay calm. I've probably seen him lose his head twice, maybe three times, in all the time I've known him. His man-management was good and he had good coaches around him. I always remember him saying, "Managers manage and coaches coach."'

That play-off semi-final defeat to Norwich City at the end of the 2001/02 season went down as one of the most desperate moments for Wolves supporters in the club's entire history. It was not a low ebb – the 80s provided that – but it was the manner of the failure that hit hard. Not so much a dagger through the heart for supporters at the hands of their arch-rivals West Bromwich Albion, who pipped them to automatic promotion, more a painfully drawn-out death. Jones's men had an 11-point lead over Albion in March, which was squandered with just seven games remaining.

West Brom had a game in hand, won it and reduced the gap to eight. Wolves' lead still looked impregnable – on the face of it – but there were cracks starting to open up in the team. On two occasions, in the space of three days, they showed their fragility. Against Nottingham Forest, on 6 March, they twice squandered the lead and had to settle for a draw. Next up, at Birmingham City, they were pegged back for a draw after going two ahead. When Kevin Muscat was sent off during a home defeat to Grimsby Town later that month, the rot had begun to set in.

Albion secured the second automatic promotion place with 89 points, finishing three clear of Wolves. Losing out to sixth-placed Norwich City – who finished 11 points behind Wolves – in the play-offs was a bitter pill to swallow. 'You've Let Us Down Again' read a banner in the South Bank as the final whistle sounded against the East Anglian club. Speaking to Dave Jones several months after that, he revealed that he took umbrage to the banner. 'How could we have let them down again, we weren't here before?' It was a fair point, but supporters had lost the ability to distinguish between this and previous failures. In their eyes, it was one more in a continuous run of setbacks.

Butler acknowledges that the manager and players had messed up in the final run-in but reveals that within the squad there was none of the resignation that had inevitably overcome supporters who had been scarred once too often. 'It was hurtful, you'd let the fans down and hadn't performed. We had played so well to get where we did and then we just let ourselves down. We came back in to training after the summer and the fans were talking about that play-off semi-final as if the chance had gone. Sometimes it does go, but we just got our heads down.'

With the summer arrivals of Denis Irwin and Paul Ince, from Manchester United and Middlesbrough respectively, Jones had acquired some serious talent and experience. But the 2002/03 season did not begin as the players hoped. A 3-1 home defeat to Sheffield United on 5 October left Wolves 14th after 11 games. The fans had not forgotten the troubled end to the previous season and the skipper was their target.

'We didn't start that well. The fans were coming for someone and they came for me. Not a problem, I'd rather they come for me than the young lads. Dave pulled me out of the team and Mark Clyde went in and did a great job.'

For a man of Butler's standing in the team and presence on the pitch, it must have been difficult to come to terms with. It was a case of dealing with not just the supporters barracking from the stands but also an omission from the side.

'It was tough. But I wasn't showing that they hurt me, I was basically out there every day just training,' he says. 'I think that's why I have a closeness with the fans now because they know I could have easily walked and gone somewhere else, but I stuck around, I accepted I wasn't playing well.

'I was the captain of the team and, if anything, Dave did well by pulling me out. It felt like bad luck after bad luck. Goals going in in the 89th minute when we were comfortable and me getting it from the fans again, but it happens – this is what football is about. It's their opinion. You don't take it personally, otherwise I wouldn't be down here doing this Wolves charity do, I loved my time here.'

It was the advice of two former team-mates that kept Butler going during his darkest hours. 'I always remember speaking to Steve Bould and Kevin Ball, two lads I played at Sunderland with and two lads I speak with to this day. They told me to get my head down and work twice as hard to get back in the team. Don't walk in and say that you want away, because that's easy. Show the manager, play your reserve games, train as captain of the club and wait for the opportunity. Clyde played well for ten or 11 games and then he got injured. The gaffer pulled me in over Christmas and said, "You've got your chance."'

It was a New Year's Day league match at home to Derby County that saw Butler restored to the starting line-up. Wolves drew the game 1-1, but it was the next Molineux fixture that supporters recall with real pride. Sir Bobby Robson's Premier League title-challenging Newcastle United were in town for an FA Cup third-round tie that proved to be the catalyst for a return to form.

'There was a lot of animosity between the players,' Butler remembers. 'Craig Bellamy was pointing to the Premier League badge on his arm. It was a real cup tie and you could sense it. The pitch was a bit heavy, not like it is now at Molineux. It was good, you had two honest teams going for it. Alan Shearer gave as good as he got. Me and Joleon [Lescott] tried to boot him up and down the pitch and he gave it back. To come out at the end of that and win 3-2, it kick-started our season because we walked off the pitch having done that to Newcastle, who were third or fourth in the Premier League. Without the gaffer needing to say anything, that started us off.'

That January five-goal thriller was the first game in a cup run that took Wolves all the way to the quarter-finals, where they lost 2-0 to Southampton on the south coast. Far from the cup providing a distraction, the team found a new lease of life in the league. From tenth place at the time of the Newcastle tie, they pushed up the table to finish fifth and secure a play-off semi-final against Reading, beginning with a first-leg clash at Molineux.

'We had a feeling for that Reading game. You count on one hand those games in your career when you know you'll be alright and that was one of them,' Butler adds. 'Training was good, you came in every day and everyone couldn't wait to train. The thing you get with a successful team is that there are never any injuries, everyone wants to play. When you're having a bad time there's always plenty out injured. We knew we were playing well because there was no one injured.

'We had this belief that we could dig it out if we wanted to because we had the characters in there. We had flair in the team with Mark Kennedy and Shaun Newton and the four strikers were unbelievable – Kenny Miller, Nathan Blake, Dean Sturridge and George Ndah. They would get in any Championship side at that time so we knew we'd score goals. But it was the belief that we were all in it together.' Newton's deflected shot and a Lee Naylor free kick earned a 2-1 first-leg victory before Alex Rae scored the only goal in a 1-0 win down in Berkshire.

The First Division play-off final at the Millennium Stadium in Cardiff against Sheffield United is still, unquestionably, the most significant day Wolves supporters have enjoyed this century. The occasion, the venue, the performance, the result, the historical context and the celebrations. Nothing has come close to the number of memories that single day has left on supporters. It was summed up by a huge banner in the Wolves supporters' end behind the goal, which read '19 years, 13 days, 22 hours, 20 minutes' in reference to the time Wolves had spent outside the top division. It had been a long wait to return. For Butler, it was not the game, the result – a 3-0 win – or the achievement that he recalls most fondly:

'The best thing about that day was seeing Sir Jack,' he reveals. 'We'd spoken about it a week before, with Dave, saying that if we did manage to get up we wanted him to come down to the pitch and lift the trophy. But Sir Jack was adamant he wouldn't come down and do it. But then, it might have been Jez Moxey [chief executive] who persuaded him, we saw him walking down after the final whistle. Sir Jack stood on the pitch by himself sticks in my mind more than anything.

'I can't remember much of the game really. I remember the Matt Murray penalty save, which he should have held, he shouldn't have pushed it round the corner, I remember that bit! And I remember the Sheffield United fans clearing out 15 minutes before the end, and I was thinking it was still only 3-0 and we could easily concede three goals. But the defining bit was seeing Sir Jack – stood on the pitch in front of masses and masses of Wolves fans. That colour of gold and him stood there.

'We walked off thinking, "He's fulfilled now. Whatever happens in his life, he's got his wish." Seeing him afterwards in the dressing room, he couldn't say anything to us, he was just stood there. I don't think it sunk in for him that we'd gone up on the day.'

Like many who found themselves in the presence of Sir Jack, the club benefactor's generosity touched Butler. 'Anything that we needed. I remember when I was first there as captain and Dave introduced me to him,' he says. 'He didn't stick his nose in to training or anything like that, he just said, "If you need anything, let me know." That was for all the players. "If I can help out let me know." He didn't want the pat on the back for that. If we went go-karting, or whatever we did, we wanted him to come with us but he kept himself out of it. You don't see many owners like that anymore, do you?'

But, of course, Sir Jack was a man of contradictions. The funding of the Molineux redevelopment and the team, and his kindness of spirit to those he came across, won him the hearts of supporters. Yet running parallel to this generosity was a failure to grasp what it took to make a real success of the club, and a nepotistic approach to the running of Wolves that ultimately caused issues.

As Sir Jack himself acknowledged, lessons were not learnt from the first two play-off failures under Taylor and McGhee in the 1990s. When Jones finally achieved Sir Jack's dream of promotion, there was shock within the squad that a summer rebuilding programme was abandoned. Jones had been speaking to representatives of established Premier League stars in preparation for the 2003/04 campaign. The former manager has since admitted that deals were being put in place to bring England internationals Robbie Fowler and Trevor Sinclair, amongst others, to the club.

'It was a strange one. I only had a year left on my contract,' Butler recalls. 'A week after we got promoted I sat down with Dave, I knew I'd been under pressure, but I was determined to come back as fit as I'd ever been. He said, "That's what I want, but I will be signing players in the summer." The calibre of player he mentioned, I thought I'd have my hands full trying to get into the team. But for some reason it never happened.

'I remember getting promoted with Sunderland with a record 105 points and that summer we went and signed Stefan Schwarz and Steve Bould – strong characters who gave you a lift for that first season to keep you in the league. We didn't do that at Wolves. No disrespect to the lads who came in before the deadline – I think we signed Oleg Luzhny and Steffen Iversen. Players like that didn't improve the squad, it was just another number. The gaffer had to bring numbers in and he knew that.'

Those two free transfers were not the worst in a terrible summer of transfer business. Isaac Okoronkwo arrived from Shakhtar Donetsk, also on a free, alongside Silas, a Portuguese midfielder of considerably less calibre than the current crop of Iberian imports. The only additions that could in any way be classed as useful were winger Henri Camara and centre-back Jody Craddock.

Wolves walked into the opening fixture against Blackburn Rovers at Ewood Park with about as much hope as a gazelle wandering into a pride of lions. They were torn apart, a 5-1 defeat clearly reflecting the gulf between the sides. With Lescott out injured for the entire season and Murray joining him after the opening game, the team was arguably weaker than the previous year's First Division side. The following game, at Molineux, was no better. A 4-0 defeat to Charlton Athletic left the players and manager visibly shocked. These were not the big beasts of the Premier League, it was the division's makeweights who were running amok.

The third game of the season was at Old Trafford in midweek under the floodlights, with some of the crueller pundits wondering whether reigning champions Manchester United could get into double figures. When John O'Shea opened the scoring after ten minutes that seemed a possibility, but to their immense credit the struggling Wolves players knuckled down and escaped with no further damage.

Back at Molineux, a 0-0 draw in the fourth game of the season was cause for celebration given what had gone on before, but there was nothing to smile about when James Beattie scored twice to sink Wolves at Southampton two weeks later. Five games in – one point, one goal scored, 12 conceded. There was to be no respite; the sixth game was at home to Claudio Ranieri's Chelsea.

'I think if we'd have won one out of the first five games we'd have been alright, but we didn't,' Butler continues. 'We were just all over the place, we didn't know where we were!

Chelsea at home and they're bringing Hernan Crespo on for Eidur Gudjohnsen. Welcome to the Premier League. You didn't know where the first win was going to be, it was so tough.'

Chelsea substitute Crespo scored the last two goals in a 5-0 rout that left Wolves rooted to the bottom after six games. To all objective observers the season had finished almost as soon as it had begun. It was not until the eighth game that Jones's side finally recorded a victory, with a rare Colin Cameron header securing a 1-0 win at home to Manchester City. It was one of very few bright spots in a campaign that limped to a predictable relegation.

'Unlike the year before, when the fans gave us a lot of stick early on, they stuck with us because they knew it was tough and they knew we were playing with a Championship team.'

After waiting almost two decades to return to the top flight, Wolves finished bottom of the Premier League that season. For Butler, although the story ended in failure, he is rightly proud of the previous season's promotion. It was achieved with a team full of characters who, surprisingly given their commitment to the cause, did not particularly mix together. The camaraderie on the pitch did not reflect feelings off it.

'Yeah, we didn't like each other,' the former skipper reveals. 'But once we crossed the white line we looked after each other. You don't have to like each other off the pitch. I won't mention names but out of the four strikers we had, some of them didn't like each other. But on a Saturday or Sunday, whenever we played, if you put them as a pair, not a problem. But then when they walked off the pitch they wouldn't talk to each other. That's your strikers!'

Butler himself was once involved in an infamous training ground bust-up with goalkeeper coach Bobby Mimms that the players and management did well to keep out of the papers at the time.

'We'd lost a game, and Michael Oakes was in goal, and he'd said something in the local newspaper, the *Express and Star*,' recalls Butler. 'He'd been interviewed on the Saturday and it had appeared on the Monday and the lads had cut out the article in the paper and kept it. It said something like "Mimms is blaming the back four for not protecting the keeper", along those lines. I started laughing, screwed up the paper and threw it on the floor. But then Nathan Blake and the others started saying, "You can't be having that!" and that sort of thing but I didn't want to get involved.

'We were getting changed at the tennis club, because it was before the Portakabins were brought in for us, and I remember seeing the keepers going out, as they used to go out early, to walk across to the far side of the pitches. There was Oakesy, Matt and Carl Ikeme, who was a young kid they brought in at the time. And the likes of Alex Rae and Colin Cameron were still in my ear saying, "I'd have a word with Mimmsy if I were you." So I did, I remember going over to him and shouting "Mimmsy, what's this piece you've done in the paper?" and I remember him laughing, asking what it had to do with me. And then he did the worst thing he could have done, he walked over to me. The lads were still in my ear, and I just hit him.

'I remember at the time, the gaffer was stood on the grass bank with Terry Connor [Jones's assistant manager] and he just looked at me, pointed his finger and shouted, "Come up here!" I went over to him and he said, "What are you doing, you're the captain of the club?" I said, "I know, but he's wound me up." I could see all the other lads laughing their heads off on the far side. That was a week's wages and all they were bothered about was me getting a fine because all the fines went in the players' kitty. I remember going down to train with them and Incey and the others were giving me loads. "Look at Mimmsy, he can't even kick a ball now!" All that sort of thing.'

Butler was relieved that Mimms saw the bigger picture and was happy to forgive and forget. 'It could have blown up, with people saying there's disharmony in the camp. Mimmsy was great, I still speak to him now. I was really sorry for what I did, but he was ok about it. I think all the lads were ok with it because I'd stuck up for them in games. I could tell you stories about things that went on in tunnels up and down the country, we stuck up for each other.'

Another memorable club fine came after a sending off during a 2-0 home defeat against Manchester City in April 2002. The big defender was so incensed he put his foot through two reinforced tunnel doors, doing thousands of pounds' worth of damage. Chief executive Jez Moxey had little sympathy and Butler reluctantly agreed to a £100-a-week fine until the repair bill had been paid off.

The moments when discipline was lost were perhaps inevitable amongst a group of such strong characters. Jones's promotion-winning team had won the fans' respect despite their short stay in the Premier League. There will always be a sense of regret from the players on the pitch and the supporters in the stands that there was no lasting legacy after the promotion. The two exiled decades outside the top division had seemed an eternity. Albeit too briefly, Wolves had finally joined the country's elite again.

Chapter 13

MICK'S MEN

The 2008/09 Championship winners

PRIOR TO the ascent of Nuno Espírito Santo's team, the previous era of Premier League football at Wolves came during Steve Morgan's boardroom regime at the turn of the decade. Between 2009 and 2012, Mick McCarthy's side survived three seasons in the top division. Promotion had been achieved in an entirely different context to the one gained under Nuno.

When outgoing manager Glenn Hoddle left Wolves in the lurch with his resignation just a month before the start of the 2006/07 season, McCarthy came in to a situation that appeared hopeless. 'MM stands for Mick McCarthy, not Merlin the Magician,' he famously said at the press conference to unveil his appointment. He arrived just 12 days before the start of the Championship season and was introduced to just 13 senior players at the club's Compton Park training ground.

Hoddle's team had finished seventh, but many of the established players had moved on, or were in the process of arranging their exit, such as Paul Ince, Joleon Lescott, Mark Kennedy, Kenny Miller, Lee Naylor and Seol Ki-Hyeon. There had to be a restructuring of finances, with Sir Jack

Hayward looking to sell up and the last of the club's Premier League parachute payments from their 2004 relegation already banked.

McCarthy started shopping in the bargain basement, looking for cast-offs and untapped talent. He acquired central defender Gary Breen from his old club Sunderland and then turned to another veteran in Jamie Clapham, who came in from neighbouring Birmingham City. Karl Henry, a local lad but unwanted at Stoke City, was brought in for just £100,000. Winger Michael Kightly was snapped up from non-league Grays Athletic for £25,000. In January, McCarthy turned to Irish side Bohemians for unknown forward Stephen Ward. The only outlay of any substance was for Andy Keogh, who arrived from Scunthorpe United for £600,000 in the same month. It was not so much chequebook spending, more the emptying of pockets in search of loose change.

Supporters feared that Wolves would be loitering in the bottom half of the table but, instead, McCarthy led his unfancied side into the Championship play-offs in May 2007, where they lost out to Black Country rivals West Bromwich Albion in the semi-finals.

That was then followed up with a near miss seventh-place finish for the 2007/08 season. New owner Morgan, who had completed the purchase of the club in August 2007, recognised the rebuilding job and backed his incumbent manager to complete the job. McCarthy rewarded supporters in his third season in charge as Wolves ran out Championship title winners for 2008/09. The side was built on a strong work ethic, with a significant contingent of young and unproven players eager to prove their worth. They led from the front during that title-winning season, going top in October and remaining there until the trophy was lifted in May.

On this Thursday evening at the end of November, three of the team are reunited at a supporters' event put on at The

Cleveland Arms in Wolverhampton. The large sports bar is situated on the Willenhall Road, just a couple of miles from Molineux. The event was sold out weeks in advance, indicating how highly regarded McCarthy's team remains.

Chris Iwelumo, Matt Jarvis and George Elokobi all filled different roles during their time at Molineux, but the trio earned the respect of fans. To witness the ovation they are given when event host, and former Wolves goalkeeper, Matt Murray welcomes them to the stage is affirmation of that.

Iwelumo is the elder statesman. His partnership in the Championship with Sylvan Ebanks-Blake was the most prolific in the division in that 2008/09 season, and went a long way to helping Wolves secure the title. Iwelumo was a journeyman forward who arrived at Molineux in July 2008 on the back of successful spells at Colchester United and Charlton Athletic. He moved from London a month before his 30th birthday and expected to fight for a place in the team.

'For the first game it was Andy Keogh and Sylvan who started, against Plymouth. They'd done ever so well the season before with each other and I think Mick was loyal and he wanted that relationship to work,' Iwelumo explains. 'I started the next game, it was a League Cup match against Accrington Stanley. I scored a brace and the gaffer told me straight after the match that I was starting on Saturday. It just went from there, I got two goals in that next game against Sheffield Wednesday.

'You won't know this, but Sylvan and I didn't speak to each other for two months. We were scoring goals for fun, winning games, sitting top of the league, and he never spoke to me. I was in the changing room at the training ground and, even if no one else was there, he would walk in and he wouldn't say anything. Then, I think I was sitting on 14 or 15 goals, and as soon as he got to 16 he was, "Alright Lumes, how's things?"

'But, you know what, that's what made him different. He had that about him that he wanted to be the main man, to be the one scoring the goals with his name up there. The way that I started, I guess I stole that kind of limelight a little bit. But you wouldn't have been able to tell on the pitch. If someone came and kicked me or was having a go he'd be the first person in there and it was the same the other way around. Those relationships were so important for that team. There were lots of little partnerships, quality throughout, and the goals came from everywhere.'

Wolves dressing rooms have always had that eclectic blend of characters, but McCarthy's seemed to thrive on the differences. Jarvis and Elokobi came into the professional game after the most contrasting upbringings imaginable. A powerful and energetic full-back during his time with Wolves, Elokobi was born in Mamfe in the south-west region of Cameroon. At the age of ten his father died, so his mother moved over to England in search of work to support the family. Elokobi went to live with one of his grandmothers whilst his mother settled into a new life in Lambeth, sending money home to support the family and pay for his school studies in Cameroon.

Then, at the age of 16, she decided to bring her son over to England to continue his education and study for his GCSEs.

'I'd never been on a plane before. I was sat in it not knowing what was going on,' Elokobi explains. 'I kept thinking, "How the hell is this big thing gonna go up there and come back down?" I was 16 years of age and it was a completely different environment from what I was used to. Everything was so new for me, I was getting confused. The life I lived in Cameroon growing up was really tough and, when I came over, it was not easy either because my mum was still working hard to get me settled into the system. I'd left all my friends back home and it was a new country. I had no friends, it was just myself and my mum.

'I found myself going into college and trying to get my education back on track. It was amazing the way everything happened after that. After losing my dad, coming to England to join my mum was the best thing that happened to me.'

Until he made the move over here, Elokobi's football had been played in a rough-and-ready environment.

'Growing up we had a saying: "Every man for themselves, God for us all." You played with your friends, there were no age groups or coaching. I had never been coached before coming to England, I was as raw as you can get. We used to just get the football, 40 kids and one football. Whoever was the bravest touched the ball – you touch the ball and see what happens to you! You would get kicked but you'd become brave.

'There were no rules, we did not have anyone to referee the game. We took it seriously and we took it personally. That's how I learned how to be quick because if you got the ball you had to outrun the other kids. We rarely played on grass, often it was barefoot on pitches lent to us by a local brewing company. There would be broken bottles lying around and we'd get lots of cuts on our feet. That's how I became brave.

'I had never heard of Wolverhampton Wanderers before I came here. I rarely had access to a television screen when I was back home. We used to peep through the windows of wealthy people's homes to get a glimpse of colour television. I knew of Manchester United, but not a club like Wolverhampton.'

In England, Elokobi studied Business and IT at college. He pursued his football dreams by joining Isthmian League Division One club Dulwich Hamlet's youth training scheme. After two years in the junior ranks he went full time with Colchester United in 2004, at the age of 18, before moving to Wolves in January 2008.

Jarvis – a winger in the traditional sense, with a nifty turn of pace and accurate crossing ability – took an entirely different route. Growing up in Guildford, Surrey, structured sport was introduced into family life at an early age.

'Both my parents were England number-one table tennis players,' he reveals. 'My mum won the European mixed doubles with Desmond Douglas, so they were pretty sporty. I had a good upbringing. During school I did football, swimming, athletics, cross country, everything really. I was a Surrey champion at swimming, cross country and athletics so I was pretty good. At swimming I was very good, even though I was a lot smaller than everyone else. I was 0.01 of a second off the national record at the time in breast stroke, which was my strength.'

Jarvis suffered an early setback in football when he was released by Millwall at the age of 15. He had been desperate to secure youth terms but was told he was not good enough to make the grade. There would be an early second chance.

'The day I got told I was being released, one of the chief scouts at Gillingham called me up saying they wanted me to come down on trial,' he adds. 'I didn't want to do it at first, but the following week I went down on trial. I was terrible, but luckily they took a chance. I think my confidence had been shot to pieces by being told I was not good enough. To then go and play with so much pressure on me to have to perform to get a contract, I was rock bottom, but luckily they took a chance on me.

'I remember I was in a science class at school when I got a text message. My phone wasn't on, but I came out and had a text from my parents to say I'd been offered a contract at Gillingham. I went in for pre-season and something just clicked after that. I was back to feeling confident and I had an unbelievable first year as a trainee. Then in my second season as a trainee I was playing with the first team. That was it, I stayed with them.'

Jarvis was 21 years old when Wolves signed him in June 2007. During his time at Wolves he would not only win promotion, but also earned an England call-up from Fabio

Capello. He made his one and only international appearance against Ghana, at Wembley, becoming the first Wolves player to represent England since Steve Bull in 1990.

Jarvis credits McCarthy and his assistant Terry Connor with every aspect of his own development as a player, from the moment he joined until the time he moved on to West Ham five years later.

'Ultimately Mick and TC were on the training pitch every single day, drilling us so that we knew exactly what we were supposed to be doing,' he says. 'Mick was out there every day. He had the biggest influence on my career. I was 21 when I arrived and I left at 26. Over that period of time and development, he and TC brought my game on tremendously and I owe them a lot for that. They put a lot of hours' work in. I still speak to both of them now.'

If Jarvis needed coaching, Iwelumo needed man-management.

'Even though he was old school, he knew how to manage me,' the Scot explains. 'Sports science had come into the game massively and Mick was very aware of that. He was listening to what his staff were saying to him. It took me a couple more days to recover from games so I'd be refereeing matches [on the training ground] instead of playing. I'd still get the yellow jersey as a ref, by the way!

'But he was great with me. He'd check how I was feeling and if he didn't want me to play he would just tell me to go in the pool or in the gym. There are a lot of managers who don't manage players properly, it's just about getting that result on the Saturday. If you're injured they don't even give you the time of day. Wolves saw the best out of me because I was managed properly.'

McCarthy would have no problem calling players out if he felt it was needed but, even in the bad times, there was an integrity to his approach that the players admired.

'What you see is what you get, he is honest as the day is long,' Iwelumo adds. 'His man-management is quality.

He doesn't bullshit. I've seen him tear up a player after the match in the dressing room but the next day he would apologise if he was wrong in that heat of the moment. That says a lot about a person, he doesn't hide or hold grudges. He earned your respect that way.'

Iwelumo left the club after the first season in the Premier League. Following a dramatic last-day escape in the second season, a third survival proved to be a step too far. Most supporters felt McCarthy's time was up by the time the board decided to dismiss him in February 2012, a day after a torrid 5-1 home defeat to bitter rivals West Bromwich Albion. During a question and answer session towards the end of the night, one fan asks how the players felt about losing the manager who had been so influential on their own careers.

'It was horrendous the day before. Coming in on Monday we just thought it was going to be a review of the game, which no one really wanted,' Jarvis recalls. 'Then Mick came in and told us that was it, he had been sacked. There was just silence in the room. Everyone was devastated. I know it's hard to believe that some people weren't pleased, but everyone I spoke to was gutted.

'Mick had brought everyone in that room to the club, so that was all we knew at Wolves: Mick McCarthy and TC. For him to come in and tell us that news, he was upset and frustrated. We were all gutted, it was really hard to get our heads around.'

Elokobi is a bit more forthcoming about the divisions that had opened up in the dressing room. With Karl Henry replaced as captain by Roger Johnson for that final Premier League season, the dynamic of the dressing room changed. Equally damaging was the change in wage structure, with many of those signed during the club's Premier League days coming in on much better terms than the players who had achieved promotion.

'Having some lads coming in on four or five times more than what we were on, we didn't take it so highly if I'm being honest,' admits Elokobi. 'Surely the club should have rewarded us a little bit more. The squad had been together such a long time, we had a leader in Karl Henry who was an amazing skipper for this football club. For that to change in the third season in the Premier League, I think that didn't go down well in the changing room. If that could happen to Karl it could happen to any one of us. It was all about doing our best for the football club but we all liked to be rewarded equally.'

The McCarthy era took two very distinct forms. The longer opening chapter was one of hope, triumph against the odds and a team which was greater than the sum of its parts. The shorter closing chapter – essentially just the 2011/12 relegation season – was wretched. Hope had been replaced with despair. The strength was no longer in the group and a major rebuilding job was required.

All three players had their regrets when leaving the club; Iwelumo went too soon, Jarvis went as a relegated player and Elokobi was sold against his wishes. But, as the three of them pose for selfies and sign autographs long into the night, there is no doubt they recall their time at Wolves with huge fondness. And that affection is reciprocated by the supporters tonight.

* * *

Several months later, in April 2019, Henry, the man who captained the side during the good times, also took the opportunity to speak to supporters. At the Wolves Former Players' Association annual dinner, the Wolverhampton-born midfielder was welcomed back to Molineux along with his former team-mate Kevin Foley. Henry arrived from Stoke City in the summer of 2006. At 23 years of age, he was at the point in his career when he needed to be playing regularly. Circumstance can throw up unique opportunities. McCarthy offered him a special pre-season trial match.

'He brought in players who were young and hungry who had maybe not done a lot in their careers,' Henry recalls. 'I spoke to Mick on a Friday. He said, "Come down, we've got a game on the pitch tomorrow." I spoke to my stepdad, who'd been a Wolves fan all his life. I rang him and said, "You're not going to believe this, I've got a trial at Wolves. I've got a game on the pitch tomorrow." He said, "It's not just a game on the pitch, it's Steve Bull's 20th anniversary testimonial match. It'll be a packed house, it's against Aston Villa." All of a sudden I went from calm to panic. I turned up and Mark Davis, unfortunately for him, got injured after about six minutes and Mick told me to get on. I had a really good game, I kicked Gareth Barry up in the air four or five times and maybe a few others as well. The Villa players were looking at me as if to say, "What the hell are you doing, this is a friendly game?" For me it was a huge opportunity. I played well and Mick offered me a deal.'

Henry, who cost Wolves just £100,000, came to epitomise the type of player McCarthy trusted. An honest, hard-working professional with an integrity about everything he did on and off the pitch, the two men were made for each other.

'I've always had a work ethic, it's been ingrained since I was a kid,' Henry adds. 'I figured from an early age that if I outrun people, I tend to have quite good games and I get another contract. It was the same when I signed here under Mick, I knew it was a rebuild job. He wanted to get us back to the Premier League, he had a plan and I knew if I worked my socks off he was the kind of manager who repaid that.

'It was really refreshing for me to have a manager like Mick. If you're crap, he tells you you're crap. And if you do that again you're not going to play for him. He tells that to every player. Everybody was treated the same whether you're the star player or not. It felt for me like a real fresh start for my career.'

Henry's insight into the role of Connor in the management structure is revealing. McCarthy's style won respect in the dressing room, and his players knew what they had to do to remain in the team. But Connor had his eye on the wider picture at all times.

'Something I remember seeing with TC when I first joined is that he worked so hard to keep all the players on board,' Henry explains. 'You can't keep everybody happy. Only 11 can start and you end up with another 13 or 14 players who are not really happy because they are not in the team. TC would put sessions on specifically for those players who weren't playing, and the rest of us would have to participate in those sessions. So he'd create a session for a player who wasn't playing and everyone respected that so much. They understood what that player was going through. I'd not seen that before. TC was phenomenal.'

Both McCarthy and Connor knew they were operating on a small budget, although McCarthy's best spending came with less money. His imprint remains in the Wolves side today. Doherty came in from Bohemians for £75,000, and has gone on to represent Republic of Ireland and establish himself in Nuno Espírito Santo's Premier League team. It was the more significant outlays of cash during McCarthy's time that never paid off. Roger Johnson was signed from Birmingham City for a reported £7million and Jamie O'Hara arrived from Spurs for £5.5million. Both were flops during the relegation season. Under Morgan and his chief executive Jez Moxey, money was always tight, but Henry puts this down to a responsible approach to spending rather than a lack of ambition at boardroom level.

'Jez always got a lot of stick from supporters but I thought he was brilliant,' Henry adds. 'I joined Queens Park Rangers after Wolves and saw the money they spent. And I have seen the situation they are in now because of how badly they spent that money. What Wolves were never going to be under Jez Moxey and Steve Morgan was a boom and bust side. You weren't going to see them down in League Two with 20 points deducted. That was really important, and Jez was brilliant at keeping the reins tight. Did Mick have as much money as he would have liked? Possibly not. But did he find some gems? He certainly did. He signed players like Matt Jarvis, Michael Kightly and Matt Doherty. He signed a lot of players with next to no money.'

Wolves may not have slipped to the bottom division during Morgan and Moxey's time at the club, but they did drop down to League One. McCarthy and Connor could only be held to account for one of those relegations. The season after their dismissal, Wolves went down again. Stale Solbakken and Dean Saunders oversaw the relegation from Championship to League One. Henry, more than any other player, felt the embarrassment that came with a double relegation.

'One hundred per cent regret and disappointment,' he says. 'We were ashamed of the situation. Certainly being local, from Wolverhampton. I was at Wolves for seven years and six of those years were good. To get relegated from the Premier League, I don't think there's any shame in that. But to get relegated from the Championship with the team we had was a disgrace and we knew that. I think it marred a really good period for us.'

In the summer of 2013, Henry was moved out of the club by manager Kenny Jackett, who went on to secure an immediate return to the Championship for Wolves. Four years at Queens Park Rangers followed, before a single season with Bolton Wanderers. One of his last games as a professional came in April 2018 at the Macron Stadium, when his Bolton side were on the end of a 4-0 rout at the hands of Wolves, a victory that secured the Championship title for Nuno's team.

The achievements of Nuno's players touched a nerve with Henry. He believes the 2008/09 Championship title winners were not appreciated as much as the two teams that won promotion either side of their title.

'It felt to me at times like we weren't really appreciated by the fans, that's how it felt,' he admits. 'It's not just me speaking, the rest of the players will tell you the same. It felt like the team that reached the play-offs five years earlier were held in higher regard. And then after we left, it becomes all about the current team and how good they are. It felt like we were up against it, but we understand that that last year ruined a really good era for the club. I'm sure Mick and TC feel the same as well.'

Context is crucial here. There is an obvious reason why the 2002/03 play-off-winning team may be more fondly remembered amongst a certain generation, and that is because of what went on before. As the famous banner on that historic May afternoon in Cardiff proclaimed, it had been more than 19 years since Wolves had last graced the top flight. A whole generation of supporters had grown up with no experience of top division football. Dave Jones's team broke through a ceiling and put to bed two decades of disillusionment and disappointment.

McCarthy's side achieved something the 2002/03 play-off winners could not manage: survival in the Premier League. Jones's team came straight back down, whereas McCarthy's lasted three seasons at the top.

Yet the blend of Jones's side was more colourful than McCarthy's, which may also go some way to explaining why they are remembered so affectionately – the up-and-coming talents of Matt Murray, Lee Naylor and Joleon Lescott mixed with the big names of British football such as Paul Ince and Denis Irwin. There were a few hotheads in there too; from captain and centre-back Paul Butler, midfield enforcer Alex Rae to fiery front-runner Kenny Miller. There was no shortage of on-field voices. They were not afraid to fall out with each other, with many of them admitting they did not particularly get on well off the pitch. But they kept the common goal in sight. These larger-than-life characters left their mark on spectators. McCarthy's players were different. The team grew together more cohesively. Perhaps they were a more humble bunch who kept a lower profile.

Times have changed again, with the club's third promotion to the Premier League. Nuno's 2017/18 promotion bears no resemblance to either of the previous achievements. Backed by Fosun's millions, the Portuguese management revolutionised the playing style. There has been a cultural shift in the way the club operate now. Perhaps the club has got it right at the third time of asking. What cannot be disputed is that Nuno has been given the backing neither Jones nor McCarthy was afforded when it came to establishing the club in the Premier League.

Henry's comments should not be interpreted as sour grapes. As a player he was under-rated during his time at Molineux. Henry turned out to be one of the most influential captains the club has ever had, at a time when they were crying out for someone to lead on the pitch. Returning to Molineux as the newest member of the Wolves Former Players' Association, he was able to understand that the team's achievements made a lasting impression on supporters. In summing up what it meant to be one of McCarthy's men, he was able to pinpoint why the class of 2008/09 was a remarkable team.

'Winning the Championship was special, we were all young and hungry,' he concludes. 'There's a number of us who are still in touch. Myself, Kevin Foley, Richard Stearman, Sylvan Ebanks-Blake, also Stephen Hunt and Kevin Doyle from the Premier League days. We are all still a tight-knit group, we all left here and realised how special it was here, how special the fan base was and the club as a whole.

'The fact you have nights like this. I appreciate being invited back and being part of the Wolves family. That is something we probably took for granted – just how good a dressing room we had. I've never had it since. I didn't have it before I came here, I didn't have it when I left. It was a real special time for us. We had a really good group and I'll remember that for the rest of my days.'

Chapter 14

A CAPTAIN'S ROLE

Sam Ricketts – leader of a revival

IT IS the third week of August, with the 2018/19 Premier League season just two games old. Sam Ricketts is sitting at a table in the lounge of a smart countryside hotel in Cheshire, not far from where he is living while he takes his first steps into management. It has been a busy introduction to the job for the former Wolves defender. Ricketts took over as manager of National League side Wrexham in May, and the Welsh club are already five games into the National League season. It has been a great start for Ricketts, with four wins and a draw putting the Red Dragons top of the fledgling table.

Ricketts gives his players every Thursday off, as opposed to the more traditional Wednesday break for professional footballers, and he has made a gap in his hectic schedule to meet up and chat about Wolves' League One campaign of 2013/14. It was just five seasons before this Premier League campaign, but the club was in a completely different state to the one it finds itself in now.

For many it feels like a distant memory, such has been the pace of change at Molineux in recent years, but it is worth recalling that Wolves were playing third-tier football not so long ago. The calamitous drop from the Premier League to League One in successive seasons was a modern-day nadir. As Mick McCarthy's tenure drifted to an unsatisfactory conclusion, followed by Terry Connor's stop-gap appointment, Stale Solbakken's arrival from overseas, and finally Dean Saunders's best-forgotten spell in charge, Wolves became a byword for mismanagement and underachievement.

A rot had set in. Fans had fallen out of love with the club and its players. The squad was divided, with rifts emerging in the dressing room. And owner Steve Morgan and his chief executive Jez Moxey had become the target of the supporters' wrath. The stability of those early years of McCarthy's reign had come crashing down with that hapless series of managerial changes.

Players such as Roger Johnson and Jamie O'Hara – the two marquee signings of the Premier League summer transfer window in 2011 – epitomised the malaise. Both were involved in separate incidents during one of the most shambolic weeks of the club's three-year Premier League stay under McCarthy.

Following a 5-0 defeat at Fulham on 4 March 2012, Johnson was sent home from training and fined £50,000 for turning up at Compton Park the next morning in an unfit state to train during Connor's temporary reign.

Johnson apologised for his actions, saying at the time, 'My conduct and approach to training on Monday was below the high standard the club rightly needs and demands from me – and what I demand from myself. I have apologised to the manager, my team-mates and the club.'

After the next game, a 2-0 Molineux defeat to Blackburn Rovers, O'Hara was involved in an altercation with supporters as he made his way up the Waterloo Road after the match. This came after supporters had gathered at the foot of the Billy Wright Statue outside the main reception to protest at the way the club was being run.

When Wolves were relegated to League One, the first-team squad was still littered with Premier League recruits on big salaries. Saunders was dismissed after Wolves could only manage a lame 2-0 defeat at Brighton and Hove Albion – a result that confirmed relegation – on the final day of the 2012/13 season. It was clear that a major rebuilding job was required; it was not only time for an overhaul but a new culture was needed to reverse the decline.

Ten years earlier, Ricketts had signed for another club just up the road from Molineux. In the summer of 2003 he joined non-league Telford United, who played in the Conference. It was the bottom rung of a ladder that would take him all the way to the Premier League.

He owed much of what followed in his career to Kenny Jackett. Jackett was manager of League Two Swansea City in 2004 when he approached Ricketts with an offer of league football. The Swans manager was rewarded for his judgement, with the defender becoming a key part of the side that won promotion to League One. Ricketts never looked back, being named in League Two's PFA Team of the Year and following that up with another promotion push the next season.

Swansea only missed out on promotion to the Championship by the narrow margin of a penalty shoot-out defeat against Barnsley in the 2006 League One play-off final. It signalled the end of Ricketts's spell in Wales, and in July of that year he moved to Hull City. There, he became a key member of the team that won promotion to the Premier League under Phil Brown, sealing their first-ever top-flight appearance with a Championship play-off final win over Bristol City in May 2008.

In just four years Ricketts had joined a select group of professionals who had played in all four divisions. He would go on to enjoy four top-flight seasons in all, one with Hull and three more with Bolton Wanderers. By the summer of 2013 he found himself looking for another move, with the

Lancashire club – now in the Championship – reaching a mutual agreement to terminate his contract. Step forward Jackett once more.

The former Swansea manager had enjoyed success of his own since the pair had last worked together. After leaving the Liberty Stadium in the summer of 2007, Jackett spent a short time on the coaching staff at Manchester City before moving to League One strugglers Millwall as manager in November that year. After guiding the London club to safety, he took them to the play-off final in his first full season in charge, losing out on promotion to Scunthorpe United.

The following season, 2009/10, Millwall finished third and returned to Wembley in the play-off final, this time winning promotion with a 1-0 victory over Swindon Town. Jackett kept Millwall in the Championship for three successive seasons before Wolves came knocking at the door for his services. Despite the drop down a division, Jackett saw the move to the better-resourced League One club as a step forward. So what persuaded Ricketts to join his old manager a division lower down too?

'Do you know what, it was a bit of everything,' he says. 'Wolves is a massive club. You have the potential to get 30,000. Kenny had just been appointed manager. I knew him, I'd worked with him before. I knew he'd be successful, which ultimately you have to be. And then there's the challenge. We – the manager, the staff and players – had a really big job on that season. It ticked an awful lot of boxes. I wanted something to really engage me, especially at that time in my career. A real challenge that would be very rewarding as well if we got it right.'

But if there was one over-riding factor it was surely the chance of working with the man who had put his career on that spectacular upward trajectory again?

'I'd been fortunate. I'd played under Kenny before. He took me out of non-league and I had two years at Swansea. I went from non-league, then under his tutelage we won

League Two. I got in the PFA Team of the Year, won the Football League Trophy, made my Wales debut and we only just got beaten in the League One play-off final too. We had a really good run under him and I just knew what he was like as a manager. I knew how meticulous he was.

'He's ruthless, but in a good way of knowing exactly what he wants to be successful. You look at the top managers now – Nuno would be the same. Nuno knows exactly what he wants to be successful with the team and Kenny was exactly the same. Different style, different methods, but to the same detail he knew exactly what he wanted to be successful and it proved to be the case.'

Jackett perfectly judged the situation Wolves were in when he drove through the gates of the club's Compton Park training base for the first time. He had prepared for the job as thoroughly as Ricketts was convinced he would, though the defender did not expect to be thrust into the spotlight as early as he was.

'Kenny threw me under the bus a bit on my first day,' he explains. 'We came together at pre-season training and we all got into a little group. Kenny said, "Lads, Sam has just signed for the club and he's the new club captain." And everyone took a step back. I only knew Dave Edwards from the Welsh set-up. I was thinking, "Cheers Gaffer, thanks for that, you've thrown me under the bus there, you could have let me settle in for a few days!"

'But he wanted to make a statement there and then and he wanted to say this is a new team. He saw me as being the figure-point of the dressing room, of the team, and he decided to move players around a little bit.'

Ricketts arrived in the first week of July but was the only signing the club made for over a month. The 2013/14 season had begun before the next recruit was secured, when Kevin MacDonald joined from Sheffield United in the second week of August. But despite the almost non-existent transfer business, massive changes were taking place at the training ground. Jackett had identified a core of academy talent that he wanted to work with ahead of many of those senior players who had come down with the club from the Premier League. The likes of O'Hara, Johnson, Stephen Ward, Karl Henry and Kevin Doyle found themselves cast aside, to the extent of being told to get changed in a separate dressing room with the academy players.

'There were certain players who trained at different times,' Ricketts explains. 'Kenny wanted to build a new squad and a new generation and really rejuvenate the club from within. He probably had ten or so players training in the afternoon. It was called Group Three at the time – they were still under contract, still getting their wages, still training correctly, but Kenny and the club had decided they weren't going to feature in the first team that year.'

The group would often train on pitch three, as it was then, which was notorious for its slope and being a little bit drier than the other pitches. It was regularly used by a nearby school and was certainly not somewhere that first-team players would expect to utilise. Henry revealed in an interview some years after leaving Wolves that it was an extremely testing period for the exiled players. 'They wanted to get rid of us and they made life difficult,' he said.

'It was a club policy to go with the new group of players, generally a lot of young players,' Ricketts adds. 'An awful lot came out of the academy that season, especially at the start of the season when I was the only signing for the first few weeks. It was a real opportunity for these academy players to stake a claim. We obviously added players to it, but it was an opportunity for all the players who were there, who would never have had a chance in the previous seasons.'

That fresh start was in evidence at Preston North End on the opening day of the season. Jackett had put his faith in the youngsters at the club. Joining captain Ricketts in the first-team squad that day were Jack Price, Zeli Ismail, Liam McAlinden, David Davis, Danny Batth and Carl Ikeme.

All of them had come through the youth set-up at the club. With Matt Doherty, Lee Evans and Jake Cassidy also in the squad that day, the emphasis was on players with their careers ahead of them. Something else remains in Ricketts's memory from the trip to Deepdale, too:

'I think we sold out the entire away section, there were 5,000 fans there. I had some friends who came to the game and I was thinking, "Wow, this is a real moment. This is a real opportunity." You go back to the question, why did I sign for Wolves? Well 5,000 away fans on the first day of the season is a pretty good reason.'

The faith Jackett showed in the young guns was illustrated with his treatment of Batth, who would eventually succeed Ricketts as club captain. Batth knew all about League One from his time out on loan at Sheffield Wednesday. He was runner-up in the Owls Player of the Season award for the 2011/12 season, when his displays at the heart of defence helped guide Wednesday to promotion.

On his return to Wolves the following season he did not find a regular place in the Championship side that went on to be relegated. He made just five league starts and seven substitute appearances. As the season drew to its ignominious close at Brighton, he sat on the bench as an unused substitute, with Johnson and the on-loan Kaspars Gorkss entrusted with a starting place.

'Well it probably was the real start for the likes of Danny to come through,' Ricketts agrees. 'Danny had been out on loan; he'd been promoted out of this league with Sheffield Wednesday, played bits for the team but nobody had ever said, "Danny – you're there, you're playing." I think Kenny did that straight away. "Danny, you are in. You are my centre-back and you're playing."

'I was signed to play alongside Danny and eventually I ended up moving out to either full-back position. Then Richard Stearman came back in. We had Carl Ikeme in goal, he was the best goalkeeper I ever played with. From that season he was that much of a man mountain. He'd come and catch crosses. His kicking was immaculate. There was so much confidence in him and he was a big reason why we were winning games. The saves he was making early on in the season, I remember against Swindon Town at home some point-blank headers. We should have been losing the game and we ended up winning 3-2 after Kemes made two or three unbelievable saves.'

Despite winning eight of the next nine matches after the Preston draw, Ricketts believes that Wolves were never actually playing good enough football to merit their lofty league position.

'This is probably the bit where Kenny is so good. We were winning games at the start of the season and to be honest we had no right to be winning those games,' he recalls. 'We just won them out of pure hunger and desire. We used to do an awful lot in training where we'd play games for five pounds a man and the games were really competitive. I saw that come out on the Saturday where there was a hunger and desire to win. We weren't playing fantastically but we were the team that didn't play well and still won, which is what you want all your teams to be, especially if you're going to be successful – you need to win those games.'

The team was not without its characters, who tested the patience of Jackett from time to time. Striker Leigh Griffiths was the club's leading scorer going into the new year. A former Wolves team-mate of the Scottish striker tells an amusing story about the first time they roomed together on an away trip. Griffiths opened up his suitcase, which was divided into two parts, on the floor of the hotel bedroom. The one half contained his clothes and toiletries for the trip, the second part was filled entirely with sweets. Haribos, lollipops and more. 'I was sat there eating an apple thinking, "What the hell is this?",' his room-mate said.

Griffiths and his collection of confectionary moved on to Celtic during the 2014 January transfer window, but Wolves continued on their quest for promotion with the bulk of the goalscoring duties shared amongst Nouha Dicko and Bakary Sako. By the last week of March, Wolves were four points clear at the top of the table going into their final game of the month away at MK Dons.

In the weeks building up to the game, supporters decided that they wanted to take as big a following as they could to the match. A social media hashtag, #10K2MK, emerged and the fans embraced the challenge of taking 10,000 fans to Stadium MK on 29 March.

'I don't know who started it up but it was a great idea, #10K2MK, it runs off your tongue and the Wolves fans were up for it,' Ricketts remembers. 'I think MK Dons reduced the ticket allocation in the end to 9,000, which was a bit of a shame as it would have been brilliant to get the 10,000 in there. But to go out at Stadium MK, a lovely new stadium which wraps around, there's no corners, to see it was half full with Wolves fans was amazing. It made for such an atmosphere in the game. It's another reason why Wolves are where they are at now. It's alright being successful in League One, but you need that fan base for the club to go on and achieve things. If you take 9,000 away to a League One match it shows you what support there is for the club.

'We actually struggled a little bit because of it. MK Dons were nothing special, they were ok, but it turned into a cup final for them, walking out in front of that crowd, and they upped their game, and we had to up ours. Eventually one of the young players, Liam McAlinden, came on and scored the goal which kept the run going for us. We snuck another 1-0 win without playing great football. Again it was that desire to be successful which came from Kenny all the way through to the players.'

The appetite to be part of Wolves was back amongst the support. Success on the pitch helped but Ricketts believes the fans had begun to identify with the team once more.

'That was one of the most satisfying things. You knew it was such a big task. It wasn't until Christmas time that we really started playing football. For the second half of the season we were head and shoulders the best team in the league. We had really good players, we were dominating the ball, dominating games, very much like Nuno did last season. We got promoted and to see the fans come back, we felt that energy from the fans.

'They probably saw it from the team. We wanted to give them a team to be proud of, a team that worked hard, a team that never gave in. Everyone makes mistakes – that will always happen in football – but if you're a fan and you see a team try everything they can to win the game, I think that's all you can ask for. I think they fell back in love with the club again that year after two really disappointing years. It was a springboard, a clean slate, a chance for everyone to come back together. Fans who'd been disheartened over a couple of years came back in their droves. We were being successful on the pitch and you build momentum, and I think that momentum is still going today.'

That togetherness was never more obvious than on the occasion of the penultimate home fixture of the season. A crowd of 30,110 flocked to Molineux for the visit of in-form Rotherham United for a Good Friday fixture that will not be forgotten by those in attendance. An astonishing 6-4 victory for Wolves was played out in front of a delirious crowd.

'Rotherham were on a really good run, they actually came up that year in the play-offs. They came from nowhere, so they came into it in really good form,' Ricketts recalls. 'We had played really well. 4-2 up with five minutes to go and everyone's cruising thinking it's alright, another win, they've rolled over now. Then all of a sudden Rotherham went bang, bang – two goals – and the atmosphere just dropped a fraction. It was the 90th minute, I hadn't scored all season. I'd come close, I'd hit the post and it was a running joke in the dressing room that everyone had scored and I hadn't.

'Then I received the ball on the right from kick-off after their fourth, and I remember laying it to Dave Edwards on the edge of the box, pointing and just shouting "Set!" Dave's a fantastic player, he doesn't always get the credit he deserves, and he just set me up. It was one of the best goals I've ever scored; left foot, underside of the bar and in.

'I remember going off to celebrate and all the fans were on the pitch. I think that's why it's so remembered. Thirty thousand turned up for the game and fans still talk to me today about that goal. I've tried to reproduce it a few times since but never done it, I've never been as accurate as that. I came into the dressing room after the game, and Kenny didn't really ever say too much, and he just gave me a little nod and said, "Good goal, that."'

The celebrations were a sight to behold, the win all but securing the title. Any added-time winner goes down well, but was it extra special because of the identity of the scorer?

'Yeah, for players and fans as well. I should have scored more and that was my downfall. I was a defender who, when I got that far upfield, was never prolific. But eventually it just happened and it was a perfect way to do it.' Kevin McDonald rattled in a sixth to spark more pitch invasions on a day that encapsulated the spirit of revival at Molineux.

Having failed to score all season, Ricketts followed up his dramatic winner with another in the final game, a 3-0 romp past Carlisle United. It took Jackett's men to 103 points for the season, a record for the division. All that remained was for the skipper to pick up the trophy.

'It's one of the best things you can do as a footballer, it doesn't matter what league you're in, to win any league is a real big ask. From a personal point of view, to do it as captain is something I'll never forget. An opportunity to lift a trophy, I don't care what it is, to lift a trophy as captain of that team knowing what we'd done that year was a huge moment for me and something I'll always remember with very fond memories.'

So was that the season which set the wheels in motion for where Wolves are today?

'Without any shadow of a doubt that is the start of where Wolves are at now,' Ricketts adds. 'It got us out of that league, first and foremost. It rejuvenated the whole club; fans, supporters. Everyone at the club, for the first time in a couple of years, was pulling in the same direction. We then only missed out on the Championship play-offs on goal difference by one goal the following season and that momentum carried on.

'I still feel that is the springboard for where the club is now and where the club want to go because that was the moment everyone fell back in love with the club. Supporters saw a team they wanted to be proud of and that they wanted to come and watch.'

It should be a source of pride amongst Wolves fans that a player of Ricketts's standing in the game has such fond memories of his time down in League One at Molineux. Above him, there was a manager who knew exactly what Wolves needed at that precise period in time. Ricketts is right to highlight the role of Jackett in the club's revival; someone who still plays a big role in his own development.

'That's why I'm such a big fan of his and why I still lean on him now for advice, because of the person he is,' Ricketts adds. 'He's a really good person. Football is a ruthless industry and a lot of people don't get a chance to be nice, but he's a good person. Ruthless when he has to make a decision, he did it with me the following season and you have to hold your hands up and accept it. He's doing what the team and the club needs.

'After that really good first year, the next year I never really played. He knew before me that my time as a player was coming to an end. I never fell out with him, just respected his decision. He brought me into the coaching set-up really, the next season. Professionalism, integrity and just a good human being.

'I played under him a lot. I have huge respect for him and I know his family from the very first time I met him at Swansea. His two boys were there and I keep bumping into them even now and I still speak to Kenny an awful lot. He's a big influence on me now, coming into management, and on how I am. He's a really nice guy but he's not your best mate. It was Joe Gallen [Jackett's assistant] who was messing about with the lads and having a bit of fun and that was their chemistry. It was what worked really well for us.'

Jackett was undoubtedly the key man in this period of Wolves' history, but he needed a dressing-room presence he could trust. When pressed, Ricketts talks about his own role as captain, but it is clear he puts the team ethos ahead of any desire to come across as the main man.

'Even now as a manager, I don't do big speeches, I lead by example. I didn't say anything to the lads, that was just the way it was,' he admits. 'I'd go about things my way and just try to help them. If I saw someone struggling I'd go and help them. Stupid things – can I make sure all the tickets are sorted on a Saturday? It used to take me an hour and a half every Saturday.

'We were successful, so I'd be going to the board asking for more tickets for the players. All the little things to try to make sure we got looked after as players. They probably bought into that knowing that I wasn't there for myself, I was there for the team. I was there to help them and I wanted the club to be successful. In due course the lads accepted me, they did on that first day in fairness, it was just the fact that Kenny said, "Here's the new signing and he's club captain now." That surprised everyone.

'My management style and style as a captain is to lead by example and make sure I work hardest, do the warm-up right, do training right, prepare right and then if someone isn't doing it I can say, "Come on we're doing it, why aren't you?" And I think that's the best way to lead.'

Speak to anyone who worked closely with Ricketts during that season and they will also tell of the role he played in ensuring that the players engaged with the community. He was not responsible for what had gone on in the seasons before, but he did his best to help the fans reconnect with their club.

'Any football club needs supporters, but we have to give something back for them to come and support us and push us on,' Ricketts explains. 'So it was a big thing, re-engaging with the fans, and it was really important that the players responded to that. At a club like Wolves it's really important that we go out to the schools, go out and do all the community events. I made sure that – every player – we went and did everything, there weren't any who didn't do that side of it.

'Danny was vice-captain at the time and subconsciously I was trying to get him ready because I knew he would be captain after me. He's carried that on. Speaking to Danny after I left, all these things that have gone on, the community visits, all the players still do it and it's really important that a club like Wolves, with its community spirit, still does it.'

It is a fitting legacy. His was a short spell, even by today's transitory standards, but Ricketts's impact on the team and the community around him was significant. Wolves were wanting for on-field leaders in the two seasons before his arrival. At his age it would have been simpler to find a more straightforward challenge than dropping to League One to join a club that had lost its way, with disharmony in the dressing room and dismay in the stands. He will go down as one of the most important captains the club has ever had.

'Now, when I chat with supporters, they say I was the right person at the right time to try and help bring the club back,' Ricketts concludes. 'I was only doing my small part, there were so many other people doing theirs as well. But just to play a small part at Wolves was great. Now I see them in the Premier League and have a smile and think I had a little part to play in that.'

Chapter 15

FAMILY

The bond between club and supporters

'YOU FEEL like you've known these people all your life.'

Jason Guy has a clipboard in his hand and is looking through his speech one last time as he prepares to host a charity fundraiser at The Mount Hotel in Tettenhall on this Thursday evening in March. Two of the club's players from the 1970s era, Steve Daley and Steve Kindon, are the guest speakers. The season has reached a fever pitch. Wolves have qualified for the last eight of the FA Cup. Two days later they will play against Manchester United in the quarter-finals at a sold-out Molineux. Tonight's gathering feels like a prelude to that. Jason is nervous, but excited, as he surveys the guests assembling in the bar. There have been several of these occasions over the past four years, each one touching the deepest place in his soul.

Wolves' End of Season Dinner was drawing to a close at the Telford International Centre on 18 May 2011 when the club's former goalkeeper Matt Murray introduced Lucy Smith to Jason. Lucy had been working at the event, looking after the club's silent auction stand in the concourse outside the main dining hall. Jason was a regular attendee at the many functions and events put on by the club. He had got to know several of the former players and had confided in Murray that he had taken a shine to Lucy during the evening.

'After we spoke that night I sent her a few texts and she didn't respond initially,' Jason recalls. 'It went on for a few months. Then out of the blue I got a text back asking if I wanted to meet up for lunch. So I played it really cool, and 30 seconds later I texted her back. We went out the next day and became inseparable.

'We'd been going out for about 12 months, then bought a house together. It was after three months of living together that she was diagnosed. We never thought it would happen to us, you read about it, but nobody in my family had ever had cancer. Nobody in Lucy's family had either. So it just wasn't in our lives.'

Lucy had been diagnosed with triple negative breast cancer, a particularly aggressive form of the disease. 'It had been business as usual in the house, the usual arguments about who was going to walk the dog or put the bins out, and then an hour or so later our lives were turned upside down.'

Although it was aggressive, it was treatable. 'The first year or so of treatment went very well. They told us that if it was going to come back it would do so in the first five years. We went to Brazil for the World Cup in 2014 and when we returned she was told it had come back.'

Lucy began a highly toxic type of chemotherapy, but after several sessions the tumour had doubled in size and spread further. The cancer was terminal. Less than two months later Jason proposed to Lucy, on her 33rd birthday. As they prepared for the wedding, Jason decided that Lucy's suffering would not be in vain. He set up 'Legacy 4 Lucy' to raise money for Breast Cancer Now. So far, through many Wolves-themed fundraisers, such as tonight's event, £185,000 has been raised.

The couple married in February 2015. 'Although we knew Lucy was terminally ill, we put a brave face on and we had some great friends there who had supported us,' Jason continues. 'Steve Bull and Andy Mutch came to the wedding, a lot of ex-Wolves players were there. Jody Craddock and Matt Murray were there too, they had shared our journey. They have all given up their time to do things for the charity.

'You learn more and more about the illness after that. What I do want to say is this: people say you lose a battle with cancer. No one loses their battle, it's an unfair fight from the start. You don't get cancer knocking on your door three months beforehand saying, "We're on our way." Nobody ever loses their battle.'

The club has played an important role in Jason's life ever since his first game, back in January 1989. 'Bristol City in the Sherpa Van Trophy, 3-0, Steve Bull scored a hat-trick. Job done. What I remember about that night is my mum saying we're going to the match. I come from a single-parent family so it was just me and Mum who went up to Molineux on the bus. I remember seeing all the Wolves fans and then walking in to the South Bank. I could hardly see any of the game but I was hooked.'

Many of the players from that era turn out for the Wolves All Stars, the club's former players' team that takes part in charity friendlies throughout the season. Jason, through his staff recruitment company, sponsors the team and helps manager Mel Eves find players.

'I'd kept in contact with a few former players at functions and charity events put on by the club and just introduced myself to them,' Jason explains. 'You exchange numbers and that sort of thing. We had 16 former players at the last Wolves All Stars game. You find out that they're quite a small number of players, they tend to be local and so we've helped them. I've had some of them living at my house when they've gone through marriage break-ups and the likes, it's been a halfway house for some of them. At first they're your heroes and then the next thing you've got them making breakfast for you in the morning, walking around in their pants. You soon go off them.'

So how big a role has Wolves played in his life over these last few years? 'Massive really, the first few events I did were with former players, just question and answer sessions where they gave up their time,' Jason recalls. 'We started to raise money that way. We even did a bucket collection at Wolves once, which raised a lot. That was the supporters being generous. Social media is huge and the ex-players help me out. On the whole, the Wolves community has really come together. When Paul Berry [the club's former communications manager] was here he would always retweet our appeals. I was also very fortunate to be chairman on Jody Craddock's testimonial committee and that really helped, opening a lot of doors. Jody has been a massive supporter of the work I do and vice versa.'

Craddock was the club's captain during their last promotion to the Premier League, as Championship title winners under Mick McCarthy in the 2008/09 season. In August 2002, whilst he was playing for Sunderland, Craddock's four-month-old son, Jake, died at his home from cot death. Ten years later, Craddock's two-and-a-half-year-old son Toby was diagnosed with Acute Lymphoblastic Leukaemia. He underwent a lengthy process of treatment at Birmingham Children's Hospital, before making it into remission.

'What Jody has been through is something else,' Jason says. 'I remember once, early on in his testimonial year, we were on a train up to the North East to watch Sunderland play Newcastle. We were on the train for about three hours together. I'd got to know him a bit but that particular time I was going through a tough moment with Lucy suffering from breast cancer and I asked him about his bad luck – it is down to luck, because if a young boy like Toby gets diagnosed with leukaemia, what has he done wrong?

Brian Law in action during the 1994/95 season

Steve Froggatt skips over a challenge from West Bromwich Albion's Paul Holmes during the Black Country derby in August 1997

[Left] *[Left] Paul Butler offers the linesman an alternative perspective during a First Division match in March 2002*

Wolves landlady Ann Schorah works her way through the day's ironing at her home

Ann's partner Arthur Benton makes a brew

Matt Murray with former team-mates Chris Iwelumo, George Elokobi and Matt Jarvis at a supporters' event at the Cleveland Arms in November 2018

Secretary Richard Skirrow watches on with chief executive Jez Moxey as Wolves are relegated from the Championship at Brighton in 2013

Danny Batth hitches a lift with Sam Ricketts as the pair celebrate the League One title win in May 2014

London Wolves on their way to a match during the 2016/17 season
Express & Star

Johnny Phillips interviews skipper Conor Coady during a break at Wolves' warm-weather training camp at the Marbella Football Centre in February 2019

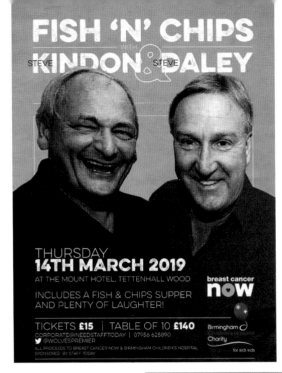

Steve Kindon and Steve Daley headlining a charity event during the 2018/19 season

Odin Henrikssen is filmed for a Sky Sports feature at his museum in Bergen, Norway, in March 2019

Supporters walk to the match under the ring road subway during the 2018/19 season

Nuno Espírito Santo heads towards supporters to celebrate Wolves' 3-1 win over Arsenal at Molineux in April 2019

'And with his other son dying through cot death, what he has been through is unimaginable. It was devastating what happened to his little boy to die like that and then for Toby to be diagnosed, I asked him how he dealt with it all. He did say he was thinking, "Why me?" But what I love about Jody is that his family is really close-knit. They just all pulled together and they showed such strength to get through it all.'

So, would it be too much of a stretch to suggest it was Wolves that helped Jason through his own tragedy? 'The reality is that Lucy passed away and the next day you wake up in an empty bed,' he says. 'There's nobody left to argue with. Wolves was a massive help in coping. Jody actually invited me to dinner that first Christmas without her. I went on holiday with him too after that, he was such a help. Steve Bull was at my wedding and after Lucy died he gave me a canvas print of the two of us. Dale Rudge was my best man. All these people were there for me when I was at my lowest point. The players have been brilliant.

'We are doing this night with Steve Kindon and Steve Daley. I bumped into Kindo at the Wolves versus Burnley game earlier this season and he was asking me how the fundraising was going and he offered to put a night on for free. He said, "You host the event and I'll drive down and do the gig." He lives over 150 miles away in Lytham St Annes. It was such a nice thing to offer to do. And then when Dales heard about it he said he'd join Steve and speak too.

'What I decided to do was get Neil involved and split the fundraising down the middle with Neil's chosen charity, the Birmingham Children's Hospital. Neil has done some amazing things. When he ran the New York marathon he split it between Birmingham Children's Hospital and Breast Cancer Now.'

Neil is 48-year-old Neil Taylor. He owns The Fox in Shipley, a well-known pub and restaurant located just a few miles west of the city, with his wife Kerry. Their daughter, Kiahna, was born in September 2006.

'We were absolutely elated,' says Neil. 'Then within 24 hours of her being born our world was blown apart when we found out she had a really serious life-threatening heart problem. She was born with a massive hole in her heart. They couldn't operate on her straight away because she was too weak, so she was put on various drugs to build her up.

'She was four months old when she had her first surgery. It was turmoil, and obviously you're worried, but at the time you just go into auto-pilot. I have had so many people ask how we coped, but we just had to. Then over the next two months she had two further operations. And since that first six months she's had two more operations.'

The Birmingham Children's Hospital became a familiar part of the Taylors' lives. 'The longest stay we had in there was around six to eight weeks. We'd be back and forth all the time, but gradually, after her last operation when she was eight, we ended up going back less and less. It took five operations to close the hole. Two years ago we were told she won't need any surgery going forward.'

After witnessing the incredible work done by the hospital, Neil decided he had to help raise funds and he has so far donated £144,000 to the hospital. Wolves proved to be a logical starting point.

'After moving into the area, at the time Don Goodman was living just up the road and he used to use The Fox,' Neil explains. 'I got to know Don that way and, through him, got to know Steve Bull. Those two, from day one when we first started the fundraising, have always got involved, either doing nights together or bringing in other players.

'I'll do the fundraising until the day I die because I've got personal reasons for it; if it wasn't for Birmingham Children's Hospital my daughter wouldn't be here. The first one we ever did was with Bully and Andy Mutch at the pub. Andy came down from Liverpool for it and we raised quite a bit of money and that's what got the ball rolling. We did one with Matt Jarvis and Bully after Matt had just won his England cap. We billed it as the last two Wolves players to play for England.'

Like Jason, Neil has found Wolves a source of support and companionship. 'It's a release from the problems you're going through,' he explains. 'I can't remember how long I've had the season ticket for, they've always been there. Wolves have always been the main go-to really. Through getting to know Paul Berry, Wolves have, without hesitation, put a piece in the programme whenever we've done our fundraisers like the marathons or Kilimanjaro. Everyone in this area is a massive Wolves fan. It was the first charity event I did, a straightforward Q and A down at The Fox. People came along who I had never met before. People like Jason, who was living across the road at the time, supported the charity. We've all become good friends.'

As well as New York, Neil's fundraising has taken in the Paris and London marathons. He has also climbed Kilimanjaro in Tanzania and Kala Patthar in the Himalayas range, as well as undertaking a cycle from John O'Groats to Land's End.

'Jason's journey began when I was training for the New York marathon,' Neil continues. 'One of the last things I did was promise Lucy that I'd run that for her. So I did the marathon in the November after Lucy died and shared the fundraising between Birmingham Children's Hospital and Breast Cancer Now. Steve Plant is another who has been an amazing supporter over the years.'

Steve Plant is the author of *They Wore The Shirt*, a definitive tome charting the history of Wolves' iconic shirts since the club's formation in 1877. The book was published in 2016 and has raised over £55,000 for Birmingham Children's Hospital. It was the culmination of a labour of love that began in 2009 when Steve's dad, John, was diagnosed with terminal pancreatic cancer. John had introduced Steve to Wolves 40 years earlier.

'My first game was in 1969 against Manchester United,' Steve recalls. 'My dad took me and my brother, Simon. I decided to follow Wolves and my brother followed United – he's had all those years winning everything. Back in those days, you used to progress from sitting on the kerbing at the front of the Waterloo Road stand at the side of the pitch, then as you got older you'd get a milk crate and stand on that. Then after that you'd go to the North Bank. I've since stood on the South Bank and had a seat in the old John Ireland Stand so I've done all four sides now.'

When doctors told John he may have as little as three months to live, the whole family was devastated. 'He never complained but he went downhill very quickly,' Steve explains. 'I decided to launch a website concentrating on Wolves memorabilia, the idea being that I would update it every day and give Dad something to look forward to. A George Elokobi shirt was the first item in the collection. It escalated very quickly after that, with every spare penny going on shirts and other memorabilia.

'Dad was proud of my collection and we talked about producing a book one day. He refused expensive operations or drugs that could have kept him alive longer, insisting the money would be better spent on those with a long life left to live. We finally lost him in July 2012, which was three years longer than he had been given. I think a lot of that was down to the shirt collection. I didn't have a single shirt when he was diagnosed, but he took a real interest and wanted to see the collection grow.'

The success of the book has taken Steve by surprise. 1,877 copies were printed, the same number as the founding year of the football club. The entire print run sold out within a year.

'I remember the first meeting I went to, it was at Wolves and they asked me if I had the money to pay for the project,' he says. 'It was the chairman of the Wolves Former Players' Association, Richard Green, who used to work at the

Express and Star, who was in the meeting and he said that he thought the book would need around £25,000 to produce.

'I excused myself and went to the toilet. I sat there thinking, "What the fuck have I done?" I thought it would cost about £5,000. But with all the photography, design and the size of it, that's what they said it would cost. I went to the bank the next day and they agreed to lend me the money, but when my brother Simon heard he wouldn't let me use the bank. He put £18,000 up front so we could get it done.'

Driven on by the success of his book, Steve found another cause close to his heart the following season. In July 2017 the club's long-serving goalkeeper Carl Ikeme was diagnosed with acute leukaemia. Just days before the start of the 2017/18 Championship season, it hit the club hard. A hugely popular 31-year-old man struck with a devastating illness in such a manner during the prime of his life.

At the time, team-mates rallied around. One of the club's youngsters, Jordan Graham, described Ikeme as 'like a second father'. David Edwards described him as 'a role model to so many'. 'One of the most genuine people you could wish to meet,' added Jed Wallace. Tony Daley, Wolves' former fitness coach, spoke of the player's fortitude for a fight. 'You've taken charge, showed courage and strength throughout your career; I know you will meet this challenge head on and win,' he wrote on hearing of the diagnosis. All those comments seemed to sum up everyone's opinion of the man. When the legendary Spanish number one Iker Casillas posted a message of support on social media it told everyone how far Ikeme's reputation reached.

The love and affection that poured in over the subsequent weeks and months meant a lot to the player, his colleagues and supporters. Many were galvanised into action. Steve took up the baton and, working closely with the Cure Leukaemia charity, organised a weekend of fundraising around the opening league match of the season against Middlesbrough in August 2017. A year of events followed, with tens of thousands of pounds raised in aid of the organisation.

'There's Only 1 Carl Ikeme' was the message throughout this time. The club put together an impressive video compilation of current and former keepers speaking or singing the message in tribute.

Ikeme retired with a proud record of service to the club. He was a quiet and calm individual who brought an air of serenity to the pressurised environment of his sport. He worked hard for everything he achieved, playing for the club over an 11-year period. In the 2013/14 season his 22 clean sheets deservedly earned him a place in the PFA League One Team of the Year. He had huge amounts of resolve that served him firstly as a player and then a person as he battled against leukaemia.

After his debut in August 2006 Ikeme suffered a knee injury that kept him out for over a year. There was no easy route back in to the first team. There were seven different loan spells after his first-team debut for Wolves. Time and time again Ikeme went out on loan before eventually winning the trust of a Wolves manager.

If ever fans thought that the fabric of the place was changing and the club was moving away from its roots then Ikeme's presence would allay those fears. He may have hailed from down the road in Birmingham, but he remained a Wolves man.

He can count all the heroes of the club's recent history as team-mates. As a 17-year-old academy graduate, Ikeme joined Paul Ince, Kenny Miller, Matt Murray and company in the first-team squad as long ago as 2003. Matt Jarvis, Michael Kightly, Kevin Doyle and many more came and went in Wolves colours alongside him too. Murray, who was Wolves' number one when Ikeme was coming through the ranks, paid him a glowing tribute on hearing the news of his retirement. 'He was 16 at the time, when I was 21 in the first team, but I always remember how brave and strong he was. He had fantastic feet and always wanted to play. He was a real athlete and he could make some absolutely unbelievable saves.

'Carl had a steely personality but was very calm as well. I was really proud to see the keeper he became. He was a one-club man but spent time at different clubs on loan in order for him to play. It seems he always had to fight for his shirt, he always had to battle, but he always ended up back in the team.'

Like Murray before him, retirement came to Ikeme at far too early a stage, but his place in the hearts of Wolves supporters is assured.

In recognition of nine months of fundraising for Cure Leukaemia that began at the start of the 2017/18 season, Steve won the Rachael Heyhoe Flint Award for outstanding service to the community at the club's End of Season Awards night in May 2018.

Steve admits that Wolves has become an all-consuming part of his life. His understanding wife, Andrea, has been at his side helping wherever possible. He is self-employed, and went weeks at a time without working in order to get his book published. But there was never a question of giving up on it.

'The most time I spent with my dad, when it was just us two, was at the football,' says Steve. 'To go to the games now, you don't forget that. I asked the club if I could scatter his ashes at Molineux but they didn't allow it. Me, being me, we had Dad's cremation on the Friday and the next day I took him down to the game and scattered the ashes myself, inside and outside the ground.'

Steve, Neil and Jason have seen Kindon and Daley perform on many occasions. Of the many after-dinner speakers on the circuit, the Wolves duo are among the most popular. Kindon has won the Soccer Speaker of the Year on five occasions. Both men have carved out successful second careers with their self-deprecating sense of humour.

There was a time when Daley was the most talked about footballer in the country. It was September 1979. A goalscoring midfielder, he had played 244 games in eight years for Wolves, most of them in the top division, scoring an impressive 43 goals. Earlier that year, in February, Trevor Francis had become the first million-pound footballer with his move from Birmingham City to Nottingham Forest. His unveiling was slightly different to today's photo calls. Forest manager Brian Clough stood over Francis wearing a tracksuit whilst brandishing a racquet, as the deal had delayed Clough on his way to play a game of squash. Seven months later, Daley had little idea that his own fee would consign Francis's record move to the history books.

'I remember I was lying in bed at two in the morning and the phone went,' Daley says. 'It was someone from the club saying I needed to be ready at nine in the morning to go up to speak to City. I met Malcolm Allison [the Manchester City manager] and when the fee was discussed I just thought it was astronomical money. One million, four hundred and thirty-seven thousand, five hundred pounds – not that it sticks in my mind or anything!'

To put the figure in context, the British transfer record was broken again only twice in the following six years; when Wolves immediately reinvested their profits from the Daley transfer in acquiring Andy Gray from Aston Villa, and then in 1981, when Bryan Robson moved from West Bromwich Albion to Manchester United for £1.5million.

Whereas Francis took the opportunity to repay some of his huge fee early on in his Forest career, with the winning goal in the European Cup Final in May 1979 against Malmo in Munich, Daley was afforded no such stage on which to parade his talents. Instead, he arrived at a club going through a major upheaval.

'When I signed for City, the club sold four players: Gary Owen, Asa Hartford, Peter Barnes and Mick Channon,' he explains. 'They sold four internationals and replaced them with me. Everyone was thinking I'd be able to replace those and make the side tick. It was a transitional time for the club with some really young players coming in like Tommy Caton, Steve MacKenzie and Nicky Reid. It was going to take time to gel together and become a team, and unfortunately it didn't work.'

City were rebuilding and Allison's spending, which included the untried MacKenzie and Michael Robinson, just didn't work out. Daley's form suffered and he became emblematic of the side's failings. Of that record transfer, Allison would later blame his chairman Peter Swales for going above his head and dealing direct with the Wolves board, which got the deal done more quickly but at an inflated cost. The nadir was probably an FA Cup third-round defeat in 1980 to Fourth Division Halifax Town at The Shay.

'First Division against Fourth Division in the cup and we're losing 1-0 with 15 minutes to go,' remembers Daley. 'I looked around our team out on the pitch and it cost about £8.5million to assemble. NASA only spent £10million getting a man to the moon and we couldn't get past Halifax.'

It is a nice line. Daley is incredibly self-deprecating about his career, which fell off a cliff with the move to Manchester City. Despite his troubles at Maine Road, he was a fine player, but he now makes a living telling everyone how bad he was.

'I'm a success now at talking about being a failure. I sat down with Kindo, who is a great pal of mine and a really accomplished after-dinner speaker, and a comedian called Gary Marshall, and we put some stories together.'

Later that evening, those stories trip off Daley's tongue. The laughter rolls around the room as Daley talks about a time in his career that would have destroyed lesser men. Twenty months after his arrival at Maine Road, and with Allison's second spell at the club also over, Daley took his leave.

'When it didn't work at Manchester City it was a low time in my career and I thought the best thing to do was to get as far away as I could and start again,' Daley adds. 'An offer came in from Seattle Sounders. I was fortunate, although I didn't realise it at the time, because a lot of other teams in the North American Soccer League had brought other foreign players in from Yugoslavia, Germany, Argentina, Brazil and Mexico, but Seattle was basically an English team, coached by Alan Hinton. We had big Joe Corrigan in goal, Bruce Rioch, David Nish, Alan Hudson, Rodger Davies, Kenny Hibbitt and Tommy Hutchison. We had a top side and it was a great two years in my career. I really enjoyed it.'

In 1983 Daley returned to England, joining Burnley, before heading back to the United States a year later to sign for the San Diego Sockers. His professional career eventually ended at Walsall in 1986. It was a career to be proud of. Despite being an unused substitute for Wolves in both legs of the 1972 UEFA Cup Final, Daley played a key role in the cup run with the winning goal in the semi-final against Ferencvaros. He was also capped six times at England 'B' level, in an era when full caps were not handed out so freely. But it was the move to City for which he is remembered. And listening to him on stage, it was a move that has eventually paid off.

'It was only when he told me I could do it,' Daley says, pointing at his former team-mate, recalling the moment he decided to give public speaking a chance. 'The two main jokers in the Wolves dressing room were myself and Kindo. He believed in me.'

Kindon's story cuts to his childhood. 'You may have notisched schomething,' he tells the audience, hamming up his affliction. 'I'm an after-dinner schpeaker, who can't fucking schpeak!' Kindon's speech impediment with the letter S has become the basis for his act. Throughout his childhood he was self-conscious in public. Then, one day, just after breaking into the Burnley first team at the age of 17, it all changed.

'It was 1968, I had just made my First Division debut in the April for Burnley,' Kindon reveals. 'That summer, as soon as the league season was over, they kept mowing the pitch and kept the posts up. Around the time of the FA Cup Final they had a schools final on Turf Moor. It was all the Burnley area schools. I was 17 and I went along to watch it on the Wednesday night. The sun was shining, and I was wearing jeans and a t-shirt. I was watching the game and this steward came over to speak to me. "Mr Potts would like to see you," he said. Harry Potts was the manager of Burnley at the time, and he was sat in the director's box and must have seen me down by the pitch.

'I went to see him and he told me to go home, have a shave and get changed because I'd be presenting the prizes. "Why me?" I said. And the gaffer said, "Another player, Brian O'Neil, was supposed to do it but he's let us down." So I ran all the way home, two miles away, got cleaned up, had a shave and put a suit on. I missed the game that I wanted to see.

'I'm just expecting it to be like the Queen when I get back, present the medals, handshake, "How do you do? Well done." That sort of thing. But Harry said, "No, no, no. There's a dinner on at the Town Hall and you're going to make a speech."'

Kindon recalls the evening event that changed his life with a near photographic memory. 'I'm 17. I'm on the top table with Bob Lord, the chairman, and his wife. This fella stands up at the end of the meal. "My lord lieutenant," he says. "Mr Mayor, Lady Mayoress, Mr Chairman, ladies and gentlemen, boys and girls." Well, that's me finished. How am I going to remember that? He did three minutes and the next person stands up, and the same thing happens.

'Then it comes to me, and I'm supposed to be doing the big speech that Brian O'Neil was down to do. I lean over to the chairman and say, "I can't do this, I'm shitting myself. I've got a speech impediment, I just can't do it." And he replies, "Stephen, look out there. What do you see? Look at the kids. Every kid in this room wants to be you. Stephen, stand up and speak to the kids. Forget the mayor, forget me. Speak to those kids and tell them what it is to live your dream." That was it, I was off.

'So I was the one at Burnley after that who went to do the hospital visits or present the school prizes. It helped me overcome the embarrassment about the lisp. Then, when I was at Wolves, the manager, Bill McGarry, decided to have a member of the coaching staff and three players go out to Wolverhampton companies and organisations one evening a week throughout the season. I went on the first one, and then a rota went up for each week. Bill had me down on every single week. I went to see him to say it wasn't fair. "But you're good at it," he said.'

It is more than 40 years since Daley and Kindon were team-mates at Wolves. But, like so many Wolves players from their era, they have remained good friends.

'I went to the Wolves Former Players' Association dinner last year,' Kindon continues. 'John Richards, Kenny Hibbitt, Willie Carr and the rest. We're all around 70 years old. We're of an age where we don't expect too many people of that generation to turn up at these things. Do you know how many of our era did? Seventeen.

'For us, it wasn't just about training together or being team-mates, we socialised together. I remember going to Norway for a summer tour one year. We played a game in Oslo, we must have travelled for three or four hours. When we got there it was 2:30am, and Alan Sunderland and I went out and played a game of tennis. The sun never sets up there in the summer, so we went out just to say we had a game of tennis at half two in the morning. We were pals. We'd turn up at Fordhouses to watch Lofty [goalkeeper Phil Parkes] play his cricket in the summer.'

Kindon is in full flow, now. 'Let me tell you something. If you say Steve Daley, the next name is Alan Sunderland. If you say Kenny Hibbitt, then it's Willie Carr. John Richards – Steve Kindon. Frank Munro – Dave Wagstaffe. Derek Parkin – John McAlle. Do you know what I'm talking about? It's room partners. We got to a hotel on an away trip and Sammy Chung [Bill McGarry's assistant manager] would shout out something like, "401 John Richards". He'd never need to say "Steve Kindon", we would just pair off. It was automatic. We were pals.

'Now, it's a different dynamic. They get off the coach with their headphones on and they all have double rooms with single occupancy, and they're on their iPads all the time. We were of an age.'

Many in the audience, such as Jason, were too young to see Kindon and Daley play. But they feel a strong affinity with them, nonetheless.

'You feel like you've known these people all your life, it is such easy conversation,' says Jason. 'These nights are great fun. London Wolves have got a table, they've come up early for the Manchester United game on Saturday. The two Steves were in the team when London Wolves first got going so it's nice that they're here tonight. It's great being able to do these things. The club is such an important part of the city, right in the centre and we are a one-club city.'

Steve Plant agrees. 'Whenever you go to anything Wolves-related, there are people and ex-players you've never met before. The likes of John Richards and Kenny Hibbitt, they're all fantastic blokes. People I watched and idolised, they feel like mates at these sort of events. Do you get that everywhere? I don't know.'

Two days later, Molineux is the stage for a match of real theatre. One of those, 'It'll be talked about for years to come' nights. Manchester United are beaten 2-1 in an FA Cup quarter-final under the floodlights. The quality and intensity of the performance on the pitch from Nuno

Espírito Santo's team is matched by the energy and passion of the supporters in the stands. Evening kick-offs bring out the fire in Wolves fans. Maybe a Saturday off in the pub had something to do with it too. The two goals are greeted with raging elation, almost primal screams. Steve and Neil were in their usual spot in the Stan Cullis Stand. Jason was over in the Steve Bull Stand. The three of them surrounded by friends, new and old.

It is tempting, also, to wonder if the links between those in the stands and the current crop on the pitch will be the same in years to come. The star names from overseas have brought so much happiness to the club's supporters. They have evoked those distant times when Wolves won trophies. João Moutinho, Raúl Jiménez and Rúben Neves are unlikely to set foot in the city ever again, once their own playing days have passed. Maybe that does not really matter. Bonds are revealed in many different ways.

'I know we're paying Moutinho and the rest of them a lot of money, but he could have been paid a lot of money in London,' says Steve. 'Neves, and this is what I love, when he has a day off, he takes his missus and kids around West Park. They all do their shopping in that new Sainsbury's on the ring road. Rui Patrício was having his picture taken in there the other day. Not Harrods in London, Sainsbury's in Wolverhampton.'

Chapter 16

HOME AND AWAY

Danny Batth – A role model for all times

IN THE summer of 2017 Danny Batth set out on a life-affirming adventure. When he travelled to Jharkhand province, in the desert region of north-east India, he was not sure what to expect. Travelling with his partner Natalie Ann Cutler, Batth was heading for a girls' school run by the Yuwa India Trust.

The project was set up in 2009 when Franz Gastler, an American who had been working in Delhi as a business consultant, moved to Jharkhand and witnessed the striking disparity between the lives of boys and girls. He began to help the girls challenge this social inequality through participation in team sports and education.

Yuwa means 'Youth' in Hindi. What began with Yuwa setting up one football team, quickly grew. Now, ten years later, there are over 300 girls playing in the project's various football teams, with 90 per cent of those teams coached by women.

The pitches are often marked out in unused agricultural fields or dusty strips of flattened land on the outskirts of villages, but that does not seem to matter to these footballers.

Six years after Yuwa was founded, the first school was opened, with the aim of empowering the girls further and giving them the tools to go on to higher education. Girls between the ages of six and 18 are taught by qualified teachers from India and abroad, and many do indeed go on to further education.

Batth spent his days there coaching football to the pupils on the dusty pitches dotted around the few trees that grow on the land. The lifestyle was as basic as he could have imagined, but the trip was an extremely rewarding one. They were two weeks of his life that will remain with him forever.

'We slept on beds that were solid boards, with just a mosquito net covering us,' Batth says. 'It was a proper experience of what it was like. It was really humbling, an unreal thing to experience.'

Batth was in the process of setting up his charity, Foundation DB, to help some of the most vulnerable in society. There were two key areas where he wanted to make a contribution: around his home in Wolverhampton and in his partial homeland, India. Batth was the first player of Indian descent to represent Wolves. His mother is English and his father is from the Punjab region of north India.

'We hadn't started the foundation at that point but, being half Indian, as well as working with a charity in England, I wanted to find an Indian one,' Batth continues. 'I was keen to work in a developing world country and I wanted it to be around sport, and particularly football, so we found a charity in India looking out for girls who were having a really tough upbringing. A lot of girls who are looked after by the charity would have been married by the age of 12, in arranged marriages. It is exploitation really. Yuwa is a school set up to take girls in who may be suffering domestic violence or at risk of being sex trafficked. It's a way of giving them confidence and a voice. In India, some women are very much silenced, especially in rural areas like these, it's a very poor area. Some of the girls have a ridiculous schedule to their lives. They're up at four in the morning walking to wells to get pails of water for the day. Then they start cooking, cleaning, looking after kids, or working in fields. Yuwa is basically delivering an education to girls who wouldn't normally get it.

'My girlfriend produced a fly-on-the-wall documentary [*Married to the Game*] following me around for the trip. We had a great time, we formed a partnership with them straight away. We support Yuwa through the foundation and last year we raised £15,000. Each little team has to save up for a football which takes a group of five or six of them ten weeks to save up for. That football means a lot to them and they value it more than we do over here. We've even had a couple of girls over recently; my girlfriend took them to the Houses of Parliament.'

Growing up in Brierley Hill, in the Black Country, Batth was aware of his Indian heritage, but it was never something that was forced upon him.

'It was weird really, growing up we'd go to a lot of Indian weddings, we'd eat the food, but my dad never taught me how to speak the language,' he explains. 'My mum and dad wanted us to have an English upbringing. At the time when they met it wasn't a common thing for an Indian man and a white woman to get together. Especially within Indian culture, to be with a white girl, it wasn't necessarily accepted straight away. They didn't want me to worry about colour, just to live a normal upbringing. We'd do the traditional things, like going to the temples, and weddings are a big thing in India, I used to love going to the weddings. I've got lots of aunties and uncles who I keep in touch with. It was only when I was 15 or 16 that I understood the politics of it a bit more.'

Batth was nine years old when he began schoolboy training with Aston Villa. But he was not enjoying his football and it placed a strain on the family, with his father having to make a work commute back from Wales before taking him to training. He began enjoying Sunday League football with Swinmoor Rangers, and a year later he represented his primary school playing as a midfielder for the Brierley Hill and Dudley District against a team from Stoke-on-Trent. It was during this representative game that he was spotted by Les Green, Wolves' schoolboy scout, who was also responsible for bringing Joleon Lescott to the club.

'From that age of ten up to 15, we attended school as normal and used to train at Aldersley Stadium on Tuesdays and Thursdays. You'd get a one-year contract each year, and about six weeks before the end of each season you'd find out if you were being kept on another year. I was made centre-back because I was taller than everyone else. I sulked for a little while, I thought I was good enough to play in midfield. But I got used to it, I was good in the air. I used to be on the free kicks when I was in midfield but the coaches soon stopped that!

'There were seven of us who went on to sign the scholarship scheme – Ashley Hemmings, Scott Malone, Kyle Bennett, Johnny Dunleavy, Sam Winnall and a goalkeeper who didn't stay in the game. I used to walk 15 minutes from home and catch two buses to get to training – it was Brierley Hill to Dudley and Dudley to Wolverhampton in those days.'

Despite the progress he was making, Batth knew he was a long way from making the grade as a professional. He had ambition and drive, though.

'I wrote a list of every centre-half who was between me and the first team, and I used to watch the next one in front of me and see what he was doing, thinking that if I could do that better I'd be ahead of him. And I literally did that all the way through until I got to Jody Craddock, who was the last one. I ended up playing with him in the reserves and started breaking into the first-team squad.

'I actually had a bit of a setback when I was a first-year scholar. On my debut I dislocated my shoulder, which put me out for three months. I came back and did it again, so that was six months out of my first year. When I finally returned I was twice the size, having done all the lifting in the gym every day. So I think that helped me in a strange way.'

Batth was part of a youth team that was called up by Mick McCarthy and Terry Connor to work with the first XI on a Friday afternoon for set piece routines. It was 2008/09, the season Wolves won the Championship.

'They used to call us the "Red Mist". The young lads were bang up for it, knocking the likes of Sylvan Ebanks-Blake around as much as we could, trying to make a bit of an impression. The first team used to hate it. The day before a game they were wrapped up in cotton wool and there we were, flying in to headers and tackles.'

Loan spells at Colchester United and Sheffield United in League One served as an introduction to professional football, but it was the year spent with Sheffield Wednesday for the 2011/12 season that proved to be the making of Batth. Under former Wolves boss Dave Jones, Wednesday won promotion to the Championship.

'I was runner-up in their Player of the Year award, I was buzzing about that,' Batth says. 'That was my breakthrough season, where I was either going to go back and play for Wolves or would have to move on elsewhere.'

Batth returned to a club in turmoil. Relegated from the Premier League, Wolves took a new direction in the Championship by appointing Norwegian coach Stale Solbakken. The camaraderie of the McCarthy era had disappeared from the dressing room.

'Stale signed seven or eight lads that we had never heard of. The best of them was Bakary Sako. There was Tongo Doumbia, Razak Boukari, Bjorn Sigurdarson, Georg Margreitter and a couple of others. Razak, Tongo and Bakary were the three we thought were decent. It looked quite promising early on, he structured the team in a way that was really European, keeping the ball, really short distances between the lines. But I remember playing a friendly against Shrewsbury Town and we were trying to use this high line and they were literally getting in every time. What he hadn't realised was that teams were taking two touches and shelling it in behind. So as we were on our way up as a back four, the strikers were already timing their runs in, going through on goal.

'We did alright for a little bit in the Championship, but there was one particular team we couldn't get near in one game. I remember going into training after that, and the captain Karl Henry and Stale had a big row about his position, whether or not Karl could go and press. I think it was a ten-metre distance that Karl wanted to come out and press, but Stale was telling him to stay. Literally, training stopped for 15 minutes while they were having a debate over it.'

Batth insists that the players did get on board with the change in style, but Solbakken was dismissed in January and replaced with Dean Saunders. 'Dean came off the back of doing well at Doncaster,' Batth recalls. 'It was a shock from the fans' point of view, but the chairman gave it him on merit, the fact he'd done well at Doncaster in League One. He probably was not the name the fans wanted, though.'

Saunders could not do enough to prevent relegation. It proved to be a testing first full season in Wolves colours for Batth, who was used sparingly.

'It was difficult but I was just trying to learn all the time,' Batth adds. 'Even with Stale, they were different methods but I felt I could get something out of it because one day I might play for a continental manager. I remember Stale bringing me on in defensive midfield a few times, so it was all a good experience really.'

With Wolves down in League One, Batth was given his chance to shine. New manager Kenny Jackett put together a young team built by the club's academy system. Youth team graduates Jack Price, Zeli Ismail, Liam McAlinden, David Davis, Carl Ikeme and Ethan Ebanks-Landell joined Batth in the first team that season. Batth was an ever-present in the side, as Wolves ran away with the League One title.

'So many young lads featured, it was great for the academy and the fans started to recognise that these lads wanted to play for the club,' Batth says. 'For us boys coming through, we were determined, we were fit, and Kenny gave us that platform to perform. The new captain Sam Ricketts was another one I learnt from. I'd learnt a lot from Karl, who had been there a long time, but Sam was almost the polar opposite to Karl in the way he led the team. Karl was quite vocal, old school. Sam was quieter but just set an example. I thought if I could be somewhere in between those two I'd be alright.'

During this time, when Batth was establishing himself in the team, Punjabi Wolves Supporters got in touch with the player. It was at the 2003 First Division play-off final in Cardiff when Punjabi Wolves first took a flag to the match, and it heralded the beginning of their supporters' group, which was officially founded in 2007. Their formation was still some years after the first two known Punjabis attended a fixture at Molineux. Laskar Singh and Lachhman Singh went to a game in 1954, the year Wolves won the first of their three league titles, and are recognised by the group as pioneers of sorts.

'We called it Punjabi Wolves because that's our background and our heritage,' says Pete Bassi, one of the co-founders. 'We wanted to let other people experience that culture, not as a religious thing, we're fans first and foremost. We just wanted to show that it was not just middle-aged Caucasians going to games, there's support across the board from BAMEs. You know Wolverhampton, it's very multicultural, but that hasn't always been represented at Molineux.'

Like all parts of the West Midlands, Wolverhampton has a large Asian community. The diversity is something to be proud of for the city. But, as with any multicultural area in the country, there have been tensions and challenges too. Enoch Powell was MP for Wolverhampton South West between 1950 and 1974. After he delivered his infamous 'Rivers of Blood' speech, strongly criticising immigration, at a Conservative Party meeting in Birmingham in April 1968, he was dismissed from Edward Heath's shadow cabinet. But opinion polls in the United Kingdom at the time revealed as much as 75 per cent of the population supported his stance. They were hard times for immigrants.

'That [Powell's speech] had been lingering on,' says Bassi. 'I was born in 1970. When we were growing up there was a bit of tension. We were the first Asian family to move to a new estate, and on one of the first days there we went over to play in the park. We were approached by a group of Caucasian lads who said, "No Pakis allowed in this park." They outnumbered us, so we just left. But then as we grew up and more of our cousins moved to the area it wasn't as bad. Nobody is born racist, it is your upbringing and who you meet. Lots of factors define how you turn out.'

The terraces of the 70s and 80s all across England were generally the preserve of the white male. Far right groups, such as the National Front, would openly recruit outside grounds and on the terraces. Stadiums have changed beyond recognition since then, along with the demographic of supporters.

'I've never personally had an issue at a football match,' Bassi continues. 'Attending games with Wolves is a really positive experience. Football is so family orientated with lots of events going on. That hooligan element seems to have gone; it still happens occasionally, but it's marginalised. Like any place that's multicultural, Wolverhampton has its problems but the vast majority of people get on. Our motto is "Local Sport, Local Pride". We are born and bred in Wolverhampton and we are proud of our local football club.'

The Punjabi Wolves Supporters number over 500 members today, with a message of inclusivity at the core of their existence.

'At the FA Cup semi-final against Watford in April this year we took four coaches, and there were 70 per cent non-Asians on board, it was fantastic, absolutely brilliant,' Bassi explains. 'We take our drum – called the dohl – with us and everyone loves it. At Wembley we contacted a pub in Hayes and had food put on and we stopped off before the match and just enjoyed the day. We got the drum out and everyone was dancing away and singing Wolves songs.'

'They contacted me quite quickly once I broke into the team,' says Batth. 'They started asking would I help out with this, or come to events, and I'd always try to be there. I still keep in touch with them now, it's a great community thing and Wolves obviously have a huge Asian following.'

'We associate ourselves with a few grassroots clubs in Wolverhampton and we always said we wanted to see an Asian footballer make it,' Bassi adds. 'We were fortunate that Danny broke through and got into the first team. He was very receptive to us, and he became an ambassador of Punjabi Wolves. When he set up his own foundation he approached us to help with his events, which we were more than happy to do. He's such a strong character, and a really good lad.'

When Ricketts was transferred out of Molineux in the summer of 2015, Batth became club captain, which brought further responsibilities in the community.

'As captain I went on a lot of the school visits, learning how to speak in public more,' he says. 'I was that kid once, and I never met anyone famous so I thought it was important to do that. There was no switching off, because I'm from the area. It took its toll a little bit, but it means a lot to be someone who has come all the way through like that, living everyone's dream really.'

As captain, Batth played a key role when Wolves went through significant upheaval during the 2016/17 campaign, Fosun's first as owners of the club. Former Italian goalkeeper Walter Zenga's brief tenure as head coach was one of the more surreal times in the club's history.

'Again, it was another learning experience. I actually thought Walter was a great, genuinely nice guy. I still keep in touch with him now. He always says, "My captain, my captain!" It's funny, and I had a good relationship with him. We had some good wins that season, Newcastle away was phenomenal. We were starting to click, then it just nose-dived. I think what happened was that the recruitment under-shot the league a bit. We signed young lads that perhaps weren't ready, there was a big overhaul of players. The club was at that transition stage.

'Walter had this great Italian mind set, he was so steely, aggressive. It was all about being aggressive in defence, I liked that bit. He was so passionate. He used to have these funny sayings as his English wasn't the best. If you passed the ball and it came bobbling in he'd say, "Take the kangaroo out of the ball." He lives on the Palm in Dubai, so home is this kind of paradise. I'm sure when it was pissing down with rain at Compton he was thinking, "This place isn't for me."'

The following season, 2017/18, was Batth's last at the club, but it proved to be the most successful. He made just 16 league appearances, but played his part in taking Wolves back into the Premier League.

'We saw the kind of players they were bringing in. Rúben Neves was the marquee signing, so we weren't sceptical,' Batth recalls. 'I remember we played the first game against Middlesbrough, and they were favourites to go up. One of their lads made a mistake at the back and we won 1-0. From there it just snowballed. By the back end of September we were really confident, shifting the ball really well, and it was totally different to what anyone else was doing. We had good players but also players playing in positions that brought them on a level, like Conor Coady and Matt Doherty.'

Coady assumed the role of on-field captain when Batth was not selected for the starting XI. The Liverpudlian missed just one league game all season. Both men lifted the Championship trophy together in front of a full house at Molineux after the final home game of the season, against Sheffield Wednesday – the club Batth had proved his credentials at six years earlier.

'We saw it coming and knew we were up, but to win the league was the big thing, winning it in the fashion we did,' he adds. 'That Wolves side were one of the best teams ever to go up, it's the benchmark. I always wanted to get the team back into the Premier League, nobody can take that away from me. In the early days, when we were going away to Morecambe and getting beaten, I was thinking, "We've got a long way to go, here."'

Batth had achieved his aim, but with his opportunities restricted in the Championship, it was inevitable he would have to look elsewhere for regular football once Wolves reached the Premier League.

'It was a gradual thing, not playing regularly. It wasn't easy, but as captain you've got to be behind the manager, and I think I was good for him like that. Some people do throw the toys out of the pram but whoever is playing in my position I respect them, it's my job to get back in.'

Batth's new challenge is at Stoke City. It is late afternoon by the time we meet up on a midweek summer afternoon ahead of the 2019/20 season, following a long pre-season training session under the club's young manager, Nathan Jones. Chatting at a restaurant just around the corner from their impressive Clayton Wood training ground, it is clear Batth has settled in well.

There is a healthy ex-Wolves contingent in the Potteries now, with Benik Afobe, Sam Vokes and Stephen Ward amongst his team-mates. 'We're all a little bit older, and a bit wiser now.'

At 28, Batth is reaching the peak of his career. His hope is to return to Molineux one day with a promoted team. He may not have played in the Premier League, but his role on and off the pitch since breaking into the first team at Molineux has been hugely appreciated.

'If you're full-hearted and honest, fans recognise that. I've had good and bad games, but when you leave they always see the bigger picture.'

So, apart from being his local club, what is it that makes Wolves so important in his life?

'Everyone is so passionate about it. It's those highs and lows, the rollercoaster that is Wolves, it's almost addictive for fans. Molineux is special in itself, an iconic stadium. The home game against Rotherham at the end of the season in League One, when we won 6-4, was everything about being a Wolves fan or a Wolves player in one single game. So good and so bad at the same time. It was just carnage, one of the maddest games I've ever played in. Those fans backing the club in League One can enjoy what's happening there now.'

The passion from the stands can sometimes boil over into frustration. Batth knows there were times when he was on the end of criticism but, as a local player living through it all, he makes an interesting observation on the relationship between players and supporters at Wolves:

'It is like a sibling relationship. You obviously love each other but at the same time you can have a big bust up every now and then, or throw the toys out of the pram. You might have a few good days or a few bad days but you're still brothers, do you know what I mean? Wolves fans see the players like that, they love the players but they'll have days when they give them a really hard time, and that's accepted.'

Batth has not left Wolverhampton behind, though. As well as the work in India, Foundation DB supports an important cause close to home.

'We founded a charity in the Black Country, YMCA Open Door, which looks after kids on the streets between the ages of 12 and 18,' Batth reveals. 'I wanted to make sure the foundation helped give opportunities to kids that they might not otherwise have. The response from Wolves fans has been really good. We've done a few events in Wolverhampton that sold out. The auctions do well, I think Rúben Neves's boots went for £800 at one event. It's great support for the foundation.

'We're also doing work now with Help Refugees [which supports the most vulnerable people at refugee centres across Europe]. It's about raising awareness. Everyone wants to know what footballers are up to, so by getting involved with this it helps the charities. It's also about raising money and helping with equipment, clothes or shelter. I can auction a shirt I've worn in a game and the money raised keeps a kid off the street for a couple of nights. One thing you can forget when playing football is just how universal it is. Every country in the world plays it, even if it's not their number-one sport.

'Every single person at some point in their family history will have been a refugee or an immigrant, that's the way I look at it. My dad emigrated to England. Football breaks down barriers because people who might never speak to each other, when you're playing a game of football you don't care, do you? You have a laugh, have a kick-around and anyone can do it. I've got so much out of this sport so why can't other people?'

Batth takes everything in his stride these days. More than any other player of his generation at Molineux, he has been aware of the hopes he carried on his shoulders, and the example he needed to set. A local talent who wanted to see his club restored to the top. A talisman for the Asian community he grew up around. A captain who understood his duties inside the dressing room and his responsibilities to the community outside. Danny Batth is a role model worth his weight in gold.

Chapter 17

A COACHING REVOLUTION

Nuno Espírito Santo's Team

FOUR GROUNDSMEN are preparing to dig up a large rectangle of turf around the edge of the 18-yard box on one of the four full-size pitches at the Marbella Football Centre. The facility on the outskirts of Puerto Banus, on Spain's Costa del Sol, is being used by Wolves for a week during a mid-season warm weather training camp in February. Nuno Espírito Santo's team has travelled out to the Mediterranean coast on the back of three successive Premier League wins. They sit seventh in the 2018/19 table.

The training session has come to an end. Most of the players have wandered off to get changed, leaving the ground staff to assess the damage. For the previous half an hour this same patch of grass was subjected to sustained and repetitive use as Nuno's first-team squad undertook a specific free-kick drill. So intensively did the players repeat the routine that the ground staff decided it was better to completely replace this section of turf, about 4x8 metres in total, rather than repair it.

It was a seemingly straightforward set piece. João Moutinho took free kicks from close to the left and right touchlines, approximately ten yards further out from the edge of the penalty area. Rúben Neves stood on the D of the box instructing the players to hold their position on the edge of the area, before shouting at them to drop back at the exact moment the ball was struck. In unison, the attackers and defenders would drop into the box and challenge for the ball.

Throughout the drill, Nuno watched from the far post, switching positions whenever Moutinho switched sides of the pitch. Goalkeeping coach Rui Barbosa watched at the near post. Assistant head coach Rui Pedro Silva observed from a position in line with the players on the edge of the box, whilst first-team coaches Ian Cathro and Julio Figueroa stood close to Moutinho. Each coach contributed to the session at various stages, making the smallest positional adjustments when necessary. To those of us watching from the stands, including a handful of Wolves fans and a couple of club media staff, it was impossible to dissect the minutiae of the exercise.

Five coaches overseeing one set piece. There is an intensity of detail and practice to everything Nuno does. He is quite often the first man on the training pitch each morning, setting up the drills himself. What has happened at Wolves since he arrived at Molineux with his assistants in June 2016 is a coaching revolution.

Conor Coady, an inspirational captain whose career was reinvigorated with the arrival of Nuno, cannot speak highly enough of the changes that have taken place. He has wandered over for a chat before heading back to the team hotel, with the groundsmen still busily working behind him.

'His attention to detail is brilliant,' Coady explains. 'His ideas are fantastic in terms of how he sets you up on the training field, how he wants you to play. We go through things over and over again. He has different ways of pressing, having possession of the ball, opening the pitch up. It's sensational and I love listening to him and his ideas.'

Moutinho, the hugely talented Portuguese international midfielder who has worked with vastly experienced coaches such as Claudio Ranieri, Carlos Queiroz and Luiz Felipe Scolari, is another who has been impressed by Nuno's outlook.

'It's my first time working with the coach, he's very good,' Moutinho agrees. 'How he thinks about football is important for us. He has passion for the things we do at training, and wants to do everything better and better, that's important.'

As a player, Nuno only ever watched football from two places. This has played an important role in defining his work as a coach. During an 18-year career, which began at Vitória Guimarães in 1992 and ended with Porto in 2010, he spent the majority of first-team games on the substitutes' bench. Here, he was in prime position to pay close attention to the work of the coaching staff who helped influence his career path. There was a three-year halcyon spell under the tutelage of Jose Mourinho, whose Porto side won the domestic Primeira Liga, on two occasions, Taca de Portugal, UEFA Cup and Champions League.

The remainder of Nuno's experience was picked up as a goalkeeper on the pitch, from the position of the goalmouth. This was perhaps the most formative part. Nuno's ideology for the shape and style of his team came from here. Even now, when analysing matches after the event, his preferred view is from a camera angle high behind the goal.

'I think, because I was a goalkeeper, the way I see the game helps me realise the space, the movement and the distance between the players,' the head coach says. 'I can really look and analyse it from there. The reality is on the side as well, but I already spend so much time on the bench.'

Nuno's employment of a three-man defence worked wonders in his first two seasons in charge at Wolves. It is a system he has enjoyed significant triumphs with. When he led Valencia to Champions League qualification in the 2014/15 La Liga season, there was a victory over Carlo Ancelotti's Real Madrid that earned widespread acclaim in Spain. Real were looking unbeatable, on the back of a 22-game winning streak. They turned up at the Mestalla with an abundance of attacking options. Cristiano Ronaldo, Karim Benzema and Gareth Bale formed a three-pronged forward line. Behind them were Toni Kroos, James Rodriguez and Isco.

Nuno fought fire with fire, entrusting defensive duties to Lucas Orban, Nicolas Otamendi and Shkodran Mustafi. He pushed the wing-backs, Pablo Piatti and Antonio Barragan, so far forward and wide that Real's midfield was dragged out of shape, giving Valencia the numbers in the middle they required to dominate the ball. After falling a goal behind, Nuno's team went on to win 2-1. Real lost La Liga by two points that season.

There is nothing revolutionary about playing three at the back. Wolves fans of a certain age will remember Mark McGhee doing so throughout most of his tenure in the mid-90s, when Ade Williams, Keith Curle and Dean Richards were the men usually found at the heart of the defence. This is something completely different, though. Watching Nuno's Wolves from behind the goal can be a far more enlightening place than from the traditional main camera angle high up on the side. It is as if all 11 players are connected by ropes, moving from side to side, up and down, in unison. To say they are well drilled is an under-statement. Key to this success has been ensuring the players buy into the plan.

During Nuno's first week at the club's Compton Park training base, club captain Danny Batth knocked on the door of the new head coach's office. Batth had seen too many managerial changes over the previous 12 months. Nuno was the fourth permanent appointment in less than a year. Batth was, quite naturally, concerned at the turnover of coaching staff. Nuno sat him down and took out a sheet of paper from his notebook.

He wrote down the word 'player' and put a circle around it. Then he marked out all the different branches coming out of the circle, representing the various coaches, departments and infrastructure at the club. 'We're here to make you better. It's all going to be around you,' Nuno said. The players bought into everything the coach asked of them. He immediately won the respect and trust of the dressing room. Even those who had featured significantly under the previous management and were marginalised early on, such as Jack Price and David Edwards, left the club bearing Nuno no grudges. The head coach quickly won supporters over, too. Now he is almost deified, such is the worship that comes down from the stands for a man who has made this impact in so short a space of time. Maybe Wolves supporters were ready for this approach. The Molineux crowd, so often keen to see the ball moved forward quickly, showed uncharacteristic patience during the opening games of Nuno's tenure. They saw what was happening.

Sitting down at the side of one of the sun-kissed pitches after training, Ryan Bennett is another who appreciates the total dedication to the job from the coaches. A free transfer from Norwich City, the central defender was the last signing under the previous manager, Paul Lambert.

'At the training ground, after lunch we usually go home. Out here you see a lot more of the work that they are doing, so you really see the time they actually put in,' Bennett explains. 'They're sitting around the hotel, always working or in meetings, always with their pens out or with an iPad on. They're always thinking about something they can do, something that can be made better. And that goes for the football and outside of the football. They're trying to do everything they can to provide the best they can for the lads.'

Nuno's devotion to his 'idea', as he calls it, has permeated right through the club. At every age group, the players are being introduced to Nuno's systems and shape so that when academy players and those from the under-23s step up into the first-team squad they are familiar with Nuno's way of working.

'From a personal point of view, I've never worked with someone who has been so consistent in their ideas,' says veteran keeper John Ruddy. 'Almost stubborn, but in a good way, having a set way of wanting to play, wanting to impose themselves on teams. We haven't come away from that, we made a little tweak at the start of the season when it wasn't quite going for us, but that showed that within the formation we could make adjustments.'

Despite the impressive work in the two seasons Nuno has been at the club, the head coach believes there is a long way to go before the coaching revolution is complete. It is more than just deciding on a formation and a shape to the team.

'An identity within the club that everyone recognises will take time,' he adds. 'The stronger that you are in your own idea, relying and believing that this is the way, even in the ups and downs, insisting and focussing on the right things, is the way to work. We have changed the shape but the idea doesn't change. The team can adapt to any opponent, whilst at the same time realising that if you have a strong identity, believing in the way you play, things turn and it is the opponent who starts to adapt to you. You just have to insist on your own beliefs. We don't change, we adapt. If the opponent decides to change it is because they think it is the best way to do it. If each and every week you change, you are not spending enough time to develop something.'

The set-piece routine at the Marbella Football Centre is not a unique example of this dedication. Every coach employed by Nuno to operate with the first team spends their time on the pitches throughout a typical session, participating in every part of training. The subtle changes and adaptations Nuno is referring to are drawn up through hours of meticulous observing, tweaking and planning.

'My biggest help is my team, the coaches,' Nuno continues. 'Their view, their opinion, the way they see things happening. Being strong as a team is very important. It's a family, we are friends, we've known each other for many years, we've shared a lot of experiences. They are the biggest source of inspiration that I can have. I have total trust and confidence in their abilities.'

Alongside the Portuguese coaches, and Figueroa, an Argentinian, is a Scot. Nuno first met Ian Cathro when the pair attended a coaching course at the Inverclyde National Sports Centre in Largs, on the west coast of Scotland, in 2009. At the age of 36, Nuno was taking his first steps into coaching. He immediately connected with the 23-year-old head of Dundee United's youth academy.

Three years later, when Nuno was appointed manager of Rio Ave, a small club based in Vila do Conde in the north of Portugal, he turned to Cathro and asked him to be his assistant. The pair oversaw incredible success with the Portuguese minnows, taking the club to three cup finals and leading the team into Europe for the first time in its history. They moved on to Valencia, where they earned Champions League qualification during their only full season at the Mestalla.

They went their separate ways when Cathro linked up with Steve McClaren, and later Rafael Benitez, at Newcastle United. There followed an unsuccessful seven-month spell as manager of Heart of Midlothian, where Cathro's coaching capabilities were questioned by a suspicious – some would say 'old school' – attitude in Scottish football and its media. After a year out of the game, he was reunited with Nuno in 2018.

'We're linked by the way that we see football, not just how it's played but the way it's played,' Cathro told the *Express and Star* on his arrival in Wolverhampton.

'It's not a materialistic or superficial thing because it looks nice. It's because we believe that's the best way of getting the team the most probability of being in control of the game and winning. In the vast majority of cases it transcends countries and leagues, although there are always small adjustments that need to be made. You have to go with what you believe in. That's the only way you can convince people to come with you.'

Fitness coach António Dias and conditioning coach João Lapa have been responsible for a similar revolution in the strength and conditioning department. Dias believes that Nuno and the collection of backroom staff he has brought to the club can be described in particular terms:

'I would say more than a package, maybe a pack,' he says. 'We believe a lot in each other, we trust a lot in what our partners do. Each one of us has a word in terms of decision-making but every one of us has a very specific role in the team and we trust ourselves a lot. We try to grow as a team, helping each other, challenging each other on a daily basis. Everything comes from the pack.

'Of course we have our philosophy, our philosophy of works, the bases of our principles stay the same, but in terms of work – even from the drills we do on the pitch – things keep changing according to the stage of the team and I think that needs to be so. It's not a static knowledge, it's not a static state of point, it's moving forward. So we need to keep on moving.'

The pack metaphor works for Nuno, too. 'Yes, because we are doing it together. We came here and tried to involve everybody because I honestly believe it is the only way that we can achieve things. We need our supporters. Creating this bond that exists, between fans, players, medics, physios, chairman, it's all the same. It's all the same ambition to improve and move forward. Knowing that you are going into a football game and you have someone behind you who believes in you makes you run more and makes you feel stronger.'

In a dressing room of mixed cultures and nationalities, the presence of Coady as captain has been worth its weight in gold. His is a fascinating story of reinvention and determination. He joined Liverpool's academy in 2005 at the age of 12, progressing through the ranks as a midfielder. It was Brendan Rodgers who gave Coady his debut, at the age of 19, in a Europa League group match in Moscow against Anzhi Makhachkala in November 2012. Later that campaign he made his only Premier League appearance for the club, at Fulham.

The following season he moved to League One Sheffield United, on loan, and enjoyed regular first-team football for the first time. On returning to Anfield after his loan spell, Coady knew that leaving his boyhood club was the only option.

'It wasn't actually that hard to leave because I knew I needed to get out of Liverpool to improve as a footballer,' he explains. 'I got to a certain point where I knew I wasn't going to play for Liverpool. I was realistic in my own head about that. I'd been on loan at Sheffield United where I'd had a great season, I loved my time there. I didn't want to go back to Liverpool and play under-23s football so I knew I had to leave. I'm just lucky that a couple of years later I found myself at this great club.'

Huddersfield Town was the first calling point in August 2014. A year later, Kenny Jackett made a move for the player and brought him to Molineux in a £2million deal. Coady was a fixture in the team during Jackett's final year at the club and continued to hold down a place in the side under both Walter Zenga and Paul Lambert during the underwhelming 2016/17 season. Throughout that period Coady never truly nailed down a particular position in the side, often moving across midfield or dropping into the full-back's position.

One game in particular stands out. On 14 February 2017, Wolves lost 1-0 at home to Wigan Athletic. It was a third successive defeat for Lambert's side, which left the club 18th in the Championship table. Coady was introduced as a late substitute, coming on for winger Ben Marshall. His match-defining contribution was to lose his opponent, Jake Buxton, at an 88th-minute corner, allowing the Wigan man to head the winning goal past goalkeeper Carl Ikeme. Leaving the pitch that night, Coady must have been wondering what sort of future he had at the club. Just two years later he had signed a new five-year contract at Molineux as captain of a Premier League side.

Few would have selected the Liverpudlian as a natural starter in Nuno's team for 2017/18. But early in pre-season the head coach identified Coady's potential as the central sweeper in a three-man defence. It was a quiet dressing room that Nuno discovered on his arrival. Aside from Coady's ability to play the ball out of defence, his effervescent and infectious character was perfect for a head coach who needed to convey his message throughout the team. Coady has never looked back. A vocal presence and natural leader, he quickly established himself as the captain of the pack when club skipper Batth was out of the side. As the team took its first steps in the Premier League, Coady came to be regarded as the talisman on the pitch.

'It's the best feeling in the world, to captain this football club. I'm the proudest man every day when I play and train with Wolves,' he concludes. 'To be part of this team with this set of lads is something I'll remember for the rest of my life. It won't stay around forever; this manager and these lads won't be here forever so we need to make the most of what we have. The manager is a huge factor in that. Since he came in he has changed the whole direction of the football club.' A head coach with an idea, and a captain perfectly designed to lead it on the pitch.

Of the foreign imports, it is unquestionably Moutinho who has made the biggest impact. Seasoned observers suggest there has never been a more accomplished talent in Wolves colours than the Portuguese midfielder. Certainly, nobody in Nuno's team is more pleasing on the eye. Nothing is clumsy, no ball ever bobbles up off him, there are no mis-kicks or slices. Moutinho's feet have their very own obsessive compulsive disorder with a football. Nothing is ever misplaced or untidy.

The respect he has for his own standards and surroundings has rubbed off on those around him. More than one young team-mate has spoken of how important the 33-year-old is to the squad. Morgan Gibbs-White is one of the youngsters to break into the first team who looks up to the 2016 European Championship winner. 'The professionalism of Moutinho is improving me as a player,' he says. 'I'm learning every single day in training, not just on the pitch but off it as well. Just him coming into the club, given what he has achieved in his career, is a massive inspiration.'

But Moutinho's keenness to absorb the qualities from the youth around him in this squad is also to be admired. Earlier in the 2018/19 season, whilst speaking at the Compton Park training ground, there was no hint that the learning process was a one-way street. He may well be a living legend in the eyes of some – only Ronaldo and Luis Figo have more caps for Portugal – but there is a good reason why he has remained at the top for so long.

'You need to be open to learn because if you think you know everything, you're going to stop,' he commented. Sport plays a big part in his life away from professional football. He is a keen player of tennis and padel – a composite of tennis and squash – and is a huge fan of basketball, keenly watching NBA matches. Moutinho believes there is much to be learnt from the mentality of sportsmen from a different field.

His father, Nélson, was an accomplished midfielder who played in Portugal's Primeira Liga. 'He is a man who played football for many years and he can tell me something,' Moutinho adds. 'If I think it is good for me to do, of course I'm going to hear and try to do that at the next game or next training session. My father, my family, sometimes my wife, they tell me, "You need to do this!" OK, I listen and if it's possible I try to do it.'

Moutinho only half jokes about taking on board advice from other members of his family. When asked who has influenced his career the most, he does not hesitate to answer. 'The family, of course the family. For me it's the most important thing. You need the support of your family to do what you like, and I like a lot of football.'

Moutinho is a well-rounded individual. He is the embodiment of just how far Wolves have come under the current management. The first Premier League season of football under Nuno delivered so many memories. The subtle changes – the adaptations – allowed Wolves to overcome a tough period before Christmas. Along with Moutinho, there are players like Diogo Jota, Raúl Jiménez and Rúben Neves who bring more overseas flair and talent; Coady, Bennett and Willy Boly provide the base of the shape; Matt Doherty and Jonny Castro Otto give the width. Names that will stand the test of time when future generations look back at this moment in history. Whatever happens in that future, Nuno has changed the way Wolves supporters appreciate football forever.

Chapter 18

BILLY WRIGHT

A hero's story to be told

'I DO remember when we went on holidays, to Liguria in Italy, we had to keep stopping for people who wanted a picture with Dad,' says Vicky Wright. 'It wasn't selfies back then, it was these great big cameras that people were setting up. And I remember thinking, "Please can we just go to the beach, I want to get to the beach." He'd get recognised anywhere, but especially in Italy as they loved their football. So I knew then that he must have been big.'

As each year passed, the picture was completed a little bit more. But it is only recently that Vicky has finally got to grips with the magnitude of her father's impact and achievements as a footballer in this country and beyond. Billy Wright was arguably the greatest player ever to represent Wolves. He was also one of England's finest. The first international footballer to win 100 caps. Nobody has captained England on more occasions than the 90 times Wright led the team out. It was a tally that included appearances at three World Cups, a feat matched by no one else.

Every Wolves fan knows who Wright is. A magnificent 9ft high bronze statue of the man who lifted three league titles and an FA Cup here was erected in his honour in 1996.

It is positioned outside the reception of the main stand that bears his name at Molineux.

Wright's legacy is that, along with his team-mates in the 1950s, he set the standards all other Wolves teams aspire to. But how much longer will first-hand stories of Wright's achievements be passed down through the generations of Wolves supporters? Vicky wants to celebrate his life in football, but also his life as a husband, father and grandfather. For two years she has been working on a project to bring this story to supporters, painstakingly gathering photos, film reel and other artefacts to produce a tribute to a remarkable life.

We meet up at a riverside pub on the banks of the Thames, not far from her Surrey home, in late June. It is a couple of months before she debuts *The Billy Wright Story* in tribute to her father. Vicky is excited and nervous about the prospect of addressing her first audience of supporters at Molineux in September.

'I have discovered all sorts of little things. It's unbelievable that he found out he was made captain of England from the bus conductor on the way back from a match,' Vicky explains. 'He also got a letter when he was selected for England telling him what time the team had to meet at Paddington station to travel to one game, it might have been up in Scotland, and the players were told to bring their own towels and soap. It was just so different then.

'For me this is a legacy project. My daughter will have it, and my sister's children. It's there forever now. We've made it with all his favourite music and there's so many quotes from people like Sir Bobby Charlton. It's beautiful. When you've got the like of Sir Tom Finney and Sir Stanley Matthews saying things such as, "He was a giant of the game, we all respected Billy," all of these words, I thought, "Hey, Dad, you kept that quiet."'

Wright grew up in the Shropshire village of Ironbridge. Whilst playing as a centre-forward at Madeley Senior

School, his teacher, Norman Simpson, wrote to Wolves alerting the club to his potential. In July 1938 Wright secured a place on the ground staff at the age of just 14. Six months later it appeared that his time in football was at an end. Wright was called in to see the manager, Major Frank Buckley, who had been watching the youngster's progress during his trial spell at Molineux. Buckley was a formidable figure. He led the side out of the Second Division and came within a whisker of overseeing the club's first league title, when Wolves finished runners-up in both the 1937/38 and 1938/39 seasons. His disciplinarian style, training methods and work with the club's youngsters laid the foundations for the success of Stan Cullis's side in the 1950s.

Wright had not made a positive impression on the manager. Buckley informed the youngster that he was too small to make the grade as a professional footballer and released him. In Norman Giller's biography, *Billy Wright; A Hero for all Seasons*, the player explained the circumstances of his dismissal and subsequent reprieve.

'All I could think was that I was a failure, and I walked out of the Major's office without a word,' said Wright. 'I was too choked with tears to be able to say anything. Twenty minutes later, as I was getting my things together, I was called back into the manager's office. Our trainer Jack Davies stood alongside him. "I have been persuaded to change my mind," the Major said. "I am assured that you are big here where it really matters. In the heart." In truth, I think one of the main reasons I was kept on was because I was so good with a broom and at cleaning boots.'

'Every day he was there, dedicated to those jobs,' says Vicky. 'Then shortly afterwards, the wartime came and all the established players went off to war. Buckley gave him a chance, so Dad started playing, and clearly he was quite good.'

With the outbreak of World War Two, aged only 15, Wright found himself elevated to the first team for a wartime league match against Notts County in October 1939. Wolves pulled out of the wartime league the following season, so, along with team-mate Jimmy Mullen, Wright joined Leicester City as a guest player. The duo won the Midland Wartime Cup, beating Walsall 2-0, before being recalled to Wolves when they re-entered the wartime league for the 1941/42 season. Wright signed professional terms at the age of 17. He played as a forward in those early days, only moving to the half-back line once he established himself in the team after the war.

All was going smoothly, with Wolves making good progress in the Wartime League Cup that season. But then, in May 1942, during the second leg of a semi-final victory over West Bromwich Albion, Wright broke his ankle. Such injuries were often career-ending during that era. For the second time in three years, the youngster feared that his life in football was finished. But he found a solution with the help of Ernest Freeman, a Wolverhampton surgeon, who suggested putting a pin in the ankle to help bind the fracture.

'It was a ground-breaking procedure, the first time they'd ever put a pin in like that to try and fix it,' Vicky explains. 'Buckley had said that players don't recover from such injuries, but Dad just had this attitude, "Let's give it a go." And then he just worked and worked at getting back to fitness.'

At the age of 18 Wright joined the army as a physical training instructor. When the Football League resumed for the 1946/47 season, after the end of the war, team-mates who had been away on service duty noticed a change in the player.

'The most obvious one was his size,' said Cullis, in Giller's biography. 'The little shrimp had become a powerfully built young man. He had also grown in confidence as a person, and all his work as a physical training instructor meant he was positively glowing with strength and good health.'

Wright never looked back. He was made captain of Wolves in August 1947, and a year later he was made captain of his country. The famous incident on the bus occurred on 28 September 1948. Wright was heading back to his digs at Mr and Mrs Colley's house in Tettenhall, where he stayed for the entirety of his playing career. On board, the conductor congratulated him on being awarded the England captaincy, having read the news in the stop press of that evening's *Express and Star* newspaper. In 1949 Wright lifted his first major honour, the FA Cup, as Wolves beat Leicester City 3-1 in the Wembley final.

'There's a lovely piece of footage of him when they returned to Wolverhampton with the cup,' Vicky reveals. 'On top of this beautiful old-fashioned bus, everyone is waving. Stan Cullis comes out and says, "Ladies and gentlemen, thank you very much for coming, I'd like to introduce to you the most popular man in all of Wolverhampton." Everyone starts cheering, and Dad comes out to speak, looking so young. He puts on this posh voice as he says, "Ladies and gentlemen." It made me laugh, he never spoke like that. He must have been trying to make a good impression. These are all magical things to look back on.'

The 50s was a trailblazing decade for Wright and Wolves. The club won three league titles and took part in the prestigious televised floodlit friendlies against top opposition from Europe and beyond. The matches were a forerunner to the European Cup. Wright led the team out at Molineux in special gold shirts made from rayon, an artificial silk, designed to shine under the lights. Television audiences were huge, and Wright was by now a household name. He had already won 64 caps by the time Hungarian giants Honved were beaten in the game that earned Wolves the tags of champions of Europe.

Wright was a role model on the pitch. Cullis had built a physically powerful, fit and ruthless side, but he needed a captain who could lead by example, never shirking a challenge. The football was direct, with long diagonal balls played out to the wing forwards. In the title-winning seasons – 1953/54, 1957/58 and 1958/59 – Wolves scored 96, 103 and 110 goals, respectively. Despite the goals, it was the half-back line that drew most admirers. In the days of the 2-3-5 formation, it was the combination of three from Wright, Eddie Clamp, Ron Flowers and Bill Slater – all England internationals – which made a formidable triumvirate. Wright switched seamlessly to the centre of the defence midway through his career, having been equally at home as a wing-half. On three occasions at the 1958 World Cup, the half-back line was made up of Clamp, Wright and Slater.

It was while preparing to lead England at a third World Cup that Wright's personal life changed forever. The Beverley Sisters were the leading female pop group of the day. The three sisters from Bethnal Green – Joy, Teddie and Babs – were regular performers at the London Palladium. It was Joy, the eldest of the three, who made a big impression on the England captain.

'There was a time when Walter Winterbottom, the England manager, used to take the team for a night at the Palladium before a match, just to relax them, then they would go home to bed,' says Vicky. 'Mum was on with the Bevs one night that the England team went down there. The Bevs knew this but never got to meet the team because they would have to leave early ahead of the game. Dad's team-mate Ron Flowers said to me years later that Dad fell for Mum there. "We all ribbed Billy, because as soon as your mum went on stage he went all funny," said Ron.'

Joy had a son, Vince, from her previous marriage. A football obsessive, Vince was touring with the Beverley Sisters during the Easter school holidays a few weeks after that performance at the London Palladium. It was during a stay in Wolverhampton, ahead of a performance in the town, that Vince asked if he could see Wright, who was a friend of another entertainer appearing on the bill with the Beverley

Sisters. Joy made a few enquiries and put a phone call in to the footballer to arrange for her son to visit the club.

'Dad remembered Mum from the Palladium show when he got the phone call from her. He couldn't believe it when she rang, he thought it was a dream come true. "Yes I'll show him around Wolves and he can see the trophies," he said. So Mum gave the address of the hotel where they were staying. When Dad went round to pick Vince up, he walked in and saw Mum and the two of them just fell in love with each other. Mum said he was very handsome; blue eyes, blonde hair, with his sleeves rolled up.' Just three months later they were married.

'Because Mum had been married before, they made it a registry office thing, they didn't want a big deal,' Vicky continues. 'So they decided to go to Poole, in Dorset, as the Bevs were appearing nearby in Bournemouth. Dad picked them up, and they were driving into Poole when they hit this terrible traffic. They saw that there were people outside lining the streets. I've got a great picture of it, it was amazing. Dad rolled the window of the car down when he saw a policeman and asked him what was happening in the town causing the traffic jam as he was in a hurry to get to the registry office. The policeman just replied, "You're getting married Mr Wright, that's what is happening." The guy who was going to marry them had leaked it to someone in the press, so it had got out. All these people were lining the streets, it was unbelievable. That was in the days before *OK! Magazine* and all that paparazzi stuff. They only had one night on honeymoon, up in Stratford-upon-Avon. The Bevs were performing the next day, so Mum had to go back to work.'

Wright has been described as the David Beckham of his day, but that does him a disservice. He was a reluctant superstar who never courted the sort of publicity witnessed in the 'Posh and Becks' era. He was happy to leave the showbiz lifestyle to his wife and her sisters.

'He was shy. He never had girlfriends, he had been to a couple of dances but he didn't really have anyone before he met Mum,' Vicky explains. 'We lived in north London. They found a place in the country called Barnet. Back then it was genuinely in the country, and that's where we grew up. At one stage our household comprised of the three Bevs, their mother, my sister, me and Dad. He was outnumbered! The Bevs were a force to be reckoned with, so Dad used to sit there and it would just be the women talking. Every now and then something would happen, and he'd drop a little comment in. I remember once Argentina was on the television, and he just said, "When I was there and I met Peron ..." We all just turned to him and shouted, "What?! You met Peron?" He just wasn't someone who boasted, he was a wonderful man.

'He used to have all these England caps and he would just give them away. Someone like the milkman would knock on the door with his little boy to meet him, and he'd invite him in for a chat and when they left he'd say, "Here, have a cap." Mum would tell him off, but he used to reply, "Don't be daft, I've got loads of them." He would talk to anyone the same way. One day he would be suited and booted at Buckingham Palace meeting the Queen and the next day he would be down at the supermarket wearing a tracksuit chatting with the man pushing the trolleys in exactly the same way.'

It is moments such as this that Vicky wants to share with a wider audience when she makes her presentation.

'It gives an insight into him as a man, as a father, a family man. A lot of people have just seen the hero, the footballer, so it's for them to get to know the other side, it's lovely to share that. He's still an idol to so many people, I still have people writing to me about him. It's a love story too, it's not just about football. Dad just adored Mum, I've never seen anything like it.'

Vicky does not hesitate when asked what her favourite piece of footage is: 'Him on his 100th cap walking out on to the pitch, it's most incredible.' England beat Scotland 1-0 with a goal from Bobby Charlton at Wembley on 11 April 1959. Wright's Wolves team-mates Ron Flowers and Peter Broadbent were also in the team.

'I was born the week before, on 5 April, at the London Clinic,' Vicky adds. 'I was induced because the gynaecologist wanted to make sure it didn't drag on for days, so he could go to the match. Mum had stayed in hospital for a week. On the day of the game Mum was still not sure if she would make it, she wasn't feeling great. But you see on the *Pathe News* footage as he walks out, a news reporter runs to Dad and points up to the crowd. Dad looks up and sees Mum and breaks into a great big smile. It was the best thing I've ever seen.'

Wright retired at the end of the 1958/59 season with 105 caps. To add to three league titles and an FA Cup, he also won the Football Writers' Association Footballer of the Year award in 1952. Many years later, Bill Slater, the man who succeeded him as captain, paid this tribute. 'Wolves have not had a more loyal or more dedicated servant. We had a saying in the dressing room: Show the Wright spirit. I played with Billy in countless matches for the club and also on several occasions for England. I can count his poor games on the fingers of one hand. He was a wonderful advertisement, not only for football, but for the human race.'

But Wright's path was not always a smooth one after the illustrious playing career came to an end. A four-year spell as manager of Arsenal, from 1962–66, brought little success.

'He was too nice, you've got to be ruthless,' Vicky reflects. 'They lost a lot of matches and, as a child, I remember he was so stressed, it was a horrible time. In saying that, he brought in all the young players that went on to win the double at Arsenal: Charlie George, Frank McLintock, Bob Wilson. They went on to form a great team and Dad was never given credit for that.'

The youth structure that Wright had witnessed Major Buckley set up at Wolves was something he took into his own management. Six of Arsenal's 1970/71 double-winning squad came through the youth ranks at Highbury. Wright left the game after his Arsenal experience to pursue a career in the media at Associated Television, which later became Central Television. He eventually headed up their sports department until his retirement in 1989. But the move to the Midlands, with his family remaining in north London, brought problems in his personal life.

'He had some difficult times as well, being up there, because we weren't with him,' Vicky admits. 'The booze, there was a little bit of that, but my mum wouldn't want me to say too much about it. I am going to mention it in my talks as he was very proud that he conquered that as well. He was in Birmingham for 18 years; it was during that period that he drank a lot. That was the lifestyle up there, it was all executives sitting around having lunches. And he was lonely going home to a little one-bedroom flat. He missed Mum and he missed us.

'He shouldn't have gone up there really, but we were at school, and the twins [Joy's sisters Teddie and Babs] lived just around the corner. They kind of regretted it a bit. It was a real downer for all of us. It was kind of in our household but nobody mentioned it and it was kept quiet, it wasn't like now when everyone who has a problem can come out with it, or go into rehab. Dad had to keep quiet about it then, and I always thought that was a bit unfair, he's human. But he came through that, he conquered it, that's the man he was, he dealt with it. Although his life reads like a fairy tale at times, and everyone loved him, he did have ups and downs like everybody else.'

Wright enjoyed a swansong at Molineux. When Sir Jack Hayward took over the club, in May 1990, he installed Wright as a director. There was a further honour when the Billy Wright Stand was opened at the start of the 1993/94 season.

'When Sir Jack came along and rebuilt Molineux, with his stand, that was the proudest day of his life,' Vicky adds. 'He was great mates with Sir Jack, who was a lovely man. Jack wrote on his wreath "Goodbye old pal". He came to see him when he was ill, too, he was a lovely guy. And the statue they put up later on, it's so like him. The forearms are the same, it's wonderful.'

Wright died at the age of 70, on 3 September 1993, just a year after the stand was opened, following a short battle with pancreatic cancer.

'He was so fit, he never had a day's illness,' Vicky adds. 'He had this backache and he went to the doctors and they couldn't work it out, and then they found this little shadow on the pancreas. He was diagnosed with cancer and three months later it was done and dusted. I suppose the one time I really discovered how big he was, and it's an awful thing to say, but it was when he died.

'We filled a room with the amount of letters that came in. Some were just addressed to "Billy Wright, England". There were bags and bags of them. We read every single one of them. I just thought, "My God, he was really famous." The flags and scarves outside Molineux on the day of his funeral, it was like a state funeral. It was so public, we were so distraught. I remember our car stopped and there was a policeman on a horse right outside the window. And there was a tear rolling down his face. It was so touching. There were people coming with shirts and putting them around Dad's statue. The notes that were left, it was wonderful.'

Twetny-five years later, Vicky still finds the funeral difficult to talk about. It brought into focus a football life that had taken place before she was born. Like most children, she had never asked her father much about his previous career, as England's record-breaking captain. 'That's the only regret. If I could go back I would, I'd love to ask him more about the football part of his life.'

This project has helped her connect with that significant chapter of his life. Even today, she stumbles across reminders of her father's eminence in the football world.

'For this presentation I had to have a lot of old photographs scanned, and I went to the local printer where I live and handed them over to the woman behind the counter. She looked at them and said, "I think I recognise him, it's Billy Wright isn't it? My brother is a huge Wolverhampton Wanderers supporter."'

Every matchday at Molineux, a supporter will walk past the Billy Wright statue for the first time. Often it will be a young child. Maybe they will ask who it is, in that pose, striding out on to the pitch with the ball tucked under his arm. Wright never set out to be a star, and at just 5ft 8in he was never going to make an imposing figure. Yet he ended his career, and remains to this day, the most decorated captain in the club's history. Vicky has spent many hours immersing herself in the life of her father at Wolves.

'How lovely for him, to be a local lad doing all that, and to be loved by Wolverhampton,' she concludes. 'It's just a shame his mum never got to see it, she died when he was in his teens. She lived in Ironbridge, working at a Wedgwood pottery painting plates. I could imagine her saying, "A statue, of my little Billy?" She wouldn't have believed what has happened to him.

'The museum at Molineux is unbelievable, with Dad's stuff everywhere. I love seeing the ground, it gives me goose bumps, especially when I see the pitch. It's so steeped in history that club, it has a feel about it that they love their heritage and history. It's quite unique. Through thick and thin, they've been through a lot. I can't describe it really, but you walk into that club and it's like going on to a Hollywood movie set, with all the stories.'

And Billy Wright played the lead role in the most successful tale of all.

EPILOGUE

A CHINESE ODYSSEY

TWELVE MONTHS on from sitting down to listen to the stories of Wolves' Sherpa Van Trophy winners at their 30th anniversary dinner at Molineux, there is a club event taking place in an entirely different setting and context. On the rooftop garden of one of Fosun International's downtown office skyscrapers in Shanghai, China, a fashion show is underway. The catwalk is positioned on a stage at the side of the garden terrace, set against a backdrop of the Huangpu River and the stunning city skyline at night. French designer Christelle Koche, whose work has been commissioned by Chanel amongst others, is sat in the front row watching the models parade her designs. Seated alongside her are the Wolves first-team squad and management.

It would have been an unimaginable scenario just a couple of years ago, but this is the landscape where Wolves, under Fosun's ownership, now reside. Koche's designs comprise entirely of Wolves-themed clothing. The club's various crests from its long history have been incorporated into the outfits. To the Western eye, the designs are outlandish, almost comical. But this is not aimed at supporters from Wolverhampton. Fosun are not preaching to the converted.

Wolves' 2019 pre-season tour of China is eye-opening on many levels. The scale of the owners' ambition is laid out for the players to see. As the tour progresses, the players learn more and more about the club they are representing.

'It's now more than a football club, it's a whole brand in itself, you can tell that today,' says goalkeeper John Ruddy as he surveys the scene. 'Fosun have done really well in the last couple of years. We know what the owners' ambitions are, we are more than aware of what they want to do and where they want to be. It's a fantastic club to be at. Events like this one are a small indication of that.'

A few hours before the fashion show, the club opened a megastore in a recently built shopping arcade also owned by Fosun. The items on display are in the high-end product range. The fashion show is being attended by senior Fosun executives as well as key 'influencers' in Chinese popular culture. The rap artist Simba and the rock band Miserable Faith, both with huge Chinese followings, are headlining the evening's entertainment.

At both the fashion show and the megastore opening there is a huge number of Chinese media in attendance.

Over the course of the week-long tour, a slick and well-organised marketing campaign takes place, with corporate partners such as Tsing Tao, Levdeo, EA Sports and Manbet X hosting events with Wolves. There are many supporter-based experiences, giving the opportunity for Chinese Wolves fans to engage with the club at all levels, including signing sessions with head coach Nuno Espírito Santo and his players. The Wolves Foundation has linked up with the Fosun Foundation to provide schools' football coaching sessions in the local Shanghai community. One group of schoolchildren have arrived here by air travel from a rural outpost of the country just to be given the opportunity to train with Wolves Foundation coaching staff. The club is determined to leave an imprint behind, with the help of owners Fosun on the ground.

An editorial in Xinhua, the state-run press agency of China, published at the end of the Asia Trophy, recognised the efforts of the club on the tour, when comparing Wolves favourably against Premier League champions Manchester City's attempts at engagement on the trip. 'For Wolverhampton Wanderers, fan interaction was the cornerstone of their trip to China, with players and coaches doing everything they could to engage with fans and show them a more personal side to the club. Wolves could not do more to engage with fans and even Newcastle, despite arriving under a cloud of off-field negativity, treated China with the utmost respect and dignity. Today those clubs leave China with a new-found respect and new fans; Manchester City leave China with neither.'

This is a watershed period for the club. Another of those moments in history, which seem to come along at regular intervals.

The direction being taken now could well dictate the future for years to come. The success of Wolves in China will directly affect long-time supporters who make the regular walk to Molineux on a matchday. There are two distinct facets to the club now.

Chairman Jeff Shi acknowledges this. He offers an interesting insight into the strength of the club's identity for a new audience. 'The name of Wolves is quite unique,' he explains. 'For example, if you are Liverpool or Manchester United it is hard to imagine we can design some high-end fashion products from that name. Wolves is quite a neutral name. Of course, it comes from the city, but all across the world the name is seen more neutralised. The logo is quite fashionable.'

Nuno quickly picked up on the wolf imagery and symbolism. He has used it regularly when speaking to the media and the Wolves fans. At the club's end of season dinner in May 2019, at the Telford International Centre, he was speaking to the local supporters, the owners and the emerging overseas fan base when he made this analogy: 'Now the pack will go up into the mountains to rest. We will be prepared when we come back down to the valley to hunt the prey again next season.'

Shi sees a Wolves which offers more than just a football team. 'In China, we are not only positioned as a hardcore club, we are trying to position us as a brand which can give you very good entertainment, very good service, good products,' he continues. 'Performance on the pitch is one of the products but it is not the only one. We can provide more. The spirit and the brand awareness behind all this is Wolves. When we talk about Wolves in the future, we are talking about not just the football team, but maybe we are talking about clothes, shoes, music, esports, games. I think around the world, the fans will feel more from the Wolves brand, not just the team on the pitch.'

This is a concept that long-time supporters on the South Bank might baulk at, but it is also one that illustrates the intent to grow the club. The pace of that growth could have profound implications for supporters. So far, there has been impressive work around Molineux and the Compton Park training ground. The structural growth has benefitted the club. The improvements to the playing squad have been more obvious and have taken the team to the next level of competition.

Fosun will not stand still. There may be more seismic shifts in the sands. Some changes will be embraced, others will unnerve supporters. The fabric of the club may be changing but the soul will never disappear. In just three years, this global investment company has learnt the value of Wolves beyond a simple investment.

'We are very strong on investments but Fosun is developing into a group who is not only about investment but will also operate key assets to keep in our hands for a long time,' adds Shi. 'The things we want to do all over the world are buy some very good assets, to give them some new strengths and to develop and grow them. Wolves is one of the examples – we are not buying and selling this asset. I think Wolves will be a permanent asset for Fosun. The only thing to do is to improve the club until we fulfil our dream. I have been saying this for a long time, we have the ambition to develop this club into one of the best in the world.'

Ruddy senses something significant about belonging to Wolves at this moment in time, when asked what the most rewarding part of being a Wolves player is. 'Being part of the initial wave, the first few steps on the ladder to where they want to be,' he explains. 'Wherever they go in the future, if it's as high as the owners are looking, then it has been an honour to be part of that, however small that part might have been in the long run. It's just a really good club to be at; a massive club, and people don't realise that.'

Where will it go from here? Supporters ended the 2018/19 campaign on a significant high. Two hugely successful seasons, delivered with a style of football Wolves have never played before, have taken fans into a new realm. Almost by the week, ambitions are being reset as those in the stands open their minds to the possibility of further success. Whatever direction Wolves take over the next year, decade and beyond, it will be a fascinating one. History has shown that predicting this particular club's future path is a pointless exercise. The management, players, owners and supporters of today have their own stories still to complete. They will join those of Graham Hughes, Kenny Hibbitt, Steve Bull, Sam Ricketts, Albert and Muriel Bates, Derek Ryan and all the others who have been bitten by Wolves. No other club in this country has been forged by such contrasting highs and lows. It is what has come to define Wolverhampton Wanderers.

BIBLIOGRAPHY

The Wolves – Tony Matthews (with Les Smith)
Bully – Rob Bishop
All Played Out – Pete Davies
Between The Golden Lines – David Instone
The Doog – David Harrison & Steve Gordos
They Wore The Shirt – Steve Plant
Billy Wright; a hero for all seasons – Norman Giller

URLs FOR BOOK REFERENCE

https://www.birminghammail.co.uk/sport/
football/football-news/wolves-new-academy-
massive-boost-8065225

https://www.independent.co.uk/sport/wolves-owner-
lambasts-mcghee-1261847.html

http://www.wolvesheroes.com/2015/01/15/sir-jack-
hayward-1923-2015/

https://www.independent.co.uk/news/football-tycoon-
sues-wasteful-son-1075002.html

https://www.bbc.co.uk/sport/football/17012933

https://www.expressandstar.com/sport/football/
wolverhampton-wanderers-fc/2012/07/20/wolves-18m-
stan-cullis-stand-nears-completion/

https://www.expressandstar.com/sport/football/
wolverhampton-wanderers-fc/2012/07/20/wolves-18m-
stan-cullis-stand-nears-completion/

https://www.wolves.co.uk/news/club/20160211-wolves-
publish-annual-accounts/

https://www.bbc.co.uk/sport/football/36852323

https://www.expressandstar.com/sport/football/
wolverhampton-wanderers-fc/2016/07/21/
wolves-takeover-fosun-international-deal-is-
complete-say-law-firm/

https://www.theguardian.com/football/2016/

jul/30/wolves-appoint-walter-zenga-new-head-coach-kenny-jackett

https://www.expressandstar.com/sport/football/wolverhampton-wanderers-fc/2016/07/23/wolves-takeover-chinese-are-urged-to-respect-clubs-traditions/

https://www.independent.co.uk/sport/football/football-league/wolves-sack-walter-zenga-87-days-part-company-resign-championship-a7379546.html

https://www.bbc.co.uk/sport/football/37839003

https://www.expressandstar.com/sport/football/wolverhampton-wanderers-fc/2017/04/08/jeff-shi-gives-full-backing-to-wolves-boss-paul-lambert/

https://www.youtube.com/watch?v=l4ceci9q-ko

https://www.independent.co.uk/sport/football/football-league/wolves-fc-news-takeover-fosun-jorge-mendes-gestifute-a7472016.html

http://www.dailymail.co.uk/sport/football/article-2111783/Roger-Johnson-fined-drinking-session-training.html

https://www.expressandstar.com/entertainment/weekend/2018/09/01/looking-back-at-the-star-studded-life-of-wolverhamptons-club-lafayette/

https://www.thepfa.com/news/2014/11/10/opening-wovles-academy-and-arena

http://www.londonwolves.com/html/compton.html

https://www.dailymail.co.uk/sport/football/article-6171959/amp/Wolves-billionaire-owners-insist-bigger-Man-City.html?__twitter_impression=true

https://inews.co.uk/sport/football/premier-league/joao-moutinho-interview-wolves-wolverhampton-wanderers-days-off/amp/?__twitter_impression=true

https://www.bbc.co.uk/sport/football/45591373

https://thisisfutbol.com/2018/08/blogs/wolves-spend-5million-on-improving-training-ground/

https://www.dailymail.co.uk/debate/article-1335485/amp/Sir-Jack-Hayward-reveals-vicious-feud-fortune-torn-family-apart.html

https://www.redrowplc.co.uk/media/1960/redrow-plc-annual-report-2016.pdf

https://www.redrowplc.co.uk/land/land-overview/compton-park-wolverhampton/

http://www.wolvesheroes.com/2009/05/18/a-promising-career-lost/

https://www.expressandstar.com/sport/football/wolverhampton-wanderers-fc/2016/07/06/from-the-archive-wolves-financial-peril-30-years-on/

http://twohundredpercent.net/100-owners-number-73-the-bhatti-brothers-wolverhampton-wanderers/

https://www.expressandstar.com/sport/football/wolverhampton-wanderers-fc/2018/11/16/from-car-park-to-compton-park-an-exclusive-tour-of-wolves-multi-million-pound-training-ground/

https://www.expressandstar.com/sport/football/wolverhampton-wanderers-fc/2015/10/19/classic-match-report-newcastle-1-wolves-4/

https://wwosc.wordpress.com/who-are-we/

https://www.11v11.com/teams/wolverhampton-wanderers/tab/leagueTables/31-december-1989/

https://www.expressandstar.com/sport/football/wolverhampton-wanderers-fc/2016/10/11/feature-golden-moments-from-50-years-of-supporting-wolves/

https://www.coachesvoice.com/my-idea/

https://www.skysports.com/football/news/11699/11564297/nuno-espirito-santo-interview-wolves-boss-explains-his-vision

https://www.skysports.com/football/news/11699/10899634/nuno-espirito-santo-to-wolves-jorge-mendes-links-underlined

http://www.londonwolves.com/wwlsc.html

https://www.youtube.com/watch?v=coDxyBTJphQ

https://www.youtube.com/watch?v=QwVGmK-Xrak

https://www.youtube.com/watch?v=Yb06sPg7FZ4

https://www.expressandstar.com/news/local-hubs/

wolverhampton/2017/08/16/how-football-prank-still-haunts-me-to-this-day/
https://www.yorkshirepost.co.uk/sport/football/non-league/when-hooligans-turned-fairytale-into-nightmare-for-scarborough-1-8701257
http://www.englandfootballonline.com/matchrsl/MatchRslTmB.html
https://www.theguardian.com/football/1999/jul/14/newsstory.sport3 https://breastcancernow.org/news-and-blogs/blogs/a-legacy-for-lucy-aims-to-reach-100000-for-breast-cancer-research
https://www.dailymail.co.uk/femail/article-3257292/Husband-s-grief-radiant-bride-loses-cancer-battle-just-four-months-dream-wedding.html
https://www.independent.co.uk/sport/football-englands-delusion-of-grandeur-1191032.html
https://www.telegraph.co.uk/sport/football/2306856/Albion-revel-in-their-invasion-of-Wolves-lair.html
https://www.independent.co.uk/sport/football-hope-for-a-marked-manager-interview-mark-mcghee-1073827.html
https://www.independent.co.uk/sport/wolves-owner-lambasts-mcghee-1261847.html
https://www.expressandstar.com/sport/football/wolverhampton-wanderers-fc/2015/11/13/from-the-archive-graham-taylor-resigns/
https://www.birminghammail.co.uk/sport/football/football-news/beginning-a-whole-new-life-of-brian-11506 https://www.theguardian.com/football/1999/nov/05/newsstory.sport1
https://www.independent.co.uk/sport/football-happy-taylor-back-in-business-at-wolves-former-england-manager-makes-smart-start-in-his-1432659.html
https://www.independent.co.uk/sport/football-wolverhampton-bids-wright-a-fond-farewell-phil-shaw-reports-on-the-funeral-of-a-football-1448579.html

https://www.independent.co.uk/sport/fan-adds-insult-to-injury-for-troubled-taylor-1616945.html

https://www.theguardian.com/football/2016/sep/27/porto-leicester-champions-league-nuno-espirito-santo

https://www.skysports.com/football/news/11699/10899634/nuno-espirito-santo-to-wolves-jorge-mendes-links-underlined

https://www.skysports.com/football/news/11699/11564297/nuno-espirito-santo-interview-wolves-boss-explains-his-vision

https://www.theguardian.com/football/2018/oct/19/nuno-espirito-santo-wolves-manager-interview

https://www.theguardian.com/football/2007/mar/13/wolverhamptonwanderersfootball

https://www.expressandstar.com/news/local-news/2015/09/02/joy-beverley-death-it-was-a-fairytale-life-says-billy-wrights-daughter/

https://www.scotsman.com/sport/football/hearts/in-full/ex-hearts-boss-ian-cathro-criticises-b-t-impression-of-him-1-4741497